The FOUNDERS *on* RELIGION
A Book of Quotations

★

The FOUNDERS *on* RELIGION

A Book of Quotations

JAMES H. HUTSON,
Editor

PRINCETON UNIVERSITY PRESS
PRINCETON AND OXFORD

Copyright © 2005 by Princeton University Press
Published by Princeton University Press, 41 William Street, Princeton,
New Jersey 08540
In the United Kingdom: Princeton University Press, 3 Market Place,
Woodstock, Oxfordshire OX20 1SY

All Rights Reserved

ISBN-13: 978-0-691-12033-1 (cloth)

ISBN-10: 0-691-12033-1 (cloth)

Library of Congress Cataloging-in-Publication Data
The founders on religion : a book of quotations / [compiled by]
James H. Hutson.
p. cm.
Includes bibliographical references and index.
ISBN-13: 978-0-691-12033-1 (cloth : alk. paper)
ISBN-10: 0-691-12033-1 (cloth : alk. paper)
1. Religion—Quotations, maxims, etc. 2. Statesmen—United States—
Quotations. I. Hutson, James H.
PN6084.R3F68 2005
200—dc22
2005015974

British Library Cataloging-in-Publication Data is available

This book has been composed in Palatino with Bauer Bodoni Display

Printed on acid-free paper. ∞

pupress.princeton.edu

Printed in the United States of America
1 3 5 7 9 10 8 6 4 2

Contents

Preface

★

In recent years "quote books" about religion and the Founding Fathers have appeared with regularity. Since they have not been published by the mainstream press, they have escaped the notice of most scholars and a considerable sector of the reading public.

The quote books have been compiled by pious citizens with conservative religious views who are distressed by what they see as the pernicious secularization of American life, caused in their view by an unremitting and illegitimate campaign to banish Christianity from all areas of the public arena as well as from the writing and teaching of American history. The perceived purging of Christianity from the history of the Founding Period has seemed to the evangelical and conservative religious community to be particularly unconscionable, because its members consider that the remarkable success of this country's republican experiment in government, launched in 1776 and constitutionalized in 1787, can be attributed in large measure to the religious convictions of the Founders. They believe that, if these convictions can be revived and restored as guiding principles in American public life, the nation can be healed of the host of social ills that afflict it.

What better way to prove that the Founders were grounded in and instructed by Christian principles than by calling the most important of them to the witness stand and letting them testify in their own words to the importance of Christianity in their lives? All quote book compilers employ this strategy, invariably focusing on Washington, Jefferson, Madison, Franklin, Adams, and a handful of lesser luminaries, culling statements from their writings that attest to the beneficent influence of Christianity on their lives and on the public welfare, and presenting these pronouncements in serial form. On the basis of the evidence offered, they assume that only the most perverse reader could deny that Christianity was the formative force in the founding of the United States.

Few compilers of the religious quote books are academic historians, although their volumes frequently contain footnotes and other trappings of scholarship. In fact, many of compilers are suspicious of the academy. Some renounce professional historians altogether as malign agents of a left-wing conspiracy, dedicated to the obliteration of Christianity from the national memory.[1] The contempt for professional historians seems, unfortunately, to have fostered a corresponding contempt for the craft of history, for some of the compilers display a cavalier attitude toward factual accuracy and the use of evidence which compromises the integrity of their work.[2] Not a few evangelical spokesmen are uncomfortable, in fact, with the undisciplined zeal of some compilers.

Convinced that the subject, Religion and the Founding, deserves better treatment than it has received in the religious quote book genre, I offer a quote book that is as objective as possible and that conforms to the canons of historical scholarship. My expectation is that readers of all religious persuasions—or of none—will find the book useful. Conservative and evangelical readers who consult the book will, I hope, be persuaded that sound scholarship is not their sworn enemy, as many have been led to believe.

I use a wider variety of sources than is employed in the quote books. Many of them rely exclusively on secondary sources and are notably incestuous, borrowing freely from one another and perpetuating in the process errors and faulty transcriptions of documents. I have examined numerous collections of original manuscripts and have quarried from them quotations that, in some cases, may be unfamiliar even to specialists. Especially fruitful were the papers of Elias Boudinot at the Princeton University Library, of John Dickinson at the Historical Society of Pennsylvania, and of Roger Sherman at the Yale University Library, as well as the microfilm editions of the papers of John Adams at the Massachusetts Historical Society and of Charles Carroll of Carrollton at the Maryland Historical Society and the recently released online edition of the papers of John Jay at the Columbia University Library. Additionally, the papers of George Washington, Thomas Jefferson, and James Madison at the Library of Congress were searched, with some surprising results. These new sources offer readers a richer and livelier selection of statements about the religion of the Founders than is now available.

A more significant difference between this volume and the conventional quote books is the organizing principle employed. Every quote book of which I am aware is organized by proper name, that is, by an alphabetical list of individuals below whose names a string of quotations is appended. The present volume will be organized alphabetically by *subject*, beginning with "addiction" and ending with "women." The advantages of using this principle will, I hope, be immediately apparent.

Organization by proper name creates a sense of incoherence, because the self-contained sections make it difficult, even with incessant page turning, to spot common threads running through the volume and to identify subjects on which there is general agreement. The quote book compilers who use the proper name design have a narrow agenda—the establishment of the religious credentials of the Founders and of their conviction that religion should have a robust role in public life—which ignores the depth and breadth of the Founders' religious interests. A book organized by subject expands the canvas and, while doing justice to the problem of religion in the public square, permits the presentation of the Founders' sentiments, as the present volume does, on more than seventy-five topics, including such perennial faith questions as the nature of God and Jesus Christ, the Trinity, the evidence for an afterlife, the untimely death of loved ones, the authority of and relationship between the Old and New Testaments, the origin of sin, the relation of faith and works and of faith and reason, the credibility of prophecy, the justice of war, the place of Islam and Judaism in the divine economy, and many others.

That the Founders had much to say about these topics should come as no surprise. With a few exceptions, Benjamin Franklin being the most conspicuous one, they were regular churchgoers, many active in the affairs of their local congregations. George Washington rarely missed an opportunity to attend divine services and took his turn on the vestry of his parish church. During his two terms as president, Thomas Jefferson, also at one time an Episcopal vestryman, "constantly attended public worship" in the House of Representatives, once riding through a cloudburst to arrive on time.[3] In retirement he regularly patronized worship services at the Albemarle County Court House, sitting on a "portable chair" of his own design.[4] As president, James Madison followed Jefferson's example by attending services in the House, making a grand appearance when he arrived in his coach and four. John Adams was a "meeting-going animal"[5] who went to church twice every Sunday. Alexander Hamilton would have been inconsolable had he not received communion, as he lay dying from Burr's bullet.[6] Roger Sherman wrote and published a sermon to give theological guidance to the members of his congregation.[7]

John Dickinson composed a catechism for Christian youth.[8] Other Founders were at least as active on behalf of their respective churches.

Mere attendance at church services is, of course, no indicator of the degree of an individual's religious commitment, a subject on which many of the Founders maintained a prickly reserve. It would, therefore, be irresponsible to attempt to read the Founders' minds and souls and offer generalizations about the firmness of their faith. There is, in fact, a debate among scholars about the degree of religious conviction, society-wide, during the Founding period, some arguing that the older estimate of popular religious "adherence" during the period is far too low and that the correct figure may be as high as 70 percent.[9] Whatever the situation in society at large, the Founders were, demonstrably, regular churchgoers, who knew their Bibles and incorporated scriptural texts into their working vocabularies.

The Founders were also interested in theological issues. They lived in an age when the medieval assumption that theology was the queen of the sciences had still not expired in America. As late as 1819 John Adams wrote that "the science of Theology is indeed the first Philosophy—the only Philosophy—it comprehends all Philosophy—and all science, it is the Science of the Universe and its Ruler—and what other object of knowledge can there be."[10] Many of the Founders were diligent students of theology. The reading of religious treatises was a principal avocation of some, certainly not of Washington and Patrick Henry, but most assuredly of John Adams, John Jay, John Dickinson, Benjamin Rush, and Roger Sherman. It would be a stretch—but not an impossible one—to include Jefferson in this company, at least in retirement, when he was a consumer of and acute commentator on theological tracts.

That many of the Founders were recognized as religious specialists is demonstrated by their continuous and many-sided correspondence, as equals, with the leading ministers of their day. No one, perhaps, eclipsed Roger Sherman, who disputed fine theological points with Samuel Hopkins, a leading spirit in the abstruse hyper-Calvinistic New Divinity movement, but many of Sherman's colleagues could have held their own with Hopkins and other leading divines of the day.

The Founders who appear in this volume were people of exceptional intelligence who fertilized their impressive religious learning with the most extensive experience in the "real" world of domestic and international politics, war, and commerce. Their opinions on religion, therefore, have an intrinsic interest which transcends the parochial subject of state-church relations, and they constitute a fund of knowledge and information on which a modern reader can draw as he or she considers the great and enduring issues of faith and practice.

Readers should be aware of two problems inherent in quote books of every description. One is the problem of timing. If an individual's views change over time, at what point are they the most authentic and, hence, quotable? Consider the case of James Madison. Fresh out of college, he wrote a friend in 1773 that "there could not be a stronger testimony in favor of Religion . . . than for men who occupy the most honorable and gainful departments and are rising in reputation and wealth, publicly to declare their unsatisfactoriness by becoming fervent Advocates in the cause of Christ."[11] Madison's religious fervor did not persist and, as the years passed, he became, according to a friend, sympathetic to Unitarianism and, if a recent scholar is to be credited, an outright skeptic.[12] If Madison's faith journey was divided against itself, which phase contained the most accurate and, therefore, quotable record of his beliefs? My policy has been to present the mature, settled opinions of the Founders, insofar as I could ascertain them.

Those who might object that this policy skews the tenor of the volume toward secularism will find that it cuts both ways. Benjamin Franklin's earliest foray into the realm of religious controversy was an atheistical tract, which he repudiated soon thereafter, settling into a long life of benign theism. Preferring the mature to the callow Franklin elevates the spiritual tone of the volume. So does offering—as I do—quotations from the mature Jefferson, who grew friendlier to Christianity as he aged. Still, the problem of deciding which of an individual's fluctuating views are his most authentic is a difficult one that is liable to error.

The other problem inherent in quote books is that of inclusiveness. A book with the title "the Founders on Religion" or some variation thereof often creates the impression that there was a collective religious "mind" of the Founding generation, which can be captured by the aggregated weight of the quotations presented. But if the definition of a Founder is expanded from a select few to the hundreds— no, thousands—of patriots who participated in state and local politics, the problems with this approach become apparent. Can the opinions of this multitude be captured by the views of a small group? Quote books solve this problem by a fiction of representation that assumes that if the few Founders quoted are carefully chosen from all sects and sections in the nation their words will express the opinions of the denominations and areas they represent and will comprise something like a national consensus on religion or at least on certain important religious issues. Securing adequate representation while keeping the number of Founders quoted to a small, manageable number is challenging because every quote book must include Washington, Franklin,

Madison, Jefferson, and Adams, all of whose religious views tracked toward the margins of the country's mainstream and were, in the case of the latter two, idiosyncratic, as they themselves admitted.

I have followed the representational strategy, just described, imperfect as it is, but have expanded the usual cast of characters to include two "Founding Mothers," Abigail Adams and Martha Washington, and one relatively unfamiliar figure, Elias Boudinot, President of the Continental Congress, Director of the United States Mint, and a prolific religious polemicist. Boudinot is of particular importance, because he was a born-again Presbyterian, whose evangelical views were probably closer to those of the majority of his countrymen than were those of most of his fellow Founders. One regrets that there were so few articulate and "quotable" political leaders like Boudinot among the Baptists, Methodists, and other disciples of evangelical religion, who after 1800 conquered the American soul, belying Jefferson's prediction that Unitarianism was the wave of the future.

During the Founding period Baptists, Methodists, and other members of evangelical sects were overwhelmingly ordinary folks, patriotic, to be sure, but not the articulate and propertied politicians and military leaders who are customarily and justly called the Founding Fathers and whose sentiments fill the religious quote books. Were these books truly inclusive they would contain topics that were of special concern to the evangelical population—the "new birth," revivals, baptism, religious "enthusiasm," and so on.[13] Whether the opinions of the ordinary people who composed this population are accessible in any form is, it should be observed, a subject that historians have vigorously debated in recent decades.

The present volume, to summarize, is a work of scholarship. It offers the views on religion of a select group of the most influential political and military leaders of the new nation, derived from a thorough examination of a large number of original and printed sources. The views of the Founders are worth presenting because they are the product of brilliantly successful men of affairs who were well informed about religion—some were experts on the subject—who spoke to issues of faith and practice that are still alive today. The Founders' views, diverse though they were, also illuminate the sentiments of important religious denominations in the Founding period and, on some issues (e.g., the power of providence), of all Americans of that generation. And, finally, the full range of the Founders' views on religion and public policy, presented here, will furnish additional grist for the mills of those involved in the current debate over this contentious issue.

Notes

1. Tim LaHaye has charged that the Christian character of the American republic was obliterated "when history was deliberately raped by left-wing scholars for hire." Tim LaHaye, *Faith of Our Founding Fathers* (Brentwood, Tenn.: Wolgemuth & Hyatt, 1987), 6.
2. See, among others, Stephen Northrop, *A Cloud of Witnesses* (Portland, Ore.: American Heritage Ministries, 1987); Steve Dawson, *God's Providence in American History* (Rancho Cordova, Calif.: Steve C. Dawson, 1988).
3. James H. Hutson, *Religion and the Founding of the American Republic* (Washington, D.C.: Government Printing Office, 1998), 84–96.
4. Thomas Jefferson to Thomas Cooper, November 2, 1822. Paul L. Ford, ed., *The Works of Thomas Jefferson*, 12 vols. (New York: G. P. Putnam's Sons, 1904–05), 12:271; *Papers of the Albemarle County Historical Society* 8 (1947–1948), 63.

5. Benjamin Rush to John Adams, August 20, 1811, Lyman H. Butterfield, *Letters of Benjamin Rush* (Princeton, N.J.: Princeton University Press, 1951), 2:1096.

6. Trevor Colbourn, ed., *Fame and the Founding Fathers: Essays by Douglass Adair* (New York: W. W. Norton, 1974), 141–59.

7. Roger Sherman, *A Short Sermon on the duty of Self Examination, preparatory to receiving the Lord's Supper* (New Haven, Conn.: Abel Morse, 1789).

8. "Religious Instruction for Youth." Several drafts may be found in the R. R. Logan Papers, Historical Society of Pennsylvania. Dickinson was evidently continuously revising the catechism for publication but no record of its appearance in print has been found.

9. For a discussion of this debate, see James H. Hutson, *Forgotten Features of the Founding: The Recovery of Religious Themes in the Early American Republic* (Lanham, Md.: Rowman & Littlefield, 2003), 111–32.

10. John Adams to Andrew Norton, November 24, 1819, Adams Papers (microfilm), reel 124, Library of Congress.

11. James Madison to William Bradford, September 25, 1773, William T. Hutchinson and William M. E. Rachal, eds., *The Papers of James Madison* (Chicago: University of Chicago Press, 1962), 1:96.

12. Frank Lambert, *The Founding Fathers and the Place of Religion in America* (Princeton, N.J.: Princeton University Press, 2003), 263. For a recent essay that stresses the obscurity of Madison's theological views, see Hutson, *Forgotten Features of the Founding*, 155–85.

13. Although Washington and Jefferson wrote memorable letters *to* Baptists, the Founders said little *about* their religious practices and convictions. An exception is Madison, who once opined that the Baptists' "religious Sentiments [were] in the main . . . very orthodox." Madison to William Bradford, January 24, 1774, Hutchinson and Rachal, *Papers of James Madison*, 1:106. Less surprising is the Founders' silence about the Methodists, who, unlike the Baptists, did not became an important force in American religious life until the beginning of the nineteenth century. In a characteristic outburst late in life John Adams inveighed against John Wesley, the "founder of the methodistical mysterys." To Adams, Wesley appeared to be "one of the most remarkable Characters that enthusiasm, superstition fanaticism ever produced. I question whether

Ignatious Loyola or any other saint in the Romish Calendar ever produced a greater effect or whether there is anything in the Acta Sanctorum more whimsical extravagant incredible galvanic or mesmerian than appears in this life. Yet what a Circle has it spread in this World wider and broader than Swedenborg himself. Will mankind be forever the credulous dupes of such vageries. When will men be rational creatures?" Adams to Francis van der Kemp, February 12, 1821, Adams Papers (microfilm), reel 124, Library of Congress. It is not clear whether other Founders shared Adams's view of Wesley and the Methodists.

Founding Generation Members
Quoted in This Volume
★

ABIGAIL ADAMS (1744–1818). Wife of John Adams, second president of the United States; mother of John Quincy Adams, sixth president of the United States. Daughter of a Congregational minister; a Unitarian in mature years.

JOHN ADAMS (1735–1826). "The Atlas of Independence." First American ambassador to Great Britain (1785–1788); first vice president of the United States (1789–1797); second president of the United States (1797–1801). A Congregationalist who became a Unitarian later in life.

ELIAS BOUDINOT (1740–1821). New Jersey politician. President of the Confederation Congress, 1782–1783; director of the United States Mint, 1795–1805; first president of the American Bible Society, 1816. A Presbyterian.

CHARLES CARROLL OF CARROLLTON (1737–1832). Influential Maryland politician. Signer of the Declaration of Independence. United States senator from Maryland, 1789–1792. A Roman Catholic.

JOHN DICKINSON (1732–1808). Leading revolutionary pamphleteer. President of Delaware, 1781, and of Pennsylvania, 1782. Defender of the Federal Constitution. Raised in a Quaker environment and married to a Quaker, Dickinson was strongly sympathetic to the Society of Friends but never became a bona fide member of his approval of defensive warfare.

BENJAMIN FRANKLIN (1706–1790). The first great American scientist. The colonies' principal agent at the British court,

1764–1775; the first American ambassador to France, 1778–
1785. President of the Supreme Executive Council of Pennsylvania, 1785–1788. Raised a Congregationalist, as an adult
Franklin was not an active member of any church.

ALEXANDER HAMILTON (1757–1804). An aide-de-camp to
Washington during the Revolutionary War. With Madi-
son, the principal author of the *Federalist*; the first
secretary of the treasury, 1789–1795. Educated as a youth by
Presbyterians, Hamilton was a member of the Episcopal
Church.

PATRICK HENRY (1736–1799). A celebrated orator of the Revolutionary Period, called by an admirer the "forest-born
Demosthenes." Governor of Virginia, 1776–1779 and 1784–
1786. Perhaps the most influential Anti-Federalist in the nation. An Episcopalian.

JOHN JAY (1745–1829). Revolutionary leader from New York
who held multiple high-level political, diplomatic and judi-
cial appointments. Appointed first American ambassador
to Spain, 1779; secretary of foreign affairs, 1784–1790; appointed first chief justice of the Supreme Court of the
United States, 1790; governor of New York, 1795–1801. An
Episcopalian.

THOMAS JEFFERSON (1743–1826). Author of the Declaration
of Independence, 1776. Governor of Virginia, 1779–1781;
ambassador to France, 1785–1789; first secretary of state under the Constitution, 1790–1793; third president of the
United States, 1801–1809. An Episcopalian (nominally) for
much of his life; in retirement he became, according to his
great-grandson, a "conservative Unitarian."

HENRY LAURENS (1724–1792). South Carolina political leader.
President of the Continental Congress, 1777–1778; a mem-

ber of the American commission to negotiate peace with Great Britain, 1782. An Episcopalian.

JAMES MADISON (1751–1836). "The Father of the Constitution." With Hamilton, the principal author of the *Federalist*. Secretary of state, 1801–1809; fourth president of the United States, 1809–1817. An Episcopalian.

BENJAMIN RUSH (1745–1813). One of the most influential physicians and social reformers of the revolutionary period, called by some the "father of modern psychiatry." A signer of the Declaration of Independence. A Presbyterian early in life, he allied for a brief time with the Episcopal Church, and later became a proponent of Universalism.

ROGER SHERMAN (1721–1793). A Connecticut politician, who served long and constructively in the Continental and Confederation Congresses and in the Congress under the Constitution. An influential member of the Federal Constitutional Convention of 1787. Also active in state politics and as a judge of the superior court of Connecticut. A Congregationalist.

GEORGE WASHINGTON (1732–1799). "The Father of his Country." Commander of the Continental Army, 1775–1783. First president of the United States, 1789–1797. An Episcopalian.

MARTHA WASHINGTON (1731–1802). The first first lady. An Episcopalian.

JOHN WITHERSPOON (1723–1794). Presbyterian pastor and president of Princeton University. Signer of the Declaration of Independence. Served on more than one hundred committees during six years of service in the Continental Congress, 1776–1782. Note that only statements made by Witherspoon during the period he was active in national politics, that is, 1776–1782, are included in this volume.

A Note on the Texts

The texts used in this book come from a variety of sources: modern documentary editions, earlier documentary editions that do not adhere to modern editorial standards, biographies and scholarly monographs, and collections of original documents in manuscript repositories and on microfilm or online. My principle of selection has been governed by the fact that, since the subject of this volume is passionately contested, readers may want to verify the accuracy and the legitimacy of the quotations presented by checking them personally. I have, therefore, chosen quotations from the source that I have judged to be most accessible to the reader. I have, for example, used an 1890–93 edition of the papers of John Jay, which was reprinted in 1971 and is, accordingly, available in most large libraries: Henry P. Johnston, ed., *The Correspondence and Public Papers of John Jay*. Most of the letters that Johnston published as well as numerous additional ones appear in an online edition of Jay's papers, recently posted by the Columbia University Library, but this edition, invaluable as it is, may challenge readers who are not accustomed to reading eighteenth-century handwriting, who may not have ready access to a computer, or who are intimated by the prospect of gleaning information online. I have, therefore, used documents from the Johnston edition, when they appear in both editions, as well as publishing numerous Jay documents which only appear in the online edition.

Similar problems are present in the published papers of other Founders such as Franklin, Jefferson, and Adams. Modern documentary editions of these Founders' papers are incomplete in the sense that some have not reached the mature years of their subjects. Earlier documentary editions publish documents from these years. When confronted with the choice of publishing these earlier printed documents and original versions of the documents, available only in a manuscript repository inaccessible to most readers, I have chosen to publish the former version.

Johnston and other early documentary editors eliminated the eccentricities of their subjects' eighteenth-century spelling and punctuation by "modernizing" both. Biographers and scholars, especially those writing in the first half of the twentieth-century, were also in the habit of "modernizing" eighteenth-century documents; items which I have selected from these biographical sources do not, therefore, replicate the originals, which, in some cases, no longer exist. In some microfilm collections I have, moreover, been obliged to rely on typed transcriptions that also feature modern spelling and punctuation of lost original documents.

The contrast between these "corrected" documents and original documents, published exactly as they appear in manuscript collections, as well as documents reprinted from modern documentary editions, whose editors strive to reproduce documents literally, will be apparent to readers, who will have the experience of moving back and forth from documents containing the oddities of eighteenth-century spelling and punctuation to documents corrected to modern grammatical and orthographic standards. To have published every document in its eighteenth-century form would have been impossible as well as imprudent, since many exist only in printed, modernized form, and since the modernized form, as in the case of John Jay's writings, is frequently more accessible to the average reader. Editorial purists may be uneasy with the heterogeneous appearance of the documents in this volume but I trust that the overwhelming majority of readers, alerted in advance to the problem, will not be troubled by these technical issues.

Short Titles

Adams, *Jefferson's Extracts*	Dickinson W. Adams, ed., *Jefferson's Extracts from the Gospels*. Princeton, N.J.: Princeton University Press, 1983.
ANB	John A. Garraty and Mark C. Carnes, eds., *American National Biography*. 24 vols. New York: Oxford University Press, 1999.
Boller, *Washington*	Paul Boller, *George Washington and Religion*. Dallas: Southern Methodist University Press, 1963.
Boyd, *Papers of Thomas Jefferson*	Julian P. Boyd, ed., *The Papers of Thomas Jefferson*. 31 vols. Princeton, N.J.: Princeton University Press, 1950–2004.
Butterfield, *Adams Family Correspondence*	Lyman H. Butterfield, ed., *Adams Family Correspondence*. 6 vols. Cambridge, Mass.: Harvard University Press, Belknap Press, 1963–93.
Butterfield, *Diary and Autobiography of John Adams*	Lyman H. Butterfield, ed., *Diary and Autobiography of John Adams*. 4 vols. Cambridge, Mass.: Harvard University Press, Belknap Press, 1961.
Butterfield, *Letters of Rush*	Lyman H. Butterfield, ed., *Letters of Benjamin Rush*. 2 vols. Princeton, N.J.: Princeton University Press, 1951.

Campbell, *Henry*

Norine Campbell, *Patrick Henry; Patriot and Statesman*. New York: Devin-Adair Co., 1969.

Cappon, *Adams-Jefferson Letters*

Lester Cappon, ed., *The Adams-Jefferson Letters*. 2 vols. Chapel Hill: University of North Carolina Press, 1959.

Corner, *Autobiography of Rush*

George W. Corner, ed. *The Autobiography of Benjamin Rush*. Princeton, N.J.: Princeton University Press, 1948.

DNB

Leslie Stephen and Sidney Lee, eds., *Dictionary of National Biography*. 23 vols. London: Oxford University Press, 1908–09.

Dreisbach, *Religion and Politics*

Daniel Dreisbach, *Religion and Politics in the Early Republic*. Lexington: University Press of Kentucky, 1996.

Fitzpatrick, *Writings of Washington*

John C. Fitzpatrick, ed., *The Writings of George Washington*. 39 vols. Washington, D.C.: Government Printing Office, 1931–44.

Haraszti, *Prophets of Progress*

Zoltan Haraszti, *John Adams and the Prophets of Progress*. Cambridge, Mass.: Harvard University Press, 1952.

Johnston, *Correspondence of Jay*

Henry P. Johnston, ed., *The Correspondence and Public Papers of John Jay*. 4 vols. New York: Da Capo Press, 1971.

Labaree, *Autobiography of Franklin*

Leonard W. Labaree, ed., *The Autobiography of Benjamin Franklin*. New Haven, Conn.: Yale University Press, 1964.

Labaree, *Papers of Benjamin Franklin*.

Leonard W. Labaree, ed., *The Papers of Benjamin Franklin* 37 vols. New Haven, Conn.: Yale University Press, 1959–2003.

Old Family Letters

Alexander Biddle, ed., *Old Family Letters*. Philadelphia: J. B. Lippincott Co., 1892.

Papers of Martha Washington

Joseph E. Fields, ed., *Worthy Partner: The Papers of Martha Washington*. Westport, Conn.: Greenwood Press, 1994.

Peden, *Notes on Virginia*

Thomas Jefferson, *Notes on the State of Virginia*, 1781. William Peden, ed., *Notes on the State of Virginia*. Chapel Hill: University of North Carolina Press, 1955.

Rakove, *Madison Writings*

Jack Rakove, ed., *James Madison: Writings*. New York: Library of America, 1999.

Richardson, *Messages and Papers of the Presidents*

James Richardson, ed., *A Compilation of the Messages and Papers of the Presidents*. 20 vols. New York: Bureau of National Literature, 1897–1924.

Rogers, *Papers of Henry Laurens*

Philip M. Hamer, ed., *The Papers of Henry Laurens*. Vols. 1–3. George C. Rogers, Jr., ed., *The Papers of Henry Laurens*. Vols. 4–16. Columbia: University of South Carolina Press, 1968–2003.

Rush, *Essays: Literary, Moral, and Philosophical*

Michael Meranze, ed., *Benjamin Rush Essays: Literary, Moral, and Philosophical*. Schenectady, N. Y.: Union College Press, 1988.

Schutz and Adair, *Spur of Fame*

John A. Schutz and Douglass Adair, eds. *The Spur of Fame;*

Dialogues between John Adams and Benjamin Rush. San Marino, Calif.: Huntington Library, 1966.

Sherman, *Short Sermon*

Roger Sherman, *A Short Sermon on the duty of Self Examination, preparatory to receiving the Lord's Supper.* New Haven, Conn.: Abel Morse, 1789.

Smyth, *Writings of Franklin*

Albert H. Smyth, ed., *The Writings of Benjamin Franklin.* 10 vols. New York: Macmillan Company, 1905–07.

Syrett, *Papers of Alexander Hamilton*

Harold C. Syrett, ed., *The Papers of Alexander Hamilton.* 27 vols. New York: Columbia University Press, 1961–87.

Taylor et al., *Papers of John Adams*

Robert Taylor et al., eds., *Papers of John Adams.* 12 vols. Cambridge, Mass.: Harvard University Press, Belknap Press, 1977–2004.

Warren-Adams Letters

Warren-Adams Letters, Being Chiefly a Correspondence among John Adams, Samuel Adams and James Warren. 2 vols. Boston: Massachusetts Historical Society, 1917–25.

Works of Witherspoon

The Works of the Rev. John Witherspoon. 2d ed., 4 vols. Philadelphia: William W. Woodward, 1802.

The Quotations

★

Addiction

Following are extracts from letters written by Charles Carroll of Carrollton to his alcoholic son, Charles Carroll, Jr. The younger Carroll, as his anguished father frequently reminded him, had been the beneficiary of everything that wealth and parental affection could provide: financial security, a good education, an impressive home. In addition, Carroll, Jr., married a model wife from an excellent Philadelphia family who presented him with attractive children. But the younger Carroll could not conquer his addiction to alcohol, which wrecked his life. Charles Adams, the second son of John and Abigail Adams, was also an alcoholic who died young and in disgrace.

It will add great comfort to the few years I may have to live to see you persevere in the resolution which you have taken. . . . If you have not the resolution of perseverance you will degrade your character, shorten a miserable life, and that of an affectionate wife, who to escape the afflicting scene she has daily witnessed and for the sake of her health has been constrained to abandon her home. I earnestly, advise you to call in religion to your aid; never rise or go to bed without humbling yourself in fervent prayer before your God, and crave his all powerful grace to overcome your vicious and intemperate habit; meditate on the end of your creation, and the dreadful consequences of not fulfilling it; keep your mind and body usefully occupied . . . avoid idle companions addicted to the same failing; which has hitherto overcome all your good resolutions of amendment, and probably theirs. Idleness, says Solomon, is the root of all evil, and St. Paul, that evil communication corrupts good morals. All your endeavours to conquer the dreadful and degrading habit you have contracted, will be of no avail unless you abstain from tasting, even from smelling all ardent spirits.

> Charles Carroll of Carrollton to Charles Carroll, Jr., April 27, 1813. Carroll Papers (microfilm), reel 2, Library of Congress.

I entreat you to comply strictly with my advice: refrain entirely from ardent spirits and strong malt liquors, and use wine with great moderation. Without a reformation you can not reasonably expect your wife to love you. I beg you will seriously reflect of an hereafter; religion will afford you the greatest of all consolations, and its powerful influence will aid you to get the better of your dreadful habit.

> Ibid., May 25, 1813, reel 2.

I need not urge the necessity of your conquering entirely the fatal habit to which you have been so many years a slave; without a perfect and complete mastery of it, you know you can enjoy no peace of mind no comfort in this life, and the thought of your dying without reformation and repentance of the consequences in the next is most dreadful.

> Ibid., June 1, 1815, reel 3.

In writing to you I deem it my duty to call your attention to the shortness of this life, the certainty of death, and of that dread judgment, which we must all undergo, and on the decision of which a happy or miserable eternity depends. The impious said in his heart, there is no God. He would willingly believe there is no God; his passions and the corruption of his heart would feign persuade him that there is not; the stings of conscience betray the emptiness of the delusion: the heavens proclaim the existence of God, and unperverted reason teaches that he must love virtue, and hate vice, and reward the one and punish the other.

Keep in mind, and reflect frequently and seriously on the passage in the Apocalypse: "Audivi Vocem de calo dicentem mihi scriebe Beati mortui qui in Domino moritentur; amodo jam dicit spiritus ut requiescant a laboribus suis; opera enim illorum sequuntureos."[1]

The wise and best of the ancients believed in the immortality of the soul, and the Gospel has established the great truth of a future state of rewards and punishments; a series of prophecies from the expulsion of Adam and Eve out of paradise to within a few hundred years of the coming of Christ announcing that event, and all fulfilled in his person, leave no room to doubt of the truth of Christianity and of the words of Christ; he foretold the approaching destruction of Jerusalem, his resurrection, the conversion of the Gentiles, and the last and general judgment: how can we doubt of the latter, when all the others have been realized? How abject, how degraded, how despicable must the mind of that man be, who wishes to persuade himself, from the dread of punishment in a future state, the inevitable consequence of vice unrepented in this, that he is not of a nature superior to that of his dog and horse, limited like them to a transitory existence, and relinquishing the hope and belief of a glorious immortality, the sure reward of a virtuous life. O! The

---

[1] Carroll is quoting (but not literally) from the Vulgate, the authorized Catholic Latin version of the Scriptures. The text he is quoting is chapter 14, verse 13, of the Apocalypse of St. John (called the book of Revelation in Protestant Bibles). In the Catholic Church's English language Challoner-Rheims version of the New Testament the passage reads: "And I hear a voice from heaven saying, 'Write: Blessed are the dead who die in the Lord henceforth. Yes, says the Spirit, let them rest from their labors, for their works follow them.'" Joseph Grispino, ed., *The New Testament . . . A Revision of the Challoner-Rheims Version Edited by Catholic Scholars under the Patronage of the Episcopal Committee of the Confraternity of Christian Doctrine* (New York: Guild Press, 1967).

fatal effect of unbridled and habitual vice, which can pervert and blind the understanding of a person well educated and instructed!

My desire to induce you to reflect on futurity, and by a virtuous life to merit heaven have suggested the above reflections, and warning: despise them not; on the making them the daily subject of your thoughts, they can not fail to impress on your mind the importance of reform and repentance. The approaching festival of Easter, and the merits and mercies of our Redeemer . . . have led me into this chain of meditation and reasoning, and have inspired me with the hope of finding mercy before my judge and of being happy in the life to come, a happiness I wish you to participate with me by infusing into your heart a similar hope. Should this letter produce such a change it will comfort me, and impart to you that peace of mind, which the world cannot give, and which I am sure you have long ceased to enjoy.

> Ibid., April 12, 1821, reel 3.

[Charles Carroll, Jr., died, April 3, 1825—Ed.]. I presume that he expressed anguish and repentance for the life he led; the course of which both of us have more cause to lament than his end. He has appeared before a judge, the searcher of hearts and most merciful. Let us pray that he has found mercy at that dread tribunal.

> Charles Carroll of Carrollton to Mrs. Charles Carroll, Jr., April 12, 1825. Ibid., reel 3.

Afterlife

When I look in my Glass I see that I am not what I was. I scarcely know a feature of my face. But I believe that this Mortal Body shall one day put on immortality and be renovated in the World of Spirits. Having enjoyed a large portion of the good things of this life and few of its miseries, I ought to rise satisfied from the feast, and be gratefull to the Giver.

> Abigail Adams to John Quincy Adams, May 10, 1817. Adams Papers (microfilm), reel 437, Library of Congress.

I too firmly believe that virtue will be rewarded and vice punished in a future state.

> John Adams to Adrian van der Kemp, January 30, 1814. Ibid., reel 95.

All Nations, known in History or in Travels have hoped, believed and expected a future and better State. The Maker of the Universe, the Cause of all Things, whether We call it, Fate or Chance or GOD has inspired this Hope. If it is a Fraud, we shall never know it. We shall never resent the Imposition, be grateful for the Illusion, nor grieve for the disappointment.

> John Adams to Thomas Jefferson, May 3, 1816. Cappon, *Adams-Jefferson Letters*, 2:471.

I know not how to prove physically that We shall meet and know each other in a future State; Nor does Revelation, as I can find give Us any positive Assurance of such a felicity. My reasons for believing, it, as I do, most undoubtedly, are all moral and divine.

I believe in God and in his Wisdom and Benevolence; and I cannot conceive that such a Being could make such a

Species as the human merely to live and die on this earth. If I did not believe a future State I should believe in no God. This Universe; this all; this . . . totality; would appear with all its swelling Pomp, a boyish Fire Work.

And if there be a future State Why should the Almighty dissolve forever all the tender Ties which Unite Us so delightfully in this World and forbid us to see each other in the next?

John Adams to Thomas Jefferson, December 8, 1818. Ibid., 2:530.

I believe enough of the Apocalypse to be perfectly convinced "that be thou faithful unto the death and thou shalt receive a crown of life."

John Adams to Louisa Catherine Adams, May 25, 1819. Adams Papers (microfilm), reel 447, Library of Congress.

I am fast approaching to that last scene which will put an end to all earthly cares and concerns. I am looking to that state from which all care all solicitude and all the passions which agitate mankind are excluded. Revelation instructs us that eternal happiness, or eternal misery will be the destiny of man in the life to come, the most pious the most exemplary have trembled at the thought of the dreadful alternative: oh! what will be the fate of those, who little think of it, or thinking square not their actions accordingly.

Charles Carroll of Carrollton to Charles H. Wharton, July 19, 1826. Carroll Papers (microfilm), reel 3, Library of Congress.

Q[uestion]. In order to encourage us to Obedience, and to deter us from Disobedience, hath not God been graciously pleased to reveal, that there will be a Day of Judgment, in which he will by Jesus Christ Our Lord judge all Mankind?

A[nswer]. Yes. "Whereof he hath given Assurance to all Men, in that He hath raised him from the Dead." "The trumpet shall sound" and "We must all appear before the

Judgment seat of Christ, that everyone may receive the Things done in his Body, according to that he hath done, whether it be good or bad." "Some shall awake to everlasting Life and some to everlasting Shame and Contempt" for "He will bring to Light the hidden Things of Darkness, and will make manifest the Counsels of the Heart" . . . "When the Son of Man shall sit upon the Throne of his Glory, then shall the King say unto them on his right Hand, Come, Ye blessed of my Father, inherit the Kingdom prepared for you from the Foundation of the World." "Eye hath not seen, nor Ear heard, neither have entered into the Heart of Man the Things, which God hath prepared for them that love him. They shall be with the Lord. They shall be like him and see him face to face." But, "the wicked and slothful servants shall go into everlasting Punishment—into outer Darkness—where there will be weeping and gnashing of Teeth—where their Worm dieth not—into the Fire that never shall be quenched."

John Dickinson, "Religious Instruction for Youth," undated.
R. R. Logan Papers, Historical Society of Pennsylvania.

Your frequently repeated Wishes and Prayers for my Eternal as well as temporal Happiness are very obliging. . . . I have my self no Doubts that I shall enjoy as much of both as is proper for me. That Being who gave me Existence, and thro' almost three score Years has been continually showering his Favours upon me, whose very Chastisements have been Blessings to me, can I doubt that he loves me? And if he loves me, can I doubt that he will go on to take care of me not only here but hereafter? This to some may seem Presumption; to me it appears the best grounded Hope; Hope of the Future; built on Experience of the Past.

Benjamin Franklin to George Whitefield, June 19, 1764. Labaree, *Papers of Benjamin Franklin*, 11:231–32.

The Body of
B. Franklin,
Printer:
Like the Cover of an old Book,
Its contents torn out,
And stript of its Lettering and Gilding,
Lies here, Food for Worms,
But the Work shall not be wholly lost:
For it will, as he believ'd, appear once more,
In a new & more perfect Edition,
Corrected and amended
By the Author.

Benjamin Franklin, *Autobiography*, 1771. Labaree, *Autobiography of Franklin*, 44.

. . . the soul of Man is immortal, and will be treated with Justice in another Life respecting its Conduct in this.

Benjamin Franklin to Ezra Stiles, March 9, 1790. Franklin Papers, Library of Congress.

Not many Weeks ago we had also a fine hearty Girl, but a violent Fever has since carried her to Heaven, where I expect one Day or other to see her much more charming and accomplished than if she had been educated either in Europe or America.

John Jay to Robert Livingston, October 6, 1780. Richard B. Morris, ed., *John Jay, The winning of the Peace: Unpublished Papers, 1780–1784* (New York: Harper & Row, 1980), 31.

Of that history . . . I have often wished that the accounts given in it of the primitive ages had been more particular. We know but little about them, and our curiosity must remain ungratified while we remain here. I say here, be-cause when we join our ancestors, we shall doubtless learn from them all that we may wish to know respecting

the affairs and events of their days. In this and other respects I promise myself much satisfaction from their society,
and that at a period which cannot be very distant. The term
of my lease has expired, and I have no reason to expect that
my continuing to hold over will be of more than ordinary
duration. It is consoling to reflect that we <u>tenants</u> are informed <u>where</u> and <u>how</u> we may go and settle in perpetuity,
and are assured that our possessions and enjoyments there,
instead of being precarious and transitory, will be certain
and permanent.

> John Jay to Gouverneur Morris, October 28, 1816. Johnston,
> *Correspondence of Jay*, 4:394–95.

The laws of nature have witheld from us the means of physical knowledge of the country of the spirits and revelation
has, for reasons unknown to us, chosen to leave us in the
dark as we were. When I was young I was fond of the speculations which seemed to promise some insight into that
hidden country, but observing at length that they left me in
the same ignorance in which they had found me, I have for
very many years ceased to read or think concerning them,
and have reposed my head on that pillow of ignorance
which a benevolent creator has made so soft for us knowing
how much we should be forced to use it. I have thought it
better by nourishing the good passions, and controuling the
bad, to merit an inheritance in a state of being of which I can
know so little, and to trust for the future to him who has
been so good for the past.

> Thomas Jefferson to the Reverend Isaac Story, December 5, 1801.
> Adams, *Jefferson's Extracts*, 325–26.

When you and I look back on the country over which we
have passed, what a field of slaughter does it exhibit! Where
are all the friends who entered it with us under all the
inspiring energies of health and hope? As if pursued by the

havoc of war, they are strowed by the way, some earlier, some later, and scarce a few stragglers remain to count the numbers fallen, and to mark yet by their own fall the last footsteps of their party. Is it a desireable thing to bear up thro' the heat of the action, to witness the death of all of our companions, and merely be the last victim? I doubt it. We have however the traveller's consolation. Every step shortens the distance we have to go; the end of our journey is in sight, the bed wherein we are to rest, and rise in the midst of the friends we have lost. "We sorrow not then as others who have no hope;" but look forward to the day which "joins us to the great majority." But whatever is to be our destiny, wisdom, as well as duty, dictates that we should acquiesce in the will of him whose it is to give and to take away, and be contented in the enjoiment of those who are still permitted to be with us.

> Thomas Jefferson to John Page, June 25, 1804. Jefferson Papers, Library of Congress.

We shall only be lookers on, from the clouds above, as we now look down on the labors, the hurry, the bustle of the ants and bees. Perhaps in that super-mundane region we may be amused with seeing the fallacy of our own guesses, and even the nothingness of those labors which have filled and agitated our own time here.

> Thomas Jefferson to John Adams, May 17, 1818. Cappon, *Adams-Jefferson Letters*, 2:524.

. . . the term is not very distant at which we are to deposit, in the same cerement, our sorrows and suffering bodies, and to ascend in essence to an ecstatic meeting with the friends we have loved and lost and whom we shall still love and never lose again.

> Thomas Jefferson to John Adams, November 13, 1818. Ibid., 2:529.

Life's visions are vanished, its dreams are no more;
Dear friends of my bosom, why bathed in tears?
I go to my fathers, I welcome the shore
Which crowns all my hopes or which buries my cares.
Then farewell my dear, my lov'd daughter, adieu!
The last pang of life is parting from you!
Two seraphs[2] await me long shrouded in death
I will bear them your love on my last parting breath.

> Thomas Jefferson, autograph poem handed to his daughter,
> Martha Randolph, July 2, 1826. Edward Boykin, *The Wisdom of
> Thomas Jefferson* (New York: Doubleday, Doran & Company,
> 1941), 212.

I believe that the souls of believers are at their death made
perfectly holy, and immediately taken to glory: that at the
end of this world there will be a resurrection of the dead,
and a final judgment of all mankind, when the righteous
shall be publickly acquitted by Christ the Judge and admitted to everlasting life and glory, and the wicked be sen-
tenced to everlasting punishment.

> Roger Sherman, "White Haven Church Confession of Faith" (draft),
> 1788. Sherman Papers, Library of Congress.

The reason why any of the human race are subjected to end-
less punishment, is, because they have sinned and voluntarily continue finally impenitent, which is wholly their
own fault.

> Roger Sherman to Samuel Hopkins, June 28, 1790. American
> Antiquarian Society, *Proceedings* 5 (October 1887–October
> 1888): 443.

[2] The "two seraphs" were Jefferson's wife, Martha (d. September 6,
1782), and his daughter, Mary (d. April 17, 1804).

But, with Cicero in speaking respecting his belief of the immortality of the Soul, I will say, if I am in a grateful delusion, it is an innocent one, and I am willing to remain under its influence.

George Washington to Annis Stockton, August 31, 1788. Fitzpatrick, *Writings of Washington*, 30:76.

I doe most sincerely lement and condole with you, on the loss of our dear departed Friend [Martha's sister—Ed.]. She has I hope made a happy exchange—and only gon a little before us the time draws near when I hope we shall meet never more to part—if to meet our departed Friends and know them was scertain we could have very little reason to desire to stay in this world where if we are at ease one hour we are in affliction days.

Martha Washington to Burwell Bassett, December 22, 1777. *Papers of Martha Washington*, 175.

Age

Your observations in your last Letter upon your Solicitude; and your reflections upon your Age and feelings, led me to a train of Reflections upon that period of Life to which we are both hastning, to that period when the wise Man hath told us, no pleasure is to be found. That Frederick[3] who was as great an unbeliever as Voltaire should experience this

---

[3] Frederick the Great (1712–1786), King of Prussia. One of the eighteenth century's most renowned freethinkers.

truth in its full force I can easily believe. How barren and imperfect that prosperity which can have no recourse to Religion to supply the insufficiency of worldly plasures. The following passage so fully expresses my own observations, that it appeard to present itself to me this day with peculiar force, upon reading your Letter.

Worldly prosperity declines with declining life. In Youth its relish was brisk and poignant. It becomes more sober as Life advances; and flattens as life descends. He who lately overflowed with Cheerfull Spirits and high hopes, begins to look back with heaviness on the days of former years. He thinks of his old companions who are gone; and reviews past Scenes, more agreable than any which are likely to return. The activity of persuit is weakened. The gaiety of amusement is fled. The gratification of Sense languishes, when his accustomed pleasures, one after another flee treacherously away. What can he who is an utter Stranger to Religion, and to the hope of Heaven, substitute in their place?

But even in that drooping period, the promises and hopes of religion support the Spirits of a Good Man till the latest hour. His Leaf, it is said shall not wither. It shall not be in the power of time to blast his prosperity. But old Age shall receive him into a quiet retreat, where if lively Sensations fail, gentle pleasures remain to sooth him. That hope of immortality which formerly improved his other enjoyments, now in a great measure supplies their absence. Its importance rises in proportion as its object draws near. He is not forsaken by the World, but retires from it with dignity; reviewing with a calm mind the part which he has acted, and trusting to the promise of God for an approaching reward. Such Sentiments and expectations shed a pleasing tranquility over the old age of the Good Man. They make the Evening of his days go down unclouded; and allow the

Stream of life, though fallen low, to run clear to the last drop.

Who would exchange these Consolations for the cold comfortless prospect of the Materilist? Even suppose it is an error, it is one which raises us above the bruits. It exalts and enobles our faculties, and the deception if it were one can do us no injury.

> Abigail Adams to John Adams, February 4, 1799. Adams Papers (microfilm), reel 393, Library of Congress.

I will not however complain. No man had ever more cause of Gratitude. In all the vicissitudes, terrors, vexations and perplexities and agitations of a long life of danger, a kind providence has preserved me to this advanced age [eighty-five—Ed.] in such a degree of health that I have rarely been incapable of business or study. I am not yet weary of life. I still enjoy it. When I cease to do so, I will pray to be discharged.

> John Adams to Louisa Catherine Adams, June 3, 1821. Ibid., reel 452.

I enjoy very good health and good spirits too, tho solitary; but it is good for man, especially an old man to be at times in solitude; it is the nurse of sense and reflection, and as I am drawing to the end of my career, it is salutary to think of a better state of existence and gradually to wean myself from the passing scenes of this bustling world.

> Charles Carroll of Carrollton to Mary Caton, April 26, 1816. Carroll Papers (microfilm), reel 3, Library of Congress.

The most undesirable of all things is a long life and there is nothing I have ever dreaded so much. Altho' subject to occasional indispositions my health is too good generally not to give me fear on that subject. I am weak indeed in body, able scarcely to walk into my garden without too much fatigue, but a ride of 6, 8, or 10 miles a day gives me none. Still however a start or stumble of my horse or some one of the accidents which constantly beset us, may cut short the thread of life and relieve me from the evils of dotage. Come when it will it will find me neither unready nor unwilling. [Jefferson was eighty-two—Ed.]

> Thomas Jefferson to Benjamin Waterhouse, January 8, 1825. Jefferson Papers, Library of Congress.

America

I always considered the settlement of America with Reverence and Wonder, as the Opening of a grand scene and design of Providence, for the Illumination of the Ignorant and the Emancipation of the slavish part of Mankind.

> John Adams, "Dissertation on the Canon and Feudal Law" (draft), February 1765. Butterfield, *Diary and Autobiography of John Adams*, 1:257.

The American Union will last as long as God pleases. It is the duty of every American Citizen to exert his utmost abilities and endeavours to preserve it as long as possible and to pray with submission to Providence "esto perpetua" [may it last forever—Ed.].

> John Adams to Charles Carroll, August 2, 1820. Adams Papers (microfilm), reel 124, Library of Congress.

I love and revere the memories of Huss Wickliff Luther Calvin Zwinglius Melancton and all the other reformers

how muchsoever I may differ from them all in many theological metaphysical & philosophical points. As you justly
observe, without their great exertions & severe sufferings
the USA had never existed.

John Adams to F. C. Schaeffer, November 25, 1821. Ibid.

Under the auspices and direction of Divine Providence,
your forefathers removed to the wilds and wilderness of
America. By their industry they made it a fruitful, and by
their virtue a happy country. And we should still have enjoyed the blessings of peace and plenty, if we had not forgotten the source from which those blessings flowed; and
permitted our country to be contaminated by the many
shameful vices which have prevailed among us.

John Jay, Address of the Convention of New York, 1776. Johnston,
Correspondence of Jay, 1:101.

I shall need, too, the favor of that Being in whose hands we
are, who led our fathers, as Israel of old, from their native
land and planted them in a country flowing with all the nec-
essaries and comforts of life; who has covered our infancy
with His providence and our riper years with His wisdom
and power, and to whose goodness I ask you to join in supplications with me that He will so enlighten the minds of
your servants, guide their councils, and prosper their measures that whatsoever they do shall result in your good, and
shall secure to you the peace, friendship, and approbation
of all nations.

Thomas Jefferson, Second Inaugural Address, March 4, 1805.
Richardson, *Messages and Papers of the Presidents*, 1:370.

The great Governor of the Universe has led us too long and
too far on the road to happiness and glory, to forsake us in
the midst of it.

George Washington to Benjamin Lincoln, June 29, 1788. Fitzpatrick, *Writings of Washington,* 30:11.

No People can be bound to acknowledge and adore the invisible hand, which conducts the Affairs of men more than the People of the United States. Every step, by which they have advanced to the character of an independent nation, seems to have been distinguished by some token of providential agency.

George Washington, First Inaugural Address, April 30, 1789. Ibid., 30:293.

American Revolution

The late revolution, my respected audience, in which we this day rejoice, is big with events, that are daily unfolding themselves, and pressing in thick succession, to the astonishment of a wondering world! It has been marked with the certain characteristics of a Divine over-ruling hand, in that it was brought about and perfected against all human reasoning, and apparently against all human hope. . . . Divine Providence, throughout the government of this world, appears to have impressed many great events with the undoubted evidence of his own almighty arm. He putteth down kingdoms, and He setteth up whom He pleaseth, and it has been literally verified in us, that "no king prevaileth by the power of his own strength."

Elias Boudinot, "Oration to the Society of the Cincinnati," July 4, 1793. Jane J. Boudinot, ed., *The Life, Public Services, Addresses, and Letters of Elias Boudinot* (New York: DaCapo Press, 1971), 361.

ALMIGHTY GOD himself will look down upon your righteous contest with gracious approbation. You will be a *"band of brothers,"* cemented by the dearest ties—and strengthened with inconceivable supplies of force and constancy, by that sympathetic ardor, which animates good men, confederated in a good cause. Your *honor* and *welfare* will be, as they now are, most intimately concerned; and besides—*you are assigned by divine providence*, in the appointed order of things, the *protectors of unborn ages*, whose *fate* depends upon your *virtue*.

> John Dickinson, *Letters from a Farmer in Pennsylvania to the Inhabitants of the British Colonies*. Paul H. Ford, ed., *The Writings of John Dickinson* (Philadelphia: Historical Society of Pennsylvania, 1895), 1:405.

The American Revolution was the grand operation, which seemed to be assigned by the Deity to the men of this age in our country.

> Patrick Henry to Henry Lee, June 27, 1795. Campbell, *Henry*.

If my endeavours to avert the evil, with which this country was threatned, by a deliberate plan of Tyranny, should be crowned with the success that is wished; the praise is due to the <u>Grand Architect</u> of the Universe who did not see fit to Suffer his Superstructures, and justice, to be subjected to the ambition of the princes of this World, or to the rod of oppression, in the hands of any power upon Earth.

> George Washington to Watson & Cassoul, August 10, 1782. Fitzpatrick, *Writings of Washington*, 24:497.

The man must be bad indeed, who can look upon the events of the American Revolution without feeling the warmest gratitude towards the great Author of the Universe whose

divine interposition was so frequently manifested in our behalf.

George Washington to Samuel Langdon, September 28, 1789. Ibid.,
30:416.

Upon the whole nothing appears to me more manifest than
that the separation of this country from Britain, has been of
God; for every step the British took to prevent, served to accelerate it, which has generally been the case when men
have undertaken to go in opposition to the course of Providence, and to make war with the nature of things.

John Witherspoon, "Sermon delivered at a Public Thanksgiving after
Peace," November 28, 1782. *Works of Witherspoon,* 3:79.

Animals

A story goes of our Universalist Murray.[4] It is said that more
than twenty years ago he preached upon the subject of Animals in a future State and asserted that they would all
be saved, even down to the Ladies Lapdogs. He told the
Ladies they need not fear the loss of their favourite animals,
for he could assure them that even Bounce should wag
his Tail in Glory. . . . Who knows but vegetables and animals
are all in a course to become rational and immortal. There is
room enough in the universe. . . . Why should we set limits
then to our benevolence, or the predominant benevolence in
the Universe. Let Sensibility, Animation, Intelligence, Virtue

[4] John Murray (1741–1815), the most influential preacher in the early
American republic of Universalism, which promised salvation to all, although the wicked must first be punished after death. *ANB.*

and Happiness be universal, with all my heart. Think not that I am laughing.

John Adams to Benjamin Rush, November 11, 1807. *Old Family Letters*, 171–72.

As "Dominion over the inferior Creatures" is *most certainly* vested in Man by THEIR KIND AND BENEVOLENT MAKER, it is *as certainly* the Duty of Man to exercise it *with gentleness* and *not in a tyrannical manner.* In the Laws, given to the *Jews,* and in other parts of The Scriptures, this Gentleness to inferior Creatures is expressly enjoined or recommended. . . . Some have been of Opinion, that when Man withdrew his Obedience from his Maker, other Animals withdrew from him that perfect Obedience which they had before rendered.

John Dickinson, *A Fragment* (Philadelphia: Thomas Dobson, 1796), 39.

I believe brutes have souls, but I *never* said nor *never* believed that they were immortal. Wiser and better men than I shall ever be have maintained the latter opinion. . . .

Benjamin Rush to Richard Peters, November 28, 1807. Butterfield, *Letters of Rush,* 2:957.

Atheism

Government has no Right to hurt a hair of the head of an Atheist for his Opinions. Let him have a care of his Practices.

John Adams to John Quincy Adams, June 16, 1816. Adams Papers (microfilm), reel 432, Library of Congress.

You strike at the Foundation of all Religion: For without the Belief of a Providence that takes Cognizance of, guards and guides and may favour particular Persons, there is no Motive to worship a Deity, to fear its Displeasure, or to pray for its Protection. . . . [W]ere you to succeed, do you imagine any Good would be done by it? You yourself may find it easy to live a virtuous Life without the assistance afforded by Religion; you having a clear Perception of the Advantages of Virtue and the Disadvantages of Vice, and possessing a Strength of Resolution sufficient to enable you to resist common Temptations. But think how great a Proportion of Mankind consists of weak and ignorant Men and Women, and of inexperienc'd and inconsiderate Youth of both Sexes, who have need of the Motives of Religion to restrain them from Vice, to support their Virtue, and to retain them in the practice of it till it becomes <u>habitual</u>, which is the great Point for its Security; and perhaps you are indebted to her originally that is to your Religious Education, for the Habits of Virtue upon which you now justly value yourself. You might easily display your excellent Talents of reasoning on a less hazardous Subject, and thereby obtain Rank with our most distinguish'd Authors. For among us, it is not necessary, as among the Hottentots that a Youth to be receiv'd into the Company of Men, should prove his Manhood by beating his Mother. I would advise you therefore not to attempt unchaining the Tyger, but to burn this Piece before it is seen by any other Person, whereby you will save yourself a great deal of Mortification from the Enemies it may raise against you, and perhaps a great deal of Regret and Repentance. If Men are so wicked as we now see them <u>with Religion</u> what would they be if <u>without it</u>.

Benjamin Franklin to ——, December 13, 1757. Labaree, *Papers of Benjamin Franklin*, 7:294–95.

Atheism is unknown there; Infidelity rare and secret; so that persons may live to a great Age in that Country, without having their Piety shocked by meeting with either an Atheist or an Infidel.

Benjamin Franklin, "Information to those who would remove to America," September [?], 1782. Smyth, *Writings of Franklin*, 8:613–14.

If we did a good act merely from the love of god, and a belief that it is pleasing to him, whence arises the morality of the Atheist? It is idle to say as some do, that no such being exists. We have the same evidence of the fact as of most of those we act on, to wit, their own affirmations, and their reasonings in support of them. I have observed indeed generally that, while in protestant countries the defections from the Platonic Christianity of the priests is to Deism, in Catholic countries they are to Atheism. Diderot, Dalembert, D'Holbach, Condorcet, are known to have been among the most virtuous of men. Their virtue then must have had some other foundation than the love of god.

Thomas Jefferson to Thomas Law, June 13, 1814. Adams, *Jefferson's Extracts*, 355–56.

Sailors, soldiers, Indians, nay more, Deists and Atheists, all pray by an unsubdued instinct of nature when in great danger or distress.

Benjamin Rush to John Adams, June 4, 1812. Butterfield, *Letters of Rush*, 2:1138.

Bible: Value of

The Bible contains the most profound Philosophy, the most perfect Morality, and the most refined Policy, that ever was conceived upon earth. It is the most Republican Book in the World, and therefore I will still revere it.

> John Adams to Benjamin Rush, February 2, 1807. *Old Family Letters,* 127–28.

. . . the Bible is the best book in the World. It contains more of my little Phylosophy than all the Libraries I have seen: and such Parts of it as I cannot reconcile to my little Phylosophy I postpone for further Investigation.

> John Adams to Thomas Jefferson, December 25, 1813, Cappon, *Adams-Jefferson Letters,* 2:412.

Must a man possess a Library equal to that mentioned by St. Luke which he says the whole world would not contain and live to the age of Methusalah before he could read half of it before he can work out his salvation with fear and trembling? I find in the old Testament and especially the new internal evidence of a philosophy a morality and a Polity which my head and heart embraces for its equity humanity and benevolence. This is my religion.

> John Adams to Adrian van der Kemp, January 23, 1813. Adams Papers (microfilm), reel 121, Library of Congress.

For near a half century, have I anxiously and critically stud ied that invaluable treasure; and I still scarcely ever take it up, that I do not find something new—that I do not receive some valuable addition to my stock of knowledge; or perceive some instructive fact, never observed before. In short, were you to ask me to recommend the most valuable book in the world, I should fix on the Bible as the most instructive, both to the wise and ignorant. Were you to ask me for one, affording the most rational and pleasing entertainment to the inquiring mind, I should repeat, it is the Bible; and should you renew the inquiry, for the best philosophy, or the most interesting history, I should still urge you to look into your Bible. I would make it, in short, the Alpha and Omega of knowledge.

Elias Boudinot, *The Age of Revelation* (Philadelphia: Asbury Dickins, 1801), xv.

"The Holy Scriptures are able to make us wise unto Salvation, through Faith which is in Jesus Christ." "All Scripture given by Inspiration of God is profitable for Doctrine, for Reproof, for Correction, for Instruction in Righteousness that the Man of God may be perfect, thoroughly furnished unto all good Works." The Scriptures give a full and ample testimony to all the principal Doctrines of the Christian Faith; and therefore no divine or inward Communication at this Day, however necessary, do or can contradict that testimony. They are the most excellent Writings in the world; therefore, very heavenly Writings and the use of them very conformable and necessary to the Church and We are bound to give Praise to God, for his wonderful Providence in preserving these Writings so pure and uncorrupted as We have them, to testify of his Truth even against those whom he made instrumental in preserving them.

John Dickinson, "Religious Instruction for Youth," undated. R. R. Logan Papers, Historical Society of Pennsylvania.

To qualify the apostles for their important task, they were blessed with the direction and guidance of the Holy

Spirit, and by him were enabled to preach the Gospel with concordant accuracy, and in divers languages: they were also endued with power to prove the truth of their doctrine, and of their authority to preach it, by wonderful and supernatural signs and miracles.

A merciful Providence also provided that some of these inspired men should commit to writing such accounts of the Gospel, and of their acts and proceedings in preaching it, as would constitute and establish a <u>standard</u> whereby future preachers and generations might ascertain what they ought to believe and to do; and be thereby secured against the danger of being misled by mistakes and corruptions incident to tradition. The Bible contains these writings, and exhibits such a connected series of the Divine revelations and dispensations respecting the present and future state of mankind, and so amply attested by internal and external evidence, that we have no reason to desire or expect that further miracles will be wrought to confirm the belief and confidence which they invite and require.

John Jay to the American Bible Society, May 12, 1825. Johnston, *Correspondence of Jay*, 4:503–4.

In like manner we daily read chapters in the Bible rich with divine truths without perceiving them. The next generation will probably perceive them and wonder at our blindness in not finding them out. "Each verse in the Bible," says Luther, "is a bush with a bird in it. But the bird will not fly from it till the bush is well beaten." I have been astonished to find how much justice there is in this observation. I never read a chapter in the Bible without seeing something in it I never saw before.

Benjamin Rush to Mary Stockton, September 7, 1788. Butterfield, *Letters of Rush*, 1:484.

By renouncing the Bible, philosophers swing from their moorings upon all moral subjects. Our Saviour in speaking of it calls it the "Truth" in the abstract. It is the only correct map of the human heart that ever has been published. It contains a faithful representation of all its follies, vices, and crimes. All systems of religion, morals, and government not founded upon it must perish, and how consoling the thought—it will not only survive the wreck of these systems but the world itself. "The Gates of Hell shall not prevail against it."

Benjamin Rush to John Adams, January 23, 1807. Ibid., 2:936.

Bible: Accuracy of the Text

What suspicions of interpolation, and indeed of fabrication, might not be confuted if we had the originals! In an age or in ages when fraud, forgery, and perjury were considered as lawful means of propagating truth by philosophers, legislators, and theologians, what may not be suspected?

John Adams, marginal note in John Disney's *Memoirs* (1785) of Arthur Sykes. Haraszti, *Prophets of Progress*, 296.

What do you call the "Bible?" The translation by King James the first. More than half a Catholick.[5] . . . "The Bible a Rule of Faith"! What Bible? King James's? The Hebrew?

---

[5] Adams's meaning is that in his opinion James I, after whom the King James Bible was named, was unduly sympathetic to the faith and practice of the Roman Catholic Church.

The Septuagint? The Vulgate? The Bible now translated or translating into Chinese, Indian, Negro and all the other Languages of Europe, Asia and Africa? Which of the thirty thousand variantia are the Rule of Faith?

John Adams to John Quincy Adams, March 28, 1816. Adams Papers (microfilm), reel 430, Library of Congress.

Did not the writers of the Gospels testify, by their whole conduct, that they were men of integrity, impartiality and virtue? Did they not teach and inculcate the most pure and strict morality ever taught to man, and that on pain of the utmost displeasure of Almighty God?

Some of these disciples who afterwards wrote the Gospels, were personally acquainted with Jesus Christ, attended him during his life, and were actually concerned in many of the events they relate. They were intimately acquainted with Joseph and Mary; and one of them took Mary to his own house after the crucifixion, at the request of his dying Lord, and she dwelt with him for fifteen years. The brothers and sisters of Jesus Christ after the flesh, were among his disciples, and several of them sealed their faith with their blood. If these circumstances did not constitute the Apostles the most proper historians to record the life, actions and doctrines of their master, and do not operate as a strong confirmation of the facts they relate, I know not what human testimony can amount to proof; neither can I see, what reason there can be, for giving credit to the most approved histories either of nations or individuals . . . .

These historians have given us the account of the birth of their Lord and master, not only as they received it from Joseph and Mary, but as they had it from him in his life time, as well as from the influence and direction of the holy spirit, with which they were so openly and publicly filled, in presence of so many witnesses. Besides it is acknowledged, that the morality they inculcate, is of the most pure and benevolent kind: and that to mislead their adherents and followers, by publishing untruths to ruin and deceive them, would have been contrary to every principle of morality and benevolence.

If you look through their whole history, every part of it bears the mark of truth and credibility. They urge in all their teachings, the strictest attention to truth, and threaten the severest displeasure of Almighty God against falsehood, dissimulation and hypocrisy.

> Elias Boudinot, *The Age of Revelation* (Philadelphia: Asbury Dickins, 1801), 56–60.

If memoirs written by men of good character, though personally unacquainted with the transactions they relate, and who did not exist till long after the times of which they write, are to receive credit in the world, what return ought our author[6] to meet with, for decrying those written by contemporaries—intimate friends—of the same family—parties to most of the transactions—their eternal all risqued on the truth of the facts—and under every possible advantage to know the truth—men of established moral characters—of devout lives, and who sacrificed their ease, comfort, fortune, and even life itself, in confirmation of the facts they relate . . . ?

Is it supposable that men of this character, should unite to hand down to posterity, with the most scrupulous and religious exactness, and from the very moment of the transactions, an account of facts and occurrences known even to themselves to be false, for no other end than to ruin themselves, and impose upon their fellow men.

> Ibid., 163–64.

---

[6] Thomas Paine. Boudinot intended his *The Age of Revelation* to be a refutation of Paine's *The Age of Reason*.

It is to be regretted but so I believe the fact to be, that except the Bible there is not a true history in the world.

John Jay to Jedidiah Morse, February 28, 1797. Johnston, *Correspondence of Jay*, 4:225.

Read the bible then, as you would read Livy or Tacitus. . . . For example in the book of Joshua we are told the sun stood still for several hours. Were we to read that fact in Livy or Tacitus we should class it with their showers of blood, speaking of statues, beasts &., but it is said that the writer of that book was inspired. Examine therefore candidly what evidence there is of his having been inspired. The pretension is entitled to your enquiry, because millions believe it. On the other hand you are Astronomer enough to know how contrary it is to the law of nature that a body revolving on it's axis, as the earth does, should have stopped, should not by that sudden stoppage have prostrated animals, trees, buildings, and should after a certain time have resumed it's revolution, and that without a second general prostration. Is this arrest of the earth's motion, or the evidence which affirms it, most within the law of probabilities?

Thomas Jefferson to Peter Carr, August 10, 1787. Boyd, *Papers of Thomas Jefferson*, 12:15–16.

We must reduce our volume to the simple evangelists, select, even from them the very words only of Jesus, paring off the Amphibologisms into which they have been led by forgetting often, or not understanding, what had fallen from him, by giving their own misconceptions as his dicta, and expressing unintelligibly for others what they had not understood themselves. There will be found remaining the most sublime and benevolent code of morals which has ever been offered to man. I have performed this operation for my own use, by cutting verse by verse out of the printed book, and arranging, the matter which is evidently his, and which is as easily distinguishable as diamonds in a dunghill.

Thomas Jefferson to John Adams, October 12, 1813. Cappon, *Adams-Jefferson Letters*, 2:384.

Nor did the question ever occur to me before Where get we the ten commandments? The book indeed gives them to us verbatim. But where did it get them? For itself tells us they were written by the finger of god on tables of stone, which were destroyed by Moses: it specifies those on the 2d. set of tables in different form and substance, but still without saying how the others were recovered. But the whole history of these books is so defective and doubtful that it seems vain to attempt minute enquiry into it: and such tricks have been plaid with their text, and with the texts of other books relating to them, that we have a right, from that cause, to entertain much doubt what parts of them are genuine. In the New testament there is internal evidence that parts of it have proceeded from an extraordinary man; and that other parts are the fabric of very inferior minds. It is as easy to separate those parts, as to pick out diamonds from dunghills. The matter of the first was such as would be preserved in the memory of the hearers, and handed on by tradition for a long time; the latter such stuff as might be gathered up, for imbedding it, any where, and at any time.

Thomas Jefferson to John Adams, January 24, 1814. Ibid., 2:421.

I believe in the truth of no history but in that which is contained in the Old and New Testaments.

Benjamin Rush to John Adams, October 17, 1809. Butterfield, *Letters of Rush*, 2:1021.

Bible: Exegesis of

And what has not been misunderstood or misrepresented? The spirit of God could not or would not dictate words that could not be misunderstood or perverted. Misinterpretations of the Scriptures of the old and new Testaments have founded Mosques and Cathedrals, have made saints Cardinals and Popes, Tyrants and Despots without Number, and deluged three quarters of the Globe I mean all Christian and Mahometan Countries at times in blood.

John Adams to Benjamin Rush, March 23, 1809. *Old Family Letters*, 226.

You have construed the word Logos to signify Power but Pythagoras has employed it to signify the Ideas, the Intellect and the Intelligence of God or the reason of God. However he taught that these ideas, this intellect, this intelligence of God, had Power over the forms inherent in Matter sufficient to arrange it into this grand and beautiful Universe. Plato took his Philosophy from Timeus so that I consider Pythagoras as the most ancient Greek Philosopher from whom we can trace the Athanasian Creed . . . . When the Pythagorician and Platonician Philonician Philosophers had once got the Word Logos into the Christian Religion they thought they might consistently or at least plausibly be converted to it and bring with them as many as they pleased of their own Philosophical or Sophistical notions.

John Adams to Andrew Norton, December 13, 1819, Adams Papers (microfilm), reel 124, Library of Congress.

I perfectly agree with you in the sentiment that our Business is to do our Duty and leave Events to him, without whose appointment and permission nothing comes to pass. That

Duty however appears to me to call particularly on all ministers of the Gospel to look more to the Author and Finisher of our Faith than to the Expositors of it; and disregarding the doubtful and mysterious doctrines by which the latter have divided Christians from Christians, to unite in defending the plain and intelligible faith delivered to us by our Redeemer and his apostles.

> John Jay to John Lathrop, March 3, 1801. Jay Papers (online edition), Columbia University Library.

. . . we know from the best Authority that all the Law and the Prophets hang upon these two commands to Love the Lord our God with all our Hearts and our Neighbors as ourselves.

A Cherokee Indian can give a clear and precise Answer to the first and the force and extent of the latter is impress'd upon the hearts of all who name the name of Jesus Christ and yet what Ship Loads of Paper is Blackened and with amazing Labor too, to darken and entangle both subjects. Thus it has been from the beginning of time, and thus it will continue unto the end.

> Henry Laurens to James Habersham, October 16, 1769. Rogers, *Papers of Henry Laurens*, 7:165–66.

His [Jesus'—Ed.] doctrine of the Cosmogony of the world is very clearly laid down in the 3 first verses of the 1st. chapter of John. . . .

Which truly translated means "in the beginning God existed, and reason (or mind) was with God, and that mind was God. This was in the beginning with God. All things were created by it, and without it was made not one thing which was made." Yet this text, so plainly declaring the doctrine of Jesus that the world was created by the supreme, intelligent being, has been perverted by modern Christians to

build up a second person of their tritheism by a mistransla-
tion of the word λογος [Logos—Ed.]. One of it's legitimate
meanings is indeed "a word." But, in that sense, it makes an
unmeaning jargon: while the other meaning "reason,"
equally legitimate, explains rationally the eternal preexis-
tence of God, and his creation of the world. Knowing how
incomprehensible it was that "a word," the mere action or
articulation of the voice and organs of speech could create a
world, they undertake to make of this articulation a second
preexisting being, and ascribe to him, and not to God, the
creation of the universe. The Atheist here plumes himself on
the uselessness of such a God, and the simpler hypothesis of
a self-existent universe. The truth is that the greatest enemies to the doctrines of Jesus are those calling themselves
the expositors of them, who have perverted them for the
structure of a system of fancy absolutely incomprehensible,
and without any foundation in his genuine words.

Thomas Jefferson to John Adams, April 11, 1823. Cappon, *Adams-
Jefferson Letters*, 2:593–94.

Bible: Old Testament

The greatest men of every age and nation since, whether
Jews, Christians or heathens, unite their testimony in favour
of Moses being the writer of these books, as the word of
God, and coming down from him; our Lord Jesus Christ
and his apostles add their attestation. The religious jealousy,
the known accuracy, indefatigable care, and curious precision of the Jews as a people, not to mention the separation

of the ten tribes by which a violent and lasting opposition and hatred arose between them, so that they became a
watch over each other, give peculiar and demonstrative
weight to the evidence, as far as it relates to these books
having been preserved and handed down to us without important alterations: and the experience of every serious and
attentive believer, in addition to the continued fulfilment of
the predictions contained in them even at this day; leaves
no reasonable doubt on their minds, with regard to their
truth and inspiration.

It is almost four thousand years since they have been
written; and never have they been denied to be the work of
Moses, as the word of God, till modern times. It is true, as
has been already observed, Aben Ezra, a Jew of considerable note, about the year 1200, first supposed that these
books had been written in the time of the kings; but then he
considered them as inspired writings, let who would be the
author of them, and received them as absolute verity. It
never entered into his head, to disbelieve the facts recorded
in them, or to doubt their being the word or commandments of God.

> Elias Boudinot, *The Age of Revelation* (Philadelphia: Asbury Dickins, 1801), 322.

The Scriptures of the Two Testaments speak in a familiar
and consonant manner of the one true God, of the Messiah
and of the Holy Spirit. The authorities being equal, we
ought in construing them, preserve that Harmony and not
raise up such a metaphysical civil war between them, that
men of common understanding and improvements may be
so perplexed, as not to know, whether they ought to take
side with the Old Testament or with the New Testament,
and at last from the doubtfulness of their Titles, fall into an
indifference and contempt for both of them.

John Dickinson, undated notes on religion. R. R. Logan Collection, Historical Society of Pennsylvania.

… you say you have never seen executed, a comparison of the morality of the old testament with that of the new. And yet no two things were ever more unlike.

Thomas Jefferson to John Adams, August 22, 1813. Cappon, *Adams-Jefferson Letters*, 2:368.

We are told, that there are many passages in the old testament, that are improper to be read by children, and that the greatest part of it is no way interesting to mankind under the present dispensation of the gospel. There are I grant, several chapters, and many verses in the old testament, which in their present unfortunate translation, should be passed over by children. But I deny that any of the books of the old testament are not interesting to mankind, under the gospel dispensation. Most of the characters, events, and ceremonies, mentioned in them, are personal, providential, or instituted types of the Messiah: All of which have been, or remain yet to be, fulfilled by him. It is from an ignorance or neglect of these types, that we have so many deists in christendom; for so irrefragably do they prove the truth of christianity, that I am sure a young man who had been regularly instructed in their meaning, could never doubt afterwards of the truth of any of its principles. If any obscurity appears in these principles, it is only (to use the words of the poet) because *they are dark, with excessive bright.*

Rush, *Essays: Literary, Moral, and Philosophical*, 60–61.

Bible: Revision of

It is now more than one hundred and seventy years since the translation of our common English Bible. The language in that time is much changed, and the style, being obsolete, and thence less agreeable, is perhaps one reason why the reading of that excellent book is of late so much neglected. I have therefore thought it would be well to procure a new version, in which, preserving the sense, the turn of phrase and manner of expression should be modern. I do not pretend to have the necessary abilities for such a work myself; I throw out the hint for the consideration of the learned; and only venture to send you a few verses of the first chapter of Job, which may serve as a sample of the kind of version I would recommend.

Old Text	New Version
Verse 6. Now there was a day when the sons of God came to present themselves before the Lord, and Satan came amongst them.	Verse 6. And it being *levee* day in heaven, all God's nobility came to court; to present themselves before him; and Satan also appeared in the circle, as one of the ministry.
7. And the Lord said unto Satan, Whence comest thou? Then Satan answered the Lord, and said, From going to and fro in the earth, and from walking up and down in it.	7. And God said to Satan, You have been some time absent: where were you? And Satan answered I have been at my country-seat, and in different places visiting my friends.

8. And the Lord said unto Satan, Hast thou considered my servant Job, that there is none like him in the earth, a perfect and upright man, one that feareth God and escheweth evil?

8. And God said, Well, what think you of Lord Job? You see he is my best friend, a perfectly honest man, full of respect for me, and avoiding every thing that might offend me.

9. Then Satan answered the Lord, and said, Doth Job feareth God for naught?

9. And Satan answered, Does your Majesty imagine that his good conduct is the effect of mere personal attachment and affection?

10. Hast thou not made an hedge about his house, and about all that he hath on every side? Thou hast blessed the work of his hands, and his substance is increased in the land.

10. Have you not protected him, and heaped your benefits upon him, till he is grown enormously rich?

11. But put forth thine hand now, and touch all that he hath, and he will curse thee to thy face.

11. Try him;—only withdraw your favor, turn him out of his places, and withhold his pensions, and you will soon find him in opposition.

Benjamin Franklin, Proposed New Version of the Bible, [1779?].
Smyth, *Writings of Franklin*, 7:432–33.

Calvinism

★

I must be a very unnatural Son to entertain any prejudices against Calvinists or Calvinism, according to your confession of faith: for my Father & Mother, my Uncles & Aunts, and all my predecessors from our common Ancestor who landed in this Country two hundred years ago, wanting five months were of that persuasion. Indeed I have never known any better people than the Calvinists. Nevertheless I must acknowledge that I can not class myself under that denomination. My opinions indeed on religious subjects ought not to be of any consequence to any but myself. To develop them and the reasons for them would require a Folio larger than Willard's body of divinity,[7] and after all I might scatter darkness rather than light.

> John Adams to Samuel Miller, July 8, 1820. Adams Papers (microfilm), reel 450, Library of Congress.

. . . Calvinism has introduced into the Christian religion more new absurdities than it's leader had purged it of old ones.

> Thomas Jefferson to Salma Hale, July 26, 1818. Adams, *Jefferson's Extracts*, 385.

I thank you, Sir, for the pamphlet you have been so kind as to send me on the reveries, not to say the insanities of Calvin and Hopkins;[8] yet the latter, I believe, is the proper

---

[7] Adams is referring to Samuel Willard's *A Compleat Body of Divinity* (Boston, 1726), a long and dense explication of the Westminster Confession, one of the classic theological statements of Calvinism.

[8] Samuel Hopkins (1721–1803), a New England Congregational minister, who propounded a form of ultra-Calvinism known as the New Divinity. *ANB*.

term. Mr. [John] Locke defines a madman to be one who has a kink in his head on some particular subject, which neither reason nor fact can untangle. Grant him that postulate, and he reasons as correctly as other men. This was the real condition of Calvin and Hopkins, on whom reasoning was wasted. The straight jacket alone was their proper remedy.

Thomas Jefferson to Thomas B. Parker, May 15, 1819. Ibid., 385–86.

I can never join Calvin in addressing *his god*. He was indeed an Atheist, which I can never be; or rather his religion was Daemonism. If ever man worshipped a false god, he did. The being described in his 5. points is not the God whom you and I acknolege and adore, the Creator and benevolent governor of the world; but a daemon of malignant spirit. It would be more pardonable to believe in no god at all, than to blaspheme him by the atrocious attributes of Calvin.

Thomas Jefferson to John Adams, April 11, 1823. Ibid., 410.

My belief in these doctrines is founded wholly upon the Calvanistical account (and which I believe to be agreeable to the tenor of the Scripture) of the person, power, goodness, mercy, and other divine attributes of the Saviour of the World.

Benjamin Rush to Richard Price, June 2, 1787. Butterfield, *Letters of Rush*, 1:419.

Calvinists do not found their faith on the authority of his [John Calvin's—Ed.] opinions, that would be to entertain an opinion contrary to his, viz., that the word of God is the only rule of faith in matters of religion.

Roger Sherman to Samuel Hopkins, June 28, 1790. American Antiquarian Society, *Proceedings* 5 (October 1887–October 1888): 444.

Catholicism

. . . the most refined, sublime, extensive, and astonishing constitution of policy, that ever was conceived by the mind of man, was framed by the *Romish* clergy for the aggrandisement of their own order. All the epithets I have here given to the Romish policy are just: and will be allowed to be so, when it is considered, that they even persuaded mankind to believe, faithfully and undoubtedly, that GOD almighty had intrusted *them* with the keys of heaven; whose gates *they* might open and close at pleasure—with a power of dispensation over all the rules and obligations of morality—with authority to license all sorts of sins and crimes—with a power of deposing princes, and absolving subjects from allegiance—with a power of procuring or withholding the rain of heaven and the beams of the sun—with the management of earthquakes, pestilence and famine. Nay with the mysterious, awful, incomprehensible power of creating out of bread and wine, the flesh and blood of God himself. All these opinions, they were enabled to spread and rivet among the people, by reducing their minds to a state of sordid ignorance and staring timidity; and by infusing into them a *religious* horror of letters and knowledge. Thus was human nature chained fast for ages, in a cruel, shameful and deplorable servitude, to him and his subordinate tyrants, who, it was foretold, would exalt himself above all that was called God, and that was worshipped.

John Adams, "A Dissertation on the Canon and Feudal Law," August 12, 1765. Taylor et al., *Papers of John Adams*, 1:112.

Indeed, Mr. Jefferson, what could be invented to debase the ancient Christianism, which Greeks Romans, Hebrews, and

Christian Factions, above all the Catholicks, have not frau-
dulently imposed upon the Publick? Miracles after Miracles
have rolled down in Torrents, Wave succeeding Wave, in
the Catholic Church from the Council of Nice, and long before, to this day.

> John Adams to Thomas Jefferson, December 3, 1813. Cappon,
> *Adams-Jefferson Letters*, 2:404.

I have long been decided in opinion that a free government
and the Roman Catholick religion can never exist together
in any nation or Country.

> John Adams to Thomas Jefferson, February 3, 1821. Ibid., 2:571.

Liberty and Popery cannot live together.

> John Adams to Louisa Catherine Adams, May 17, 1821. Adams
> Papers (microfilm), reel 451, Library of Congress.

Do not suppose that I am so void of Christian Charity, or so
ignorant of the Principles & practices of thousands of the
Roman Church, as to suppose that a Man may not, under
the influence of them, lead a life of holiness and devotion to
God—indeed may not arrive to the highest grade of Christian character. No, I am satisfied that the grace of God is not
confined to sect or party, but that every person of whatever
nation or language, that serveth God and worketh righteousness, is accepted of him for Christ's sake.

> Elias Boudinot to John Caldwell, May 2, 1790. Boudinot Papers,
> Princeton University Library.

I am a warm friend to Toleration. I execrate the intollerating
spirit of the Church of Rome, and of other Churches—for
she is not singular in that.

> Charles Carroll of Carrollton to William Graves, August 15, 1774.
> Ronald Hoffman et al., eds., *Dear Papa, Dear Charley* (Chapel Hill:
> University of North Carolina Press, 2001), 2:726.

. . . do not forsake the faith in which you have been educated. I am no bigot, and I have charity for all men: but if the Christian religion be true it can be but one: for if revealed of God, he could not reveal different and inconsistent doctrines and variant: now all the . . . reform Churches have varied and departed from the doctrine with which they set out. The Catholic Roman and Apostolic Church is the only one whose doctrine has been uniform from the origin. I do not say that some abuses may not have crept into the practice of that Church during the dark ages; but discipline and doctrine are two different things. I have said this much on this subject to induce you to study the grounds of the Catholic Faith, for I am persuaded from what I have heard occasionally dropped from you, that you are not well grounded in the principles of the Cath. or indeed of Christianity.

> Charles Carroll to Charles Carroll, Jr., December 13, 1801. Carroll Papers (microfilm), reel 2, Library of Congress.

Being persuaded that there can be but one true religion taught by Christ, and that the R[oman] C[atholic] is that religion, I conceive it to be my duty to have my grandchildren brought up in it. I feel no ill will or illiberal prejudices against sectarians which have adandon[ed] that faith: if their lives be conformable to the duties and morals prescribed by the Gospel, I have the charity to hope and believe they will be rewarded with eternal happiness, though they may entertain erroneous doctrines in point of faith.

> Charles Carroll to Harriet Carroll, August 29, 1816. Joseph Gurn, *Charles Carroll of Carrollton, 1737–1832* (New York: P. J. Kennedy & Sons, 1932), 191.

Our ancestors from Catholic became first Church of England men, and then refined into Presbyterians. To change

now from Presbyterianism to Popery seems to me refining
backwards, from white sugar to brown.

Benjamin Franklin to Jonathan Williams, April 13, 1785. Smyth,
Writings of Franklin, 9:303.

The Protestants have concurred in considering the Pope
as the great Antichrist mentioned in the Scriptures. It is said
there are many antichrists and he has been the most conspicuous among them.

John Jay to Jedidiah Morse, September 4, 1798. Jay Papers (online
edition), Columbia University Library.

As the Commander in Chief has been apprized of a design
form'd for the observance of that ridiculous and childish
custom of burning the Effigy of the pope[9]—He cannot help
expressing his surprise that there should be Officers and
Soldiers in this army so void of common sense, as not to
see the impropriety of such a step at this Juncture; at a Time
when we are solliciting, and have really obtain'd, the
friendship and alliance of the people of Canada, whom
we ought to consider as Brethren embarked in the same
Cause. The defence of the general Liberty of America: At
such a juncture, and in such Circumstances, to be insulting
their Religion, is so monstrous, as not to be suffered or ex-
cused; indeed instead of offering the most remote insult, it
is our duty to address public thanks to these our Brethren,
as to them we are so much indebted for every late happy
Success over the common Enemy in Canada.

George Washington, General Orders, November 5, 1775. Fitzpatrick,
Writings of Washington, 4:65.

[9] Especially in New England "Pope's Day" was celebrated on November
5 of each year, the anniversary of Guy Fawkes's attempt to blow up the English parliament in 1605; the populace indulged in various kinds of anti-
Catholic revelry and vandalism.

I presume that your fellow-citizens will not forget the patriotic part which you took in the accomplishment of their revolution and the establishment of their government; or the important assistance which they received from a nation in which the Roman Catholic religion is professed.

And may the members of your Society in America, animated alone by the pure spirit of Christianity, and still conducting themselves as the faithful subjects of our free government, enjoy every temporal and spiritual felicity.

> George Washington to American Roman Catholics, March 1790. Washington Papers, Library of Congress.

Catholicism: Jesuits

★

I do not like the late Resurrection of the Jesuits. They have a General, now in Russia, in correspondence with the Jesuits in the U.S. who are more numerous than every body knows. Shall We not have Swarms of them here? In as many shapes and disguises as ever a King of the Gypsies, Bamfield More Carew himself, assumed? In the shape of Printers, Editors, Writers School masters etc. I have lately read Pascalls Letters[10] over again, and four Volumes of the History of the Jesuits. If ever any Congregation of Men could merit, eternal Perdition on Earth and in Hell, According to these Histori-

---

[10] Blaise Pascal (1623–1662), French mathematician and religious writer, whose *Los Provinciales* (1657) was one of the most influential anti-Jesuit tracts ever written. *The New Encyclopaedia Britannica*, 15th ed. (Chicago: Encyclopaedia Britannica, Inc., 1979), 13:1041–43.

ans though like Pascal true Catholicks, it is this Company of Loiola [Ignatius Loyola—Ed.]. Our System however of Religious Liberty must afford them an Assylum. But if they do not put the Purity of our Elections to a severe Tryal, it will be a Wonder.

John Adams to Thomas Jefferson, May 6, 1816. Cappon, *Adams-Jefferson Letters*, 2:474.

I can not but concide with the Parlia[men]t: in Judging dangerous to the state a body of men who implicitly believe the dictates of one Superior, & are <u>carried on to the execution of his orders with a blind impetuosity of will & eagerness to obey without the least enquiry or examination.</u> Reason was not given to man merely to restrain his passions, or merely to regulate his own actions, but to weigh & examin wether the actions he is sollicited or commanded by others to perform, are such as can stand the scrutiny & sentence of an unerring, if unprejudiced, Judge. . . . No one has a greater regard for the Jesuits than myself; I revere the virtue, I esteem the learning, I respect the apostollic labours of individuals but am forced to acknowledge their institute & plan of government liable to great abuses: let it be granted, that no such abuses have yet crept into it, that its members are disinterested, unambitious, strict observers of their vow of poverty & that other vow, which secludes them from all worldly concerns, from power, from sway, from the intrigues of courts & ministerial influence. Abuses are easier to be prevented, than when once introduced, eradicated. I have said enough, perhaps too much on this subject.

Charles Carroll of Carrollton to Charles Carroll of Annapolis, October 22, 1761. Carroll Papers, Maryland Historical Society.

Chaplains

Is the appointment of Chaplains to the two Houses of Congress consistent with the Constitution, and with the pure principles of religious freedom?

In strictness the answer on both points must be in the negative. The Constitution of the U.S. forbids everything like an establishment of a national religion. The law appointing Chaplains establishes a religious worship for the national representatives, to be performed by Ministers of religion, elected by a majority of them; and these are to be paid out of national taxes. Does not this involve the principle of a national establishment, applicable to a provision for a religious worship for the Constituent as well as of the representative Body, approved by the majority, and conducted by Ministers of religion paid by the entire nation.

The establishment of the chaplainship to Congs is a palpable violation of equal rights, as well as of Constitutional principles: the tenets of the chaplains elected shut the door of worship agst the members whose creeds & consciences forbid a participation in that of the majority. To say nothing of other sects, this is the case with that of Roman Catholics & Quakers who have always had members in one or both of the Legislative branches. Could a Catholic clergyman ever hope to be appointed a Chaplain? To say that his religious principles are obnoxious or that his sect is small, is to lift the evil at once and exhibit in its naked deformity the doctrine that religious truth is to be tested by numbers, or that the major sects have a right to govern the minor.

If Religion consist in voluntary acts of individuals, singly, or voluntarily associated, and it be proper that public functionaries, as well as their Constituents shd discharge their religious duties, let them like their Constituents, do so at their own expense. How small a contribution from each member of Congs wd suffice for the purpose? How just wd it be in its principle? How noble in its exemplary sacrifice to the genius of the Constitution; and the divine right of conscience . . . ?

Better also to disarm in the same way, the precedent of Chaplainships for the army and navy than erect them into a political authority in matters of religion. The object of this establishment is seducing; the motive to it is laudable. But is it not safer to adhere to a right principle, and trust to its consequences, than confide in the reasoning however specious in favor of a wrong one.

James Madison, Detached Memoranda, [1819?]. Rakove, *Madison Writings*, 762–64.

I have long had it on my mind to mention to Congress, that frequent applications had been made to me respecting Chaplain's pay, which is too small to encourage men of Abilities. Some of them who have left their Flocks, are Obliged to pay the parson acting for them more than they receive. I need not point out the great utility of Gentlemen whose lives and conversation are unexceptionable, being employed for that service in this Army. There are two ways of making it worth the Attention of such; one is, an advancement of their pay, the other, that one Chaplain be appointed to two regiments; this last I think may be done without Inconvenience.

George Washington to the President of Congress, December 31, 1775. Fitzpatrick, *Writings of Washington*, 4:197–98.

Children

Great learning and superior abilities, should you ever posses them, will be of little value and small Estimation, unless Virtue, Honour, Truth and integrety are added to them. Adhere to those religious Sentiments and principals which were early instilled into your mind and remember that you are accountable to your Maker for all your words and actions. Let me injoin it upon you to attend constantly and steadfastly to the precepts and instructions of your Father as you value the happiness of your Mother and your own welfare. His care and attention to you render many things unnecessary for me to write which I might otherways do, but the inadvertency and Heedlessness of youth, requires line upon line and precept upon precept, and when inforced by the joint efforts of both parents will I hope have a due influence upon your Conduct, for dear as you are to me, I had much rather you should have found your Grave in the ocean you have crossd, or any untimely death crop you in your Infant years, rather than see you an immoral profligate or a Graceless child.

> Abigail Adams to John Quincy Adams, June [10?], 1778, Butterfield, *Adams Family Correspondence*, 3:37.

John has Genius and so has Charles. Take care that they dont go astray. Cultivate their Minds, inspire their little Hearts, raise their Wishes. Fix their Attention upon great and glorious Objects, root out every little Thing, weed out every Meanness, make them great and manly. Teach them to scorn Injustice, Ingratitude, Cowardice, and Falshood. Let them revere nothing but Religion, Morality and Liberty.

> John Adams to Abigail Adams, April 15, 1776. Ibid., 1:384.

When will men be convinced that the Universe is too large and too old for Sparrows Wrens and Humbirds to comprehend its Cause its Author its Original, its Evil, its Liberty and Necessity: And that their Duties are contained in a narrow compass obvious and easily understood.

> John Adams to John Quincy Adams, June 16, 1816. Adams Papers (microfilm), reel 432, Library of Congress.

This Year compleats a Century since my Uncle Boylston introduced the practice of Inoculation into the English Dominions; but what improvements have been made since 1720, partly by experience, but much more by the accidental discovery of Dr. Jenner. The history of this Distemper is enough to humble human pride! Enough to demonstrate what ignorant Puppets we are! How we grope in the Dark! And what empty Phantoms we chase! You are not singular in your suspicions that you know but little. The longer I live, the more I read, the more patiently I think, and the more anxiously I inquire, the less I seem to know. Why should the "Vaccine" have been concealed from all Eternity and then instantaneously revealed? Why should the material World have slept in Non Entity from Eternity, and then created or awakened into Existence. Worm! Ask no such question! Do justly: Love Mercy Walk humbly: This is enough for you to know and to do. The World is a better one than you deserve; strive to make yourself more worthy of it.

> John Adams to Caroline de Windt (granddaughter), January 24, 1820. Ibid., reel 124.

My child you may search forever the depths of this science [metaphysics—Ed.] and you will never find a bottom. The secrets of eternal wisdom are not to be fathomed by our narrow understandings.

> John Adams to George Washington Adams (grandson), February 10, 1822. Ibid., reel 454.

Remember then, and oh! let me repeat it over and over again my beloved Child; and may you never forget it one Moment of your Life, that you was most solemnly and sincerely devoted to God in Jesus Christ, before you was born. That as solemnly and sincerely, you have been given up to him, a thousand Times since, by the most express declarations and Covenants, that Flesh and Blood could devise. Our baptismal Vows for you were public and formal, and they have been daily renewed before God, from that day to this.

These indeed have been the Acts of your Parents, between God and them on your Behalf, but it will avail but little as to you, if they are not confirmed and ratified by your express assent and voluntary renewal, now you have come to the Years of Maturity. What will it avail you, that your parents have delivered their own Souls, if those Obligations should add weight, aggravated weight, to your Condemnation, in case you should now neglect to bind your own Soul, forever to the Lords. Be not surprised, my dearest Child, that having given you a temporal Being, we labour as it were a second Time in Birth for you, that you be born again in Christ Jesus. It can no otherwise be a real Happiness to us, that we have been you parents in the flesh, than as it shall be the means of raising you to a spiritual Life, and giving you an interest in that blessed Redeemer, who has brought Life and Immortality to light thro' the Gospel.

We call God to witness for us, this Day, that we have not failed to give you the Knowledge of God, as it is in Jesus Christ, that we have been instant in season and out of season, by Reproofs, Exhortations, Example and Warnings, labouring that Jesus Christ might be formed within you, your and our hope of Glory.

The Application and Improvement must remain (under God) with you. We have set before you times without number, the awful State you are in by Nature, as well as the glorious Benefits and Effects of redeeming Love. We have endeavoured to convince you of the propriety, as well as necessity, of giving yourself to God, a living Sacrifice holy and acceptable, which was but your reasonable Service, and that the foundation of everlasting Happiness hereafter, must be laid in Holiness of Life here.

Elias Boudinot to Susan Boudinot, October 3, 1784. Boudinot Papers, Princeton University Library.

Remember your God. The fear of the Lord, says the wise man is the beginning of wisdom; without virtue there can be no happiness, and without religion no virtue: consider yourself as always in the presence of the Almighty; if this sentiment be strong and vivid you will never sin, or commit any action you would be ashamed to commit before man.

Charles Carroll of Carrollton to Charles Carroll, Jr., January 30, 1801. Carroll Papers (microfilm), reel 2, Library of Congress.

I hope we have been faithful to parental obligation in the education of our dear children; and there is a promise, that the fruits will be acceptable. That they may be is my allmost ceaseless prayer. My best love to them. Assure them once more that they must every day of their whole lives be constant in the practice of reading at least two chapters in the New Testament and of offering their prayers. If they neglect either of these duties, tell them from their aged parent that—The Time will come—when they will grieve for the omission. They know the earnestness with which I have en joined these things, ever since they have arrived at the age of discretion.

John Dickinson to Mary Dickinson, November 25, 1797. Loudoun Papers, Historical Society of Pennsylvania.

Your aunt informs me that you are learning to write and has sent me one of your Copies which is very well done. I hope you will have so far advanced by the time that this Letter arrives, as to be able to read it. She also tells me that you love your Books, and that you daily read in the Bible and have learned by Heart some Hymns in the Book I sent you. These Accounts give me great pleasure, and I love you for being such a good Boy. The Bible is the best of all Books, for it is the Word of God, and teaches us the way to be happy in this world and in the next. Continue therefore to read it, and to regulate your life by its precepts.

> John Jay to Peter Jay, April 8, 1784. Jay Papers (online edition), Columbia University Library.

Now is the time for you to lay the foundations of your future characters. Virtue and Religion must be the corner stones and if with these you connect useful knowledge, mildness of temper and prudence and good manners, you will not only have great reason to expect happiness here, but what is of more importance be certain of it hereafter. After a few years we must all quit this world but in the next we are to abide forever.

> John Jay to Maria and Ann Jay, June 1, 1792. Ibid.

I hope you will have good sense enough to disregard those foolish predictions that the world is to be at an end soon. The almighty has never made known to any body at what time he created it, nor will he tell any body when he means to put an end to it, if ever he means to do it. As to preparations for that event, the best way is for you to be always prepared for it. The only way to be so is never to do nor say a bad thing. If ever you are about to say any thing amiss or to do any thing wrong, consider before hand. You will feel something within you which will tell you it is wrong and ought not to be said or done: this is your conscience, and be sure to obey it. Our maker has given us all, this faithful internal Monitor, and if you always obey it, you will always be prepared for the end of the world: or for a much more certain event which is death. This must happen to all: it puts an end to the world as to us, and the way to be ready for it is never to do a wrong act.

Thomas Jefferson to Martha Jefferson, December 11, 1783. Boyd, *Papers of Thomas Jefferson*, 6:380–81.

Your affectionate mother requests that I would address to you, as a namesake, something which might have a favorable influence on the course of the life you have to run. Few words are necessary with good dispositions on your part. Adore God. Reverence and cherish your parents. Love your neighbor as yourself; and your country more than life. Be just. Be true. Murmur not at the ways of providence and the life into which you have entered will be a passage to one of eternal and ineffable bliss. And if to the dead it is permitted to care for the things of this world, every action of your life will be under my regard.

Thomas Jefferson to Thomas Jefferson Grotjan, January 10, 1824. Jefferson Papers, Library of Congress.

Don't neglect my request that your Brother should daily read the Bible & be so often exercised in the Catechism of the Church of England as to get it perfectly by Heart. . . . Gracious God! Paul may Plant. Apollos may Water, but thou alone cans't give the Increase. Thy will be done.

Henry Laurens to John Laurens, July 1, 1772. Rogers, *Papers of Henry Laurens*, 8:389.

Put your whole trust in God. Resign yourself to his Will. Act well your part in Life and be not afraid of any thing that

Man can do to hurt you. The greatest Evils in this Life are comparatively but of Short continuance, a good Conscience will carry a Man of Spirit chearfully through and give him the inexpressible Satisfaction of dying in full hope and prospect of being for ever happy in the presence of his Creator. And even in this Life, Comforts and Consolations are the attendants of Virtue and rectitude of manners.

"I have been Young and now am Old yet have I not Seen the Righteous forsaken, nor his Seed begging Bread."

These were the words of King David, a Man of great experience, and his pious observation has been Since confirmed by the experience of almost every Man who has attended to the course of Gods providence. You will find these words in the 37th Psalm in the Bible version, read that Psalm over and get the whole of it by heart, and repeat it to your Uncle when you meet. The Salutary admonitions and encouragements, to patience and affiance in God Almighty contained in that divine Song, will Sustain your Spirit in Some future hour of tribulation—for such you must look for and expect, no Man can pass through this Life in perfect peace and felicity—this is not even to be hoped for, by Men, who are "born to trouble as the Sparks fly upward."

Henry Laurens to James Laurens, May 24, 1775. Ibid., 10:140.

The late bereaving stroke of divine Providence in our family [the death of Sherman's son, William—Ed.] is very afflicting to me. . . . It is my earnest prayer that this Providence may be suitably regarded by me and all the family and especially the surviving children of our family and his child, that they may be excited to be always in an actual readiness for death. Our children have all been brought up under the bond of the covenant of baptism, but those of them who are come to years of discretion should consider that it is indispensably necessary for them to give their cordial consent to the covenant of grace and that it is their duty to make a public profession of religion and attend all the ordinances of the gospel and in order to understand how this should be done in a proper manner they should search the scripture and attend all the public preaching. The sermon that I agreed with Mr. Moses to print will give much light on that subject.

> Roger Sherman to Rebecca Sherman, January 29, 1789. Sherman Papers, Yale University Library.

Christianity

However we may live there is not any religion by which we can die but the Christian which gives us the glorious prospect of life eternal. If says the Apostle in this Life only we have hope; we are of all men the most miserable.

> Religion! Providence! an after state!
> Here is firm footing: here is solid rock
> This can support us
> His hand the good man fastens on the skies
> And bids earth roll nor feels her idle whirl.

> Abigail Adams to John Quincy Adams, January 26, 1811. Adams Papers (microfilm), reel 411, Library of Congress.

Every tyro knows that heathen philosophy and Jewish ceremonies have been intermixed with Christianity. But what then? If Christianity has been corrupted? What then? What has not?

John Adams, marginal note on Bolingbroke's essay, "Concerning Authority in Matters of Religion," n.d. Haraszti, *Prophets of Progress*, 70.

My religion you know is not exactly conformable to that of the greatest part of the Christian World. It excludes superstition. But with all the superstition that attends it, I think the Christian the best that is or has been.

John Adams to Abigail Adams, January 28, 1799. Adams Papers (online edition), Massachusetts Historical Society.

The Christian Religion was intended to give Peace of Mind to its Disciples in all cases whatsoever: but not to send civil or political Peace upon earth but a sword, and a sword it has sent: and peace of Mind too to Millions, by conquering death and taking away his sting.

John Adams to Benjamin Rush, November 29, 1812. *Old Family Letters*, 320.

In the heavenly doctrines of Christianity, reduced to its primitive simplicity, you and I agree as well, I believe, as any two christians in the world.

John Adams to Francis van der Kemp, October 4, 1813. Adams Papers (microfilm), reel 95, Library of Congress.

The Christian is the religion of the heart: but the heart is deceitful above all things; and unless controuled by the dominion of the head will lead us into Salt Ponds.

John Adams to Benjamin Waterhouse, December 19, 1815. Ibid., reel 122.

Christianity is an active, affectionate and social religion, chiefly consisting in a discharge of duties to our fellow creatures. It therefore requires no separation from them. Tho enjoining that we "be not conformed to the world," in following this direction, the utmost attention is necessary lest distinctions from others by plainness of manners and customs assume the place of virtues, and become snares. Such distinctions are not in the least value in themselves because they are no part of the Divine Laws.

> John Dickinson, "Religious Instruction for Youth," undated.
> R. R. Logan Papers, Historical Society of Pennsylvania.

History will also afford frequent Opportunities of showing . . . the Excellency of the CHRISTIAN RELIGION above all others antient or modern.

> Benjamin Franklin, "Proposals Relating to the Education of Youth in Pennsylvania," 1749. Labaree, *Papers of Benjamin Franklin*, 3:413.

Amongst other strange things said of me, I hear it is said by the deists that I am one of the number; and, indeed, that some good people think I am no christian. This thought gives me much more pain than the appellation of tory; because I think religion of infinitely higher importance than politics; and I find much cause to reproach myself, that I have lived so long, and have given no decided and public proofs of my being a christian. But, indeed, my dear child, this is a character which I prize far above all this world has or can boast.

> Patrick Henry to Betsy Aylett, August 20, 1796. William Wirt, *The Life of Patrick Henry* (New York: M'Elrath & Bangs, 1831), 402–3.

I have long been of opinion that the Evidence of the Truth of Christianity requires only to be carefully examined to produce conviction in candid minds.

> John Jay to Uzal Ogden, February 14, 1796. Jay Papers (online edition), Columbia University Library.

One of them [a French philosopher—Ed.] asked me if I believed in Christ. I answered that I did, and that I thanked God that I did. Nothing further passed between me and them or any of them on that subject.

John Jay to John Bristed, April 23, 1811. Ibid.

I am a *real Christian*, that is to say, a disciple of the doctrines of Jesus, very different from the Platonists, who call *me* infidel, and *themselves* Christians and preachers of the gospel, while they draw all their characteristic dogmas from what it's Author never said nor saw. They have compounded from the heathen mysteries a system beyond the comprehension of man, of which the great reformer of the vicious ethics and deism of the Jews, were he to return on earth, would not recognise one feature.

Thomas Jefferson to Charles Thomson, January 9, 1816. Adams, *Jefferson's Extracts*, 365.

Our saviour did not come into the world to save metaphysicians only. His doctrines are levelled to the simplest understandings and it is only by banishing Hierophantic mysteries and Scholastic subtleties, which they have nick-named Christianity, and getting back to the plain and unsophisticated precepts of Christ, that we become <u>real</u> Christians.

Thomas Jefferson to Salma Hale, July 26, 1818. Ibid., 385.

Had the doctrines of Jesus been preached always as purely as they came from his lips, the whole civilised world would now have been Christian.

Thomas Jefferson to Benjamin Waterhouse, June 26, 1822. Ibid., 405.

I am looking with anxiety to see the dawn of primitive Christianity here, where, if it once appears, it will soon beam like the rising sun and restore reason to her day! "Thy kingdom come" is therefore my prayer; and my confidence is that it will come.

Thomas Jefferson to Benjamin Waterhouse, October 15, 1822. Jefferson Papers, Library of Congress.

The best & purest religion, the Christian Religion itself.

James Madison to Jasper Adams, September 1833. Dreisbach, *Religion and Politics*, 117.

. . . christianity is the only true and perfect religion, and that in proportion as mankind adopts its principles, and obeys its precepts, they will be wise, and happy.

Benjamin Rush, "A Defense of the Use of the Bible as a School Book." Rush, *Essays: Literary, Moral, and Philosophical*, 55.

In spreading the blessings of liberty and religion, our Divine Master forbids us, in many of his parables and precepts, to have either friends or country. The globe is the native country, and the whole human race the fellow citizens of a Christian.

Benjamin Rush to Granville Sharp, August 1791. Butterfield, *Letters of Rush*, 1:609.

Christianity: Christian Nation

A veneration for the religion of a people who profess and call themselves Christians, and a fixed resolution to consider a decent respect for Christianity among the best recommendations for the public service.

John Adams, Inaugural Address, March 4, 1797. Richardson, *Messages and Papers of the Presidents*, 1:222.

Providence has given to our people the choice of their rulers, and it is the duty as well as the privilege and interest of our Christian nation to select and prefer Christians for their rulers.

John Jay to John Murray, Jr., October 12, 1816. Johnston, *Correspondence of Jay*, 4:393.

Whether our religion permits <u>Christians</u> to vote for <u>infidel</u> rulers, is a question which merits more consideration than it seems yet to have generally received, either from the clergy or the laity. It appears to me, that what the prophet said to Jehoshaphat about his attachment to Ahab affords a salutary lesson. . . . *

*"Shouldest thou help the ungodly, and love them that hate the Lord?" 2 *Chron.* xix, 2.

John Jay to Jedidiah Morse, January 1, 1813. Ibid., 4:365.

Church and State

New England has in many Respects the Advantage of every other Colony in America, and indeed of every other Part of the World, that I know any Thing of . . . . The Institutions in New England for the Support of Religion, Morals and Decency, exceed any other, obliging every Parish to have a Minister, and every Person to go to Meeting.

John Adams to Abigail Adams, October 29, 1775. Butterfield, *Adams Family Correspondence*, 1:318–19.

Religion and Government are certainly very different Things, instituted for different Ends; the design of one being to promote our temporal Happiness; the design of the other to procure the Favour of God, and thereby the Salvation of our Souls. While these are kept distinct and apart, the Peace and welfare of Society is preserved, and the Ends of both are answered. By mixing them together, feuds, animosities and persecutions have been raised, which have deluged the World in Blood, and disgraced human Nature.

> John Dickinson, writing over the signature "A.B." *Pennsylvania Journal*, May 12, 1768.

. . . that the impious presumption of legislators and rulers, civil as well as ecclesiastical, who, being themselves but fallible and uninspired men, have assumed dominion over the faith of others, setting up their own opinions and modes of thinking as the only true and infallible, and as such endeavoring to impose them on others, hath established and maintained false religions over the greatest part of the world and through all time: That to compel a man to furnish contributions of money for the propagation of opinions which he disbelieves and abhors, is sinful and tyrannical . . . that the opinions of men are not the object of civil government, nor under its jurisdiction; that to suffer the civil magistrate to intrude his powers into the field of opinion and to restrain the profession or propagation of principles on the supposition of their ill tendency is a dangerous falacy, which at once destroys all religious liberty . . . that it is time enough for the rightful purposes of civil government for its officers to interfere when principles break out into overt acts against peace and good order.

> Thomas Jefferson, "A Bill for Establishing Religious Freedom," 1777. Boyd, *Papers of Thomas Jefferson*, 2:545–46.

The legitimate powers of government extend to such acts only as are injurious to others. But it does me no injury for my neighbour to say there are twenty gods, or no god. It neither picks my pocket nor breaks my leg . . . . It is error alone which needs the support of government. Truth can stand by itself . . . . Subject opinion to coercion: whom will you make your inquisitors? Fallible men; men governed by bad passions, by private as well as public reasons. And why subject it to coercion? To produce uniformity. But is uniformity desireable? No more than face and stature. . . . Is uniformity attainable? Millions of innocent men, women, and children, since the introduction of Christianity, have been burnt, tortured, fined, imprisoned: yet we have not advanced one inch towards uniformity.

> Thomas Jefferson, *Notes on the State of Virginia*, 1781. Peden, *Notes on Virginia*, 159–60.

I contemplate with sovereign reverence that act of the whole American people which declared that <u>their</u> legislature should make no law respecting an establishment of religion, or prohibiting the free exercise thereof, thus building a wall of eternal[11] separation between church and state.

> Thomas Jefferson, draft letter to the Danbury Baptist Association, January 1, 1802. Jefferson Papers, Library of Congress.

In matters of religion, I have considered that its free exercise is placed by the constitution independent of the powers of the general government. I have therefore undertaken, on no occasion, to prescribe the religious exercises suited to it; but have left them, as the constitution found them, under the direction and discipline of state or church authorities acknowledged by the several religious societies.

> Thomas Jefferson, Second Inaugural Address, March 4, 1805. Paul

---

[11] The adjective eternal was deleted in Jefferson's final version of his letter to the Danbury Baptists as were several other phrases. For a careful study of the composition of this famous letter, see Daniel Dreisbach, *Thomas Jefferson and the Wall of Separation between Church and State* (New York: New York University Press, 2002), 30–49.

Leicester Ford, ed., *The Works of Thomas Jefferson*, 12 vols. (New York: G. P. Putnam's Sons, 1904–05), 10:131.

We maintain therefore that in matters of Religion, no mans right is abridged by the institution of Civil Society and that Religion is wholly exempt from its cognizance. . . .

The Bill implies either that the Civil Magistrate is a competent Judge of Religious Truth; or that he may employ Religion as an engine of Civil policy. The first is an arrogant pretension falsified by the contradictory opinions of Rulers in all ages, and throughout the world: the second an unhallowed perversion of the means of salvation. . . .

To say that . . . is a contradiction to the Christian Religion itself, for every page of it disavows a dependence on the powers of this world: it is a contradiction to fact; for it is known that this Religion both existed and flourished, not only without the support of human laws, but in spite of every opposition from them, and not only during the period of miraculous aid, but long after it had been left to its own evidence and the ordinary care of Providence. . . .

During almost fifteen centuries has the legal establishment of Christianity been on trial. What have been its fruits? More or less in all places pride and indolence in the Clergy, ignorance and servility in the laity, in both, superstition, bigotry and persecution. Enquire of the Teachers of Christianity for the ages in which it appeared in its greatest lustre; those of every sect, point to the ages prior to its incorporation with Civil policy.

James Madison, "Memorial and Remonstrance against Religious Assessments," June 20, 1785. Rakove, *Madison Writings*, 30–33.

There remains in others [American states—Ed.] a strong bias towards the old error, that without some sort of alliance or coalition between Govt. & religion neither can be duly supported. Such indeed is the tendency to such a coalition, and such is the corrupting influence on both parties, that the danger cannot be too carefully guarded ag[ain]st. . . . Every new & successful example therefore of a perfect separation between ecclesiastical and civil matters, is of importance. And I have no doubt that every new example, will succeed, as every past one has done, in shewing that religion & Govt. will both exist in greater purity, the less they are mixed together. . . . I cannot speak particularly of any of the cases excepting that of Virg[ini]a where it is impossible to deny that Religion prevails with more zeal, and a more exemplary priesthood than it ever did when established and patronised by Public authority. We are teaching the world the great truth that Govts. do better without Kings & Nobles than with them. The merit will be doubled by the other lesson that Religion flourishes in greater purity, without than with the aid of Govt.

James Madison to Edward Livingston, July 10, 1822. Ibid., 788–89.

I must admit, moreover, that it may not be easy, in every possible case, to trace the line of separation, between the rights of Religion & the Civil authority, with such distinctness, as to avoid collisions & doubts on unessential points. The tendency to a usurpation on one side, or the other, or to a corrupting coalition or alliance between them, will be best guarded against by an entire abstinence of the Government from interference, in any way whatever, beyond the necessity of preserving public order, & protecting each sect against trespasses on its legal rights by others.

James Madison to Jasper Adams, September 1833. Dreisbach, *Religion and Politics*, 120.

In the United States we view your religious establishment with horror, and the man who would attempt to defend it publicly or privately would be consigned to a physician, instead of a casuist or politician, to be cured of his error.

Benjamin Rush to Richard Price, April 24, 1790. Butterfield, *Letters of Rush*, 1:564.

Were it possible for St. Paul to rise from his grave at the present juncture, he would say to the clergy who are now so active in settling the political affairs of the world: "Cease from your political labors—your kingdom is not of <u>this</u> world. Read my Epistles. In no part of them will you perceive me aiming to depose a pagan emperor or to place a Christian upon a throne. Christianity disdains to receive support from human governments. From this it derives its preeminence over all the religions that ever have or ever shall exist in the world. Human governments may receive support from Christianity, but it must be only from the love of justice and peace which it is calculated to produce in the minds of men. By promoting these and all other Christian virtues by your precepts and examples, you will much sooner overthrow errors of all kinds and establish our pure and holy religion in the world than by aiming to produce by your preaching or pamphlets any change in the political state of mankind."

A certain Dr. Owens, an eminent minister of the Gospel among the dissenters in England, and a sincere friend of liberty, was once complained of by one of Cromwell's time serving priests, "that he did not preach to the *times*." "My business and duty," said the disciple of St. Paul, "is to preach to *Eternity*, not to the times."

Benjamin Rush to Thomas Jefferson, October 6, 1800. Ibid., 2:824.

Clergy

I rejoice in a preacher who has some warmth, some energy, some feeling. Deliver me from your cold phlegmatick Preachers, Politicians, Friends, Lovers and Husbands. I thank Heaven I am not so constituted my-self and so connected.

> Abigail Adams to John Adams, August 5, 1776. Butterfield, *Adams Family Correspondence*, 2:79.

My Friend, the Clergy have been in all ages and Countries as dangerous to Liberty as the Army. Yet I love the Clergy and the Army. What can we do without them in this wicked world.

> John Adams to Benjamin Rush, September 1, 1809. *Old Family Letters*, 240.

Was there ever a country, in which philosophers, politicians, and theologians believed what they taught to the vulgar?

> John Adams, marginal note in Joseph Priestley's *The Doctrines of Heathen Philosophy Compared with those of Revelation*. Haraszti, *Prophets of Progress*, 290.

All religions have something good in them: but the Ambition and Avarice of Priests and Politicians have introduced into all of them, monstrous Corruptions and Abuses, and into none more cruel bloody and horrible than into the Christian.

> John Adams to John Quincy Adams, May 10, 1816. Adams Papers (microfilm), reel 431, Library of Congress.

I have wished, among other improvements in Theological Studies, a professorship of Common Sense and Prudence was established in our Seminaries. I really have known so many ruinous Errors in practice, among our pious and zealous Ministers, for want of this celestial quality, that I am sure it is of more importance than is generally believed.

Elias Boudinot to Edward Griffin, October 24, 1809. Boudinot Papers, Princeton University Library.

I wish we had never sent for a priest: they are troublesome animals in a family and occasion many chops and changes.

Charles Carroll of Carrollton to Charles Carroll of Annapolis, October 30, 1769. Carroll Papers, Maryland Historical Society.

It is not more lamentable, than true, that the Clergy of all denominations, and in every Age, have discovered a Fondness for Power, and have seldom been scrupulous about the means of procuring it: nor have they used it with Moderation, when obtained.

John Dickinson, writing over the signature of "A.B." *Pennsylvania Journal*, April 28, 1768.

Yet I do not mean that you shou'd despise Sermons even of the Preachers you dislike, for the Discourse is often much better than the man, as sweet and clear Waters come to us thro' very dirty Earth.

Benjamin Franklin to Sally Franklin, November 8, 1764. Labaree, *Papers of Benjamin Franklin*, 11:450.

I rather approv'd his giving us good Sermons compos'd by others, than bad ones of his own Manufacture; tho' the latter was the Practice of our common Teachers.

Benjamin Franklin, *Autobiography*, post-1788. Labaree, *Autobiography of Franklin*, 168.

Altho' the mere <u>expediency</u> of public measures may not be a proper subject for the pulpit, yet, in my opinion, it is the right and duty of our pastors to press the observance of all moral and religious duties, and to animadvert on every course of conduct which may be repugnant to them.

John Jay to Jedidiah Morse, January 1, 1813. Johnston, *Correspondence of Jay*, 4:365–66.

. . . but a short time elapsed after the death of the great reformer of the Jewish religion [Jesus Christ—Ed.] before his principles were departed from by those who professed to be his special servants, and perverted into an engine for enslaving mankind, and aggrandizing their oppressors in church and state: that the purest system of morals ever before preached to man has been adulterated and sophisticated, by artificial constructions, into a mere contrivance to filch wealth and power to themselves, that rational men not being able to swallow their impious heresies, in order to force them down their throats, they raise the hue and cry of infidelity, while themselves are the greatest obstacles to the advancement of the real doctrines of Jesus, and do in fact constitute the real anti-Christ.

Thomas Jefferson to Thomas Baldwin, January 19, 1810. Adams, *Jefferson's Extracts*, 345.

In every country and every age the priest has been hostile to liberty. He is always in alliance with the despot abetting his abuses in return for protection to his own. It is easier to acquire wealth and power by this combination than by deserving them: and to effect this they have perverted the purest religion ever preached to man, into mystery and jargon unintelligible to all mankind and therefore the safer engine for their purposes.

Thomas Jefferson to Horatio Spafford, March 17, 1814. Jefferson Papers, Library of Congress.

You judge truly that I am not afraid of the priests. They have tried upon me all their various batteries of pious whining, hypocritical canting, lying and slandering, without being able to give me one moment of pain. I have contemplated their order from the Magi of the East to the Saints of the West, and I have found no difference of character, but of more or less caution, in proportion to the information or ignorance of those on whom their interested duperies were to be plaid off.

> Thomas Jefferson to Horatio Spafford, January 10, 1816. Ibid.

No doctrine of his [Jesus'—Ed.] lead to schism. It is the speculations of crazy theologists which have made a Babel of a religion the most moral and sublime ever preached to man, and calculated to heal, and not to create differences. The religious animosities I impute to those who call themselves his ministers, and who engraft their casuistries on the stock of his simple precepts. I am sometimes more angry with them than is authorised by the blessed charities which he preached.

> Thomas Jefferson to Ezra Stiles Ely, June 25, 1819. Adams, *Jefferson's Extracts*, 387.

I expect our principle contributions [for building a black church—Ed.] will come from the Deists, swearing captains of vessels, and brokers of our city. The clergy and their faithful followers of every denomination are too good to do good. The Quakers objected to the blacks' making a temporary use of one of their schoolhouses as a place of worship because part of their worship consisted in singing psalms.

> Benjamin Rush to Julia Rush, July 16, 1791. Butterfield, *Letters of Rush*, 1:600.

Communion

A religious remembrancer of Jesus Christ, of his atoning sacrifice and precious benefit. . . . An impenitent communicant is a monster, no better than a traitor at his master's table. And there is the greatest absurdity, as well as impiety, in celebrating an ordinance in memorial of a crucified Jesus, who died a sacrifice for sin, without a relenting heart, which sincerely hates, mourns for, and turns from that accursed thing which occasioned his deep humiliation and bitter agonies.

Sherman, *Short Sermon*, 5–6.

Conscience: see Liberty of Conscience

Consolation

Whilst I mingle my tears with yours over the remains of your much loved sister, I would lead your mind to the only source of consolation, from whence you can draw comfort to sooth and calm your agitated bosom. To that resignation which teaches submission to the will of heaven and that confidence in the supream being which assures us that all his ways are just and right, however hidden in mazes and perplexed to us short sighted mortals. It becomes us to say of love divine

> Teach us the hand of love divine
> In evils to discern
> Tis the first lesson which we need
> The latest which we learn

Abigail Adams to Louisa Catherine Adams, February 18, 1811.
Adams Papers (microfilm), reel 411, Library of Congress.

Of your dear and only sister I can only say that she has been and still is a patient sufferer under severe and afflicting pain [terminal breast cancer—Ed.] .... I fear her constitution was essentially injured by the operation she past through and which to my inexpressible grief has not freed her from a similar complaint upon the other side. Heaven only knows to what sufferings she may yet be reserved. My Heart bleeds. I can not get to her, nor she to me. I am too infirm myself to undertake such a journey.

Into the will and disposal of our heavenly Father I commit her. "Safe in the hand of one disposing power; or in the natal or the mortal hour."

My only source of satisfaction, says Dr. Priestley,[12] "and it is a never failing one, is my firm persuasion that everything—and our oversights and mistakes among the rest—are parts of the great plan, in which everything will in time appear to have been ordered and conducted in the best manner. Who finds not providence all good and wise; alike in what it gives and what denies."

---

[12] Joseph Priestley (1733–1804), British scientist and Unitarian minister, who emigrated to the United States in 1794 and became estranged from the Adams family with whom he had warm relations when John Adams was American minister to Great Britain, 1785–88. *DNB.*

Altho I sometimes feel my own insignificance in the creation, especially when contemplating the first Good, first perfect and first fair, I derive pleasure and assurance from the word of inspiration—that not a swallow falleth without notice.

Abigail Adams to John Quincy Adams, July 1, 1813. Ibid., reel 416.

Although I sincerely condole with you and your Lady [on the death of an infant—Ed.] and feel a deep affliction in my own Breast for the loss of a lovely Rose, which I might probably have never seen, yet we ought all, to collect ourselves, and reflect that the constitution and course of Nature in the physical, moral and social, as well as intellectual World, is inscrutable and incomprehensible to Us. While you and I believe that the whole system is under the constant and vigilant direction of a Wisdom infinitely more discerning than ours and a benevolence to the whole and to us in particular greater even than our own self love; we have the highest consolation that Reason can suggest or Imagination conceive. The same general Laws that at times afflict us, are in your Neighbourhood bereaving Millions, of their Fathers Brothers and Sons and Millions of their Food and their Shelter. In our own country how many deprivations do we read and how many savage cruelties. What Grounds have we to expect or to hope to be excepted from the general Lot. Indeed if all such considerations were out of the question, there is another which ought to compose us, viz that the Event is irreversible. Sorrow can make no alteration; afford no relief to the departed, to survivors or to ourselves. You remember the Verses of Cleanthes in the bungling translation of Bolingbroke.

> Parent of Nature! Master of the World!
> Where e'er thy Providence directs, behold
> My Steps with cheerful resignation turn
> Fate leads the willing, draggs the backward on

Why should I grieve? When grieving I must bear
And take with guilt, what guiltless I might share?
Grief Sorrow and Mourning for irremediable Events are
Useless to the living as to the dead, except as they produce
Reflection, Consideration and correct Errors or reform
Vices. Remember the best of Philosophy. The beloved are
chastened.

John Adams to John Quincy Adams, March 11, 1813. Ibid., reel 415.

What can I say to you, on this distressing and truly melancholy occasion [the death of a child—Ed.]. There can be
but one Consolation, "the Lord liveth and blessed be
his Name." Our God is a merciful God! He has come out
against us in severe afflictions again and again, but oh! what
a happiness is it to be assured that it is for our best Interest
and for his own Glory. Our place of safety is at the foot of
the Throne, crying for Mercy for Jesus' sake. We are guilty
Creatures and deserve his frowns, but glory be to his Name
thro' Jesus Christ, this transitory word is the only place we
can be punished, and that punishment is for our refinement
for Glory. Alas! We want much purifying. Our Faith is too
weak. We lye too much groveling to the Earth. Could we
but see with an Eye of true faith, we should see those things
daily fulfilling around us foretold by our Master 2000 years
ago, when we are commanded to rejoice knowing that our
Redemption is drawing nigh. The time in every view, is but
short! This Vale of Tears cannot detain us long. We are to be
made perfect thro' sufferings, and if we are then brought to
an absolute, a total resignation of will, to the will of him
who doeth all things in Heaven and Earth according to his
own good pleasure, we shall know of a truth that it was
good for us to be afflicted.

Elias Boudinot to Elisha Boudinot, October 9, 1797. Boudinot Papers,
Princeton University Library.

I condole with you, we have lost a most dear and valuable relation [Franklin's brother, John—Ed.] . . . . Our friend and we are invited abroad on a party of pleasure—that it to last for ever. His chair was first ready and he is gone before us. We could not all conveniently start together, and why should you and I be grieved at this, since we are soon to follow, and we know where to find him.

Benjamin Franklin to Elizabeth Hubbart, February 22, 1756. Labaree, *Papers of Benjamin Franklin*, 6:406–7.

The death of an excellent daughter last spring was an afflicting event, and I feel it. Convinced that her happiness was augmented by it, I had no reason to grieve on <u>her</u> account. I derived consolation, as well as resignation, from reflecting that unerring wisdom had directed that dispensation.

John Jay to Richard Peters, January 25, 1819. Johnston, *Correspondence of Jay*, 4:425.

The public papers, my dear friend, announce the fatal event [the death of Abigail Adams—Ed.] of which your letter of Oct. 20 had given me ominous foreboding. Tried myself, in the school of affliction, by the loss of every form of connection which can rive the human heart, I know well, and feel what you have lost, what you have suffered, are suffering, and have yet to endure. The same trials have taught me that, for ills so immeasurable, time and silence are the only medecines. I will not therefore, by useless condolances, open afresh the sluices of your grief nor, altho' mingling sincerely my tears with yours, will I say a word more, where words are vain, but that it is of some comfort to us both that the term is not very distant at which we are to deposit, in the same cerement, our sorrows and suffering bodies, and to ascend in essence to an ecstatic meeting with the friends we have loved and lost and whom we shall still love and never lose again. God bless you and support you under your heavy affliction.

Thomas Jefferson to John Adams, November 13, 1818. Cappon, *Adams-Jefferson Letters*, 2:529.

Shall we receive Good Things? And Shall we not receive evil Things also? But none of the Gifts of God, who giveth us <u>all Things</u>, are Evil. Afflictions, Mortifications, Disappointments, Reproaches, and the Attempts of Envying, all seem to be Evils, but by a right Application, turning our Eyes inward, pondering these Things in our Heart and considering & comparing our own Demerits, we may convert all that Poison into Salutary Medicine, and nutritive Food. Oh Gracious God! How abundantly do thy Mercies and thy loving Kindness outweigh the Afflictions, the Crosses which thou art pleased to lay upon me! Altho' the Fig Tree shall not blossom, &ca., yet I will rejoice in the Lord, I will joy in thee O God! the God of my Salvation.

Henry Laurens to James Laurens, December 12, 1771. Rogers, *Papers of Henry Laurens*, 8:86.

That we sympathize in the misfortune, and lament the decree which has deprived you of so dutiful a child, and the world of so promising a young lady, stands in no need, I hope, of argument to prove; but the ways of Providence being inscrutable, and the justice of it not to be scanned by the shallow eye of humanity, nor to be counteracted by the utmost efforts of human power or wisdom, resignation, and as far as the strength of our reason and religion can carry us, a cheerful acquiescence to the Divine Will, is what we are to aim; and I am persuaded that your own good sense will arm you with fortitude to withstand the stroke, great as it is, and enable you to console Mrs. Bassett, whose loss and feelings are much to be pitied.

George Washington to Burwell Bassett, April 25, 1773. Fitzpatrick, *Writings of Washington*, 3:133.

When the mind is deeply affected by those irreparable losses [the death of Washington—Ed.] which are incident to humanity the good Christian will submit without repining to the Dispensations of Divine Providence and look for consolation to that Being who can alone pour balm into the bleeding Heart and who has promised to be the widows god.

For myself I have only to bow with humble submission to the will of God who giveth and who taketh away looking forward with faith and hope to the moment when I shall be again united with the Partner of my life.

Martha Washington to Jonathan Trumbull, January 15, 1800. *Papers of Martha Washington*, 339.

Constitution of the United States

Our constitution was made only for a moral and religious people. It is wholly inadequate to the government of any other.

John Adams to the Officers of the First Brigade of the 3rd Division of the Massachusetts Militia, October 11, 1798. Adams Papers (microfilm), reel 119, Library of Congress.

I beg I may not be understood to infer, that our General Convention was divinely inspired, when it form'd the new federal Constitution . . . yet I must own I have so much faith in the general Government of the world by *Providence*, that I can hardly conceive a Transaction of such momentous Importance to the Welfare of Millions now existing, and to exist in the Posterity of a great Nation, should be suffered to pass without being in some degree influenc'd, guided, and governed by that omnipotent, omnipresent, and beneficent Ruler, in whom all inferior Spirits live, and move, and have their Being.

> Benjamin Franklin, "A Comparison of the Conduct of Ancient Jews and Anti-federalists in the United States of America," 1788. Smyth, *Writings of Franklin*, 9:702.

Would it be wonderful if, under the pressure of all these difficulties, the convention should have been forced into some deviations from that artificial structure and regular symmetry which an abstract view of the subject might lead an ingenious theorist to bestow on a Constitution planned in his closet or in his imagination? The real wonder is that so many difficulties should have been surmounted, and surmounted with a unanimity almost as unprecedented as it must have been unexpected. It is impossible for any man of candor to reflect on this circumstance without partaking of the astonishment. It is impossible for the man of pious reflection not to perceive in it a finger of that Almighty hand which has been so frequently and signally extended to our relief in the critical stages of the revolution.

> James Madison, *Federalist* 37, January 11, 1788. Edward M. Earle, ed., *The Federalist* (New York: Modern Library, 1937), 231.

Many pious people wish the name of the Supreme Being had been introduced somewhere in the new Constitution. Perhaps an acknowledgement may be made of his goodness or of his providence in the proposed amendments.

> Benjamin Rush to John Adams, June 15, 1789. Butterfield, *Letters of Rush*, 1:517.

. . . we may, with a kind of grateful and pious exaltation, trace the finger of Providence through those dark and mysterious events, which first induced the States to appoint a general Convention and then led them one after another (by such steps as were best calculated to effect the object) into an adoption of the system recommended by that general Convention; thereby, in all human probability, laying a lasting foundation for tranquility and happiness; when we had but too much reason to fear that confusion and misery were rapidly coming upon us. That the same good Providence may still continue to protect us and prevent us from dashing the cup of national felicity just as it has been lifted to our lips, is the earnest prayer of My Dear Sir, your faithful friend, &c.

> George Washington to Jonathan Trumbull, July 20, 1788. Fitzpatrick, *Writings of Washington*, 30:22.

We have reason to rejoice in the prospect that the present national Government, which by the favor of Divine Providence, was formed by the common counsels and peaceably established with the common consent of the People, will prove a blessing to every denomination of them.

> George Washington to the Religious Society Called Quakers, September 1789. Washington Papers, Library of Congress.

Creeds

When will Mankind be convinced that true Religion is from the Heart, between Man and his Creator and not the Imposition [of] Man or creeds and tests.

> Abigail Adams to Louisa Catherine Adams, January 3, 1818. Adams Papers (microfilm), reel 442, Library of Congress.

Where do we find a praecept in the Gospell, requiring Ecclesiastical Synods, Convocations, Councils, Decrees, Creeds, Confessions, Oaths, Subscriptions and whole Cartloads of other trumpery, that we find Religion incumbered with in these Days?

> John Adams, Diary, February 18, 1756. Butterfield, *Diary and Autobiography of John Adams*, 1:8.

I do not however attach so much attention to creeds because I believe that his can not be wrong whose life is in the right.

> John Adams to Louisa Catherine Adams, November 15, 1821. Adams Papers (microfilm), reel 453, Library of Congress.

I set at defiance all ecclesiastical authority—all their creeds, confessions & excommunications; they have no authority over me more than I have over them .... I thank them for all their good advice they give me & am willing to pay them for it but I choose to judge for myself whether it is good or not.

> John Adams to Alexander B. Johnson, April 22, 1823. Ibid., reel 124.

I think vital Religion has always suffer'd, when Orthodoxy is more regarded than Virtue. And the Scripture assures me, that at the last Day, we shall not be examin'd [on] what we

<u>thought</u>, but what we <u>did</u>; and our Recommendation will not be that we said <u>Lord, Lord</u>, but that we did GOOD to our Fellow Creatures. See Matth. 26.

Benjamin Franklin to Josiah and Abiah Franklin, April 13, 1738. Labaree, *Papers of Benjamin Franklin*, 2:204.

I put down from time to time on Pieces of paper such Thoughts as occur'd to me. . . . Most of these are lost; but I find one purporting to be the Substance of an intended Creed, containing as I thought the Essentials of every known Religion, and being free of every thing that might shock the Professors of any Religion. It is express'd in these Words. viz

That there is one God who made all things.

That he governs the World by his Providence.

That he ought to be worshipped by Adoration,
    Prayer and Thanksgiving.

But that the most acceptable Service of God is doing
    Good to Man.

That the Soul is immortal.

And that God will certainly reward Virtue and
    punish Vice either here or hereafter.

Benjamin Franklin, *Autobiography,* post-1788. Labaree, *Autobiography of Franklin*, 162.

In forming and settling my Belief relative to the Doctrines of Christianity, I adopted no Articles from Creeds, but such only as on careful Examination I found to be confirmed by the Bible.

John Jay to Samuel Miller, February 18, 1822. Jay Papers (online edition), Columbia University Library.

I never told my own religion, nor scrutinized that of another. I never attempted to make a convert, nor wished to

change another's creed. I have ever judged of the religion of
others by their lives. . . . For it is in our lives, and not from
our words, that our religion must be read.

> Thomas Jefferson to Margaret Bayard Smith, August 6, 1816. Adams,
> *Jefferson's Extracts*, 376.

I have never permitted myself to meditate a specified creed.
These formulas have been the bane and ruin of the Christian church, it's own fatal invention which, thro' so many
ages, made of Christendom a slaughter house, and at this
day divides it into Casts of inextinguishable hatred to one
another.

> Thomas Jefferson to Thomas Whittemore, June 5, 1822. Ibid., 404.

I have often lamented the squeamishness of my . . . mind
upon the subject of religious creeds and modes of worship.
But accustomed to think for myself in my profession . . . I
have ventured to transfer the same spirit of inquiry to religion, in which, if I have no followers in my opinions (for I
hold most of them secretly), I enjoy the satisfaction of living
in peace with my conscience, and, what will surprise you
not a little, in peace with all denominations of Christians,
for while I refuse to be the slave of any sect, I am the friend
of them all. In a future letter I may perhaps give you my
creed. . . . It is a compound of the orthodoxy and hetero-
doxy of most of our Christian churches.

> Benjamin Rush to John Adams, April 5, 1808, Butterfield, *Letters of
> Rush*, 2:962–63.

Crime and Punishment

The moral Law, which binds all mankind, having been or-
dained by infinite wisdom and goodness, must be perfect
and consequently unchangeable. I therefore believe that it
has continued, and will continue the same, from the Beginning to the End of the World. I also believe that if war and
capital Punishment had been forbidden by the moral Law,
the Divine Legislator would never have commanded, nor
authorized, nor encouraged any of the human Race, to en-
gage in war nor to put criminals to death. As to murderers, I
think it is not only lawful for Governments, but that it is the
Duty of Governments to put them to Death. The Gospel has
mercifully provided Relief for us from the Penalties of the
moral Law, but I cannot find that it has made a single alteration to it.

> John Jay to Eleazer Lord, February 7, 1817. Jay Papers (online
> edition), Columbia University Library.

The conduct and discourses of our Saviour should outweigh every argument that has been or can be offered
in favour of capital punishment for any crime. When the
woman caught in adultery was brought to him, he evaded
inflicting the bloody sentence of the Jewish law upon her.
Even the maiming of the body appears to be offensive in his
sight; for when Peter drew his sword, and smote off the ear
of the servant of the high priest, he replaced it by miracle,
and at the same time declared, that "all they who take the
sword, shall perish with the sword." He forgave the crime
of murder on his cross; and after his resurrection, he commanded his disciples to preach the gospel of forgiveness,
first at Jerusalem, where he well knew his murderers still

resided. These striking facts are recorded for our imitation, and seem intended to shew that the Son of God died, not only to reconcile God to man, but to reconcile men to each other. There is one passage more, in the history of our Saviour's life which would of itself overset the justice of the punishment of death for murder, if every other part of the Bible had been silent upon the subject. When two of his disciples, actuated by the spirit of vindictive legislators, requested permission of him to call down fire from Heaven to consume the inhospitable Samaritans, he answered them, "The Son of Man is not come to <u>destroy</u> men's <u>lives</u> but to save them." I wish these words composed the motto of the arms of every nation upon the face of the earth. They inculcate every duty that is calculated to preserve, restore, or prolong human life. They militate alike against war—and capital punishments—the objects of which, are the unprofitable destruction of the lives of men. How precious does a human life appear from these words, in the sight of heaven! Pause, Legislators, when you give your votes for inflicting the punishment of death for any crime. You frustrate in one instance, the design of the mission of the Son of God into the world, and thereby either deny his appearance in the flesh, or reject the truth of the gospel. . . . "The Son of Man came not to <u>destroy</u> men's lives, but to <u>save</u> them . . . ," while I am able to place a finger, upon this text of scripture, I will not believe an angel from heaven, should he declare that the punishment of death, for <u>any</u> crime, was inculcated, or permitted by the spirit of the gospel.

Benjamin Rush, "An Enquiry into the . . . Punishment of Murder by Death." Rush, *Essays: Literary, Moral, and Philosophical*, 101–2.

Death

I am certainly very near the end of my life. I am far from trifling with the idea of Death which is a great and solemn event. But I contemplate it without terror or dismay, "aut transit, aut finit" [either it is a transformation, or it is the end—Ed.], if finit, which I cannot believe, and do not believe, there is then an end of all but I shall never know it, and why should I dread it, which I do not; if transit I shall ever be under the same constitution and administration of Government in the Universe, and I am not afraid to trust and confide in it.

> John Adams to Thomas Jefferson, January 14, 1826. Cappon, *Adams-Jefferson Letters*, 2:613.

What is life but a vapour, and how soon must we who are now mourning in the dust, be mourned over in our turn and if we are but found with our lamps trimmed and burning, waiting and watching for the coming of the bridegroom, of what small consequence is it, whether the cry happens at midnight or cockcrowing, if we are ready with our loins girt to go out to meet him.

> Elias Boudinot to Elisha Boudinot, February 17, 1796. Boudinot Papers, Princeton University Library.

We are spirits. That bodies should be lent to us, while they can afford us pleasure, assist us in acquiring knowledge, or doing good to our fellow creatures, is a kind and benevolent act of God—when they become unfit for these purposes and afford us pain instead of pleasure—instead of an aid, become an incumbrance and answer none of the intentions for which they were given, it is equally kind and benevolent that a way is provided by which we may get rid of them. Death is that way. We ourselves prudently choose a partial death. In some cases a mangled painful limb, which can not be restored, we willingly cut off. He who plucks out a tooth, parts with it freely since the pain goes with it, and he that quits the whole body, parts at once with all the pains and possibilities of pains and diseases it was liable to, or capable of making him suffer.

Benjamin Franklin to Elizabeth Hubbart, February 22, 1756. Labaree, *Papers of Benjamin Franklin*, 6:407.

When all our faculties have left, or are leaving us, one by one, sight, hearing, memory, every avenue of pleasing sensation is closed, and atrophy, debility and malaise left in their places, when the friends of our youth are all gone, and a generation is risen around us whom we know not, is death an evil?

When one by one our ties are torn,
And friend from friend is snatched forlorn
When man is left alone to mourn,
Oh! then how sweet it is to die!
When trembling limbs refuse their weight,
And films slow gathering dim the sight,
When clouds obscure the mental light
Tis nature's kindest boon to die!

Thomas Jefferson to John Adams, June 1, 1822. Cappon, *Adams-Jefferson Letters*, 2:577.

O, may we never forget amidst all our hurries and amusements the awful realities of the Eternal World—"the deep dampt vault, the mattock, and the grave," ensigns of Death which so often strike a damp upon us and make us shun

the gloomy chamber of the dead, where such pensive med-
itations intrude. A sudden death is the greatest blessing a
good man can enjoy. Dr. Cotton Mather and the good
Mr. Rowe[13] always prayed for it, and we find their prayers
were answered, for we read that they both expired without
a groan. Death is so much the King of Terrors that even pious men shrink from it. Perhaps the knowledge they have
of the purity and holiness of that God before whose tribunal they are about to appear, and their humble sense of
their own infirmities, together with the thoughts of leaving
a beloved wife and a family of weeping children and relations, may not a little conduce to this. But how awful is a
sudden death to the wicked!—O let me die the death of the
righteous.

> Benjamin Rush to Ebenezer Hazard, June 27, 1765. Butterfield, *Letters
> of Rush*, 1:16.

Deism

I have long observed that men may be Deists, and yet be
warmly attached to the forms of the Sects in which they have
been educated. . . . Mr. Hurt informed me that Judge Burke[14]
had assured him that he was made a Roman Catholic and a

---

[13] Thomas Rowe (1657–1705), a British dissenting clergyman and teacher
of philosophy. Ibid.

[14] Aedanus Burke (1743–1802). South Carolina soldier and judge; member of the First Federal Congress, 1789–91. *ANB*.

Deist nearly at the same time by two different priests in one of the colleges in France.

Benjamin Rush, "Commonplace Book," July 1792. Corner, *Autobiography of Rush*, 223–24.

Divorce

Our Saviour condemns the law of Moses for permitting <u>easy</u> divorces. They favor domestic infelicity, for where marriages are originally unhappy the annihilation of <u>all hope</u> of their becoming otherwise by a separation often removes the cause of their unhappiness. He then turns their attention from the law of Moses to the law of nature made in the Garden of Eden. "From the beginning," he says, "it was not so." That is, a plurality of wives was unknown in the first institution of matrimony. God made only one female for man, and to dignify the holy ceremony of marriage as much as possible he represents God himself as <u>joining them together</u>. Let no man, let no rash vow, and let no mistaken interpretation of Scripture therefore ever separate them from each other. Nay further, let no law ever be enacted for this purpose except for adultery, in which case the end of matrimony is frustrated by the introduction of sin and by a breach in the order of society.

Benjamin Rush to Mary Stockton, September 7, 1788. Butterfield, *Letters of Rush*, 1:485.

The moral and legal aspects of divorce were of more than academic interest to Roger Sherman, whose two sons and sister experienced

marital difficulties, resulting in divorces and "estrangement" from
their spouses. John Witherspoon, from whom Sherman sought ad-
vice, was the president of Princeton and one of the new republic's
leading Presbyterian theologians. He and Sherman served together
in the Continental Congress during the crucial, early years of the
Revolution.

I herewith send you Mr. Trumbull's appeal to the public respecting divorce.[15] Upon reading of which you will see that
he supposes that divorce is not lawful in any case except for
incontinency. The law of this State admits of divorce, for
fraudulent contracts, adultery, or three years wilful desertion and total neglect of duty.

Herein it agrees with the Westminster confession of Faith
article 24th. The late President Edwards[16] was also of the
same opinion, as appears by the enclosed note extracted
from his writings. As the subject is important and interesting to the public as well as to individuals, I should esteem it
a favor to know your opinion respecting it.

It is evident that those who admit wilful desertion as
a sufficient ground for divorce, found their opinion on 1
Cor[inthians] 7:15, which they suppose contains an apostolic direction in a case not mentioned by our Lord in the
Evangelists, and perfectly consistent with what he has said
on the subject. They suppose that what is contained in the
Evangelists, and referred to in Cor[inthians] 7:10,11 as said
by the Lord, imports no more than that no separation or voluntary departing or putting away except for incontinency, is
lawful, or if the wife should accept a bill of divorce from the

[15] Benjamin Trumbull, *An Appeal to the Public, especially to the learned, with
respect to the Unlawfulness of Divorces* . . . (New Haven: J. Meigs, 1788).

[16] Jonathan Edwards (1703–1758), the great theologian; president of
Princeton for a brief period in 1758. *ANB.*

husband, and thereupon voluntarily leave him, it would not dissolve the bond of matrimony, and either party that should marry another in consequence of such a separation would be guilty of adultery. But in case there should be a wilful desertion of one party, either by going away and leaving the other, or by cruelty and abuse compelling the other to go away, this conduct obstinately persisted in, so as totally to deprive the other of all the benefits and comforts of the marriage state; the innocent party, after using all proper means to reclaim the other, and waiting a reasonable time, and there appearing no prospect of a reconciliation, may, upon application to public authority be lawfully declared free from the bond of marriage, and be at liberty to marry another. This distinction they suppose is evident from what the apostle says in the 12th verse, "To the rest speak I , not the Lord." This was therefore a new case on the same subject, about which our Lord had not given any direction. As Mr. Trumbull has fully stated the arguments in support of one side of the question, I thought it might be proper to give these few hints of what has been said in support of the other side, and submit the whole to your consideration.

> *Your humble servant,*
> *Roger Sherman*

I received a few days ago your favor of the 10th inst. with [a] copy of Mr. Trumbull's Discourse relating to Divorce. I have read it over with attention and am fully of opinion with Dr. Edwards that the declaration of our Saviour against frivolous decrees ought not to be so interpreted that it should be impossible to liberate an innocent party any other way. As all contracts are mutual and this of marriage in a particular manner, an obstinate and perpetual refusal of performance on one side seems in the nature of things to liberate the other. Therefore the Protestant Churches in general and ours in particular have always admitted wilful or obstinate desertion as a cause of divorce, and have supposed the passage of the Apostle Paul to be a confirmation of this by a particular instance. This ought not to be considered as any contradiction to our Saviour's declaration; on the contrary it may be considered as falling under it for in the law of obstinate desertion adultery may be very justly questioned in law, as the person cannot be supposed to desert in order to live the life of a monk or nun, but from alienated affection, especially as in most cases of this kind they withdraw themselves out of reach of observation or proof. . . .

Your most humble and obedient servant,
John Witherspoon

Roger Sherman to John Witherspoon, July 10, 1788; John Witherspoon to Roger Sherman, July 25, 1788. Lewis H. Boutell, *The Life of Roger Sherman* (Chicago: A. C. McClurg and Company, 1896), 277–80.

Ecumenicism

In one thing we agree that he who feareth God, and worketh righteousness shall be accepted of him and his Faith cannot be wrong whose life is in the right.

Abigail Adams to Louisa Catherine Adams, April 15, 1818. Adams Papers (microfilm), reel 443, Library of Congress.

I know of no Philosopher, or Theologian, or Moralist ancient or modern more profound; more infallible than Whitefield,[17] if the Anecdote that I have heard be true.

He began; "Father Abraham"! With his hands and Eyes gracefully directed to the Heavens as I have more than once seen him; "Father Abraham," "who have you there with you"? "have you Catholicks?" No. "Have you Protestants". No. "Have you Churchmen". No. "Have you Dissenters". No. "Have you Presbyterians"? No. "Quakers?" No. "Anabaptists"? No. "Who have you then?" "Are you alone"? No.

"My Brethren! You have the Answer to all these questions in the Words of my Text, 'He who feareth God and worketh Righteousness, shall be accepted of him.'"

John Adams to Thomas Jefferson, December 3, 1813. Cappon, *Adams-Jefferson Letters*, 2:406.

As you advance in Life, you will find the Christian World, unhappily split into a Multitude of Denominations, Professions and Names. Each will tell you that his is the only right Way, as those mentioned in the Scriptures, who tell you, lo! Here is Christ, or there is Christ, but believe them not. The true Catholicism of the Scriptures will teach you to take them all into the Arms of your Charity, and to look upon all as the servants of the same Master, as far as they follow his Example, remembering that he who is not against us, is for us.

Elias Boudinot to Susan Boudinot, November 22, 1777. Boudinot Papers, Princeton University Library.

[17] George Whitefield (1714–1770), the British evangelical preacher who was a leader in promoting the first major revival in American history, the Great Awakening, ca. 1735–1745. Ibid.

I have always acted consistent with my own ideas of religion which were that there was no necessity to become a member of any particular sect as the intent of each sect is the same and I suppose that in less than a century there will be no such distinctions but that, people thinking on a larger scale, all religions will unite under one head.

John Dickinson to Richard Penn Hicks, September 13, 1788. Logan Papers, Historical Society of Pennsylvania.

It is well known, that both cathedrals and meetinghouses have heretofore exhibited individuals who have been universally and justly celebrated as real and useful Christians; and it is also well known, that at present not a few, under similar circumstances and of similar characters, deserve the like esteem and commendation. As real Christians are made so by Him without whom we "can do nothing," it is equally certain that He receives them into His family, and that in His family mutual love and uninterrupted concord never cease to prevail. There is no reason to believe or suppose that this family will be divided into separate classes, and that separate apartments in the mansions of bliss will be allotted to them according to the different sects from which they had proceeded.

John Jay to the American Bible Society, May 13, 1824. Johnston, *Correspondence of Jay*, 4:495.

Our particular principles of religion are a subject of accountability to our god alone. I enquire after no man's, and trouble none with mine: nor is it given to us in this life to know whether your's or mine, our friend's or our foe's are exactly the right. Nay, we have heard it said that there is not a quaker or a baptist, a presbyterian or an episcopalian, a catholic or a protestant in heaven: that, on entering that gate, we leave those badges of schism behind, and find ourselves united in those principles only in which god has united us all. Let us not be uneasy then about the different roads we may pursue, as believing them the shortest, to that our last abode: but, following the guidance of a good conscience, let us be happy in the hope that, by these different paths, we shall all meet in the end. . . .

> Thomas Jefferson to Miles King, September 26, 1814. Adams, *Jefferson's Extracts*, 360–61.

Were I to be the founder of a new sect, I would call them Apriarians, and, after the example of the bee, advise them to extract the honey of every sect.

> Thomas Jefferson to Thomas B. Parker, May 15, 1819. Ibid., 386.

It would seem as if one of the designs of Providence in permitting the existence of so many Sects of Christians was that each Sect might be a depository of some great truth of the Gospel, and that it might by that means be better preserved. . . . Let the different Sects of Christians not only bear with each other, but love each other for this kind display of God's goodness whereby all the truths of their Religion are so protected that none of them can ever become feeble or be lost. When united they make a great whole, and that whole is the salvation of all men.

> Benjamin Rush, "Commonplace Book," August 14, 1811. Corner, *Autobiography of Rush*, 339–40.

Being no bigot myself to any mode of worship, I am disposed to indulge the professors of Christianity in the church, that road to Heaven, which to them shall seem the most direct plainest easiest and least liable to exception.

> George Washington to the Marquis de Lafayette, August 15, 1787. Fitzpatrick, *Writings of Washington*, 29:259.

Education

I have a thousand fears for my dear Boys as they rise into Life, the most critical period of which is I conceive, at the university; there infidelity abounds, both in example and precepts, there they imbibe the speicious arguments of a Voltaire a Hume a Mandevill. If not from the fountain, they receive them at second hand. These are well calculated to intice a youth, not yet capable of investigating their principals, or answering their arguments. Thus is a youth puzzeld in Mazes and perplexed with error untill he is led to doubt, and from doubting to disbelief. Christianity gives not such a pleasing latitude to the passions. It is too pure, it teaches moderation humility and patience, which are incompatable, with the high Glow of Health, and the warm blood which riots in their veins. With them, "to enjoy, is to obey." I hope before either of our children are prepaird for colledge you will be able to return and assist by your example and advise, to direct and counsel them; that with undeviating feet they may keep the path of virtue.

> Abigail Adams to John Adams, November 11, 1783. Butterfield, *Adams Family Correspondence*, 5:268.

He said nothing about law, but examined me more severely in Metaphysicks. We had Clark and Leibnitz, Descartes, Malbranche and Lock, Baxter, Bolinbroke and Berkley, with many others on the Carpet, and Fate, foreknowledge, Eternity, Immensity, Infinity, Matter and Spirit, Essence and Attribute, Vacuum and plenum, Space, and duration, Subjects which neither of Us understood, and which I have long been convinced, will never be intelligible to human Understanding. I had read at Colledge and afterwards a great deal on these Subjects: but would not advise any one to study longer than to convince him, that he may devote his time to more satisfactory and more usefull pursuits. We may know more in a future State: but many of these Subjects may well be suspected to be comprehensible only by the Supream Intelligence.

John Adams, *Autobiography*, post–November 30, 1804. Butterfield, *Diary and Autobiography of John Adams*, 3:272–73.

. . . the only foundation for a useful education in a republic is to be laid in Religion. Without this there can be no virtue, and without virtue there can be no liberty, and liberty is the object and life of all republican governments.

Benjamin Rush, "Of the Mode of Education Proper in a Republic." Rush, *Essays: Literary, Moral, and Philosophical*, 6.

However great the benefits of reading the scriptures in schools have been, I cannot help remarking, that these benefits might be much greater, did schoolmasters take more pains to explain them to their scholars. Did they demonstrate the divine original of the bible from the purity, consistency, and benevolence of its doctrines and precepts . . . and above all, did they often enforce the discourses of our Saviour, as the best rule of life, and the surest guide to happiness, how great would be the influence of our schools upon the order and prosperity of our country! Such a mode of instructing children in the christian religion, would convey knowledge into their <u>understandings</u>, and would therefore be preferable to teaching them creeds, and catechisms, which too often convey, not knowledge, but <u>words</u> only, into their <u>memories</u>. I think I am not too sanguine in believing, that education, conducted in this manner, would, in the course of two generations, eradicate infidelity from among us, and render civil government scarcely necessary in our country.

Benjamin Rush, "A Defence of the Use of the Bible as a School Book." Ibid., 65–66.

There is nevertheless much reason to hope and expect that the Exertions which are making in this and some other Countries, to promote and extend the influence of the Gospel on the Education and Conduct of the rising Generation, will increase the Number of virtuous Individuals, and thereby augment the General Welfare.

> John Jay to Noah Worcester, June 21, 1819. Jay Papers (online edition), Columbia University Library.

Episcopalians

There is something more cheerful and comfortable in an Episcopalian than in a Presbyterian Church. I admire a great Part of the divine Service at Church very much. It is very humane and benevolent, and sometimes pathetic & affecting: but rarely gloomy, if ever. Their creeds I could dispense with very well because, the Scriptures being before Us contain the Creed the most certainly orthodox.

> John Adams to Abigail Adams, October 27, 1799. Adams Papers (microfilm), reel 396, Library of Congress.

No clear headed Man; no Man who sees all the consequences of a proposition can be an orthodox Church of England Man without being a Roman Catholic.

> John Adams to Benjamin Rush, August 17, 1812. *Old Family Letters*, 420.

Most men indeed as well as most sects in Religion, think themselves in possession of all truth, and that whereever others differ from them it is so far error. Steele,[18] a Protestant in a Dedication tells the Pope, that the only differences between our Churches in their opinions of the certainty of their doctrines is, the Church of Rome is infallible and the Church of England is never in the wrong.

> Benjamin Franklin, speech at the Federal Constitutional Convention, September 17, 1787. Max Farrand, ed., *The Records of the Federal Convention of 1787* (New Haven, Conn.: Yale University Press, 1937), 2:642.

For a considerable time past, we have observed . . . the gradual introduction and industrous propagation of high church doctrines. Of late years, they have frequently been seen lifting up their heads and appearing in places where their presence was neither necessary nor expected. There never was a time when those doctrines promoted peace on earth or good-will among men. Originating under the auspices and in the days of darkness and despotism, they patronized darkness and despotism down to the Reformation. Ever encroaching on the rights of governments and people, they have constantly found it convenient to incorporate, as far as possible, the claims of the clergy with the principles and practice of religion; and their advocates have not ceased to preach for Christian doctrines the commandments and devices of men.

To you it cannot be necessary to observe, that high church doctrines are not accommodated to the state of society, nor to the tolerant principles, nor to the ardent love of liberty which prevail in our country. It is well known that our church was formed after the Revolution with an eye to what was then believed to be the truth and simplicity of the Gospel; and there appears to be some reason to regret that

[18] Possibly Richard Steele (1672–1729), the essayist and author, with Addison, of the *Tatler. DNB.*

the motives which then governed have since been less operative. . . .

We have done our duty, in thus explicitly protesting against measures and proceedings which, if persevered in, must and will, sooner or later, materially affect the tranquility and welfare of the Church.

> John Jay to the Corporation of Trinity Church, post-1800. Johnston, *Correspondence of Jay*, 4:513–15.

There are but two ways of preserving visible religion in any country. The first is by establishments. The second is by the competition of different religious societies. The revival of the Episcopal Church in our own country will produce zeal and a regard to the ordinances of religion in every other society.

> Benjamin Rush to Granville Sharp, April 27, 1784. Butterfield, *Letters of Rush*, 1:330–31.

The Episcopal clergy and laity have held a convention in this city and agreed on such alterations in their discipline, worship, and articles as will render the Episcopal Church the most popular church in America. They have adopted a form of ecclesiastical government purely republican. A church judicatory is to consist of a bishop, three presbyters, and two or three laymen. They have reduced their thirty-nine articles to nineteen and have reserved from their creeds only the Apostles'. Their baptism, their marriage and burial services are likewise made more consonant to common sense as well as true Christianity.

You will perceive from their prayer book that their Articles, though reduced in number, are equally Calvanistical with the Articles of the old English Church.

> Benjamin Rush to Richard Price, October 15, 1785; May 25, 1786. Ibid., 371–72; 389.

Faith

Q. What is Faith?

A. An humble and hearty Assent to the Truths of Revelation—"the substance (confidence) of things hoped for, the Evidence of Things not seen"—so that we firmly believe in the Power and will of God to save Us from the Guilt and dominion of Sin, and accept Jesus Christ as he is proposed to us for our Saviour.

John Dickinson, "Religious Instruction for Youth," undated. R. R. Logan Papers, Historical Society of Pennsylvania.

Morality or Virtue is the End, Faith only a Means to obtain that End: And if the End be obtained, it is no matter by what Means. . . . Faith in Christ, however, may be and is of great Use to produce a good Life, but that it can conduce nothing towards Salvation where it does not conduce to Virtue is, I suppose, plain. . . . St. James, in his second Chapter, is very zealous against these Cryers-up of Faith, and maintains that Faith without Virtue is useless, <u>Wilt thou know, O vain Man,</u> says he, <u>that Faith without Works is dead;</u> and, <u>shew me your Faith without your Works, and I will shew you mine by my Works.</u> Our Saviour, when describing the last Judgment, and declaring what shall give Admission into Bliss, or exclude from it, says nothing of <u>Faith</u> but what he says against it, that is, that those who cry <u>Lord, Lord,</u> and profess to have <u>believed</u> in his Name, have no Favour to expect on that Account; but declares that 'tis the Practice, or the omitting the Practice of the Duties of Morality, <u>Feeding the Hungry, cloathing the Naked, visiting the Sick</u> &. In short, 'tis the Doing or not Doing all the Good that lies in our Power, that will render us the Heirs of Happiness or Misery.

Benjamin Franklin, "Dialogue between Two Presbyterians," April 10, 1735. Labaree, *Papers of Benjamin Franklin*, 2:30.

My fundamental principle would be the reverse of Calvin's, that we are to be saved by our good works which are within our power, and not by our faith which is not within our power.

Thomas Jefferson to Thomas B. Parker, May 15, 1819. Adams, *Jefferson's Extracts*, 386.

Again, do we rightly understand the way in which we are to obtain deliverance out of this our ruined and miserable condition. viz. by faith in Jesus Christ, which implies a firm belief of the Gospel report concerning him, a hearty approbation of the whole method of salvation thro' him, a cheerful consent and desire to be saved in this way, and a reliance of soul on his merits, and the mercy of God thro' him, for the whole of salvation, both from sin and hell, to be made holy as well as happy; acknowledging the whole to be of mere grace, and testifying our acceptance thereof, by a life of holy obedience to his commands.

Roger Sherman, *Short Sermon*, 5.

Fast and Thanksgiving Days

The National Fast,[19] recommended by me turned me out of office. It was connected with the general assembly of

---

[19] During his presidency Adams proclaimed two national fasts: May 9, 1798, and April 25, 1799. See Richardson, *Messages and Papers of the Presidents*, 1:259, 274–75.

the Presbyterian Church, which I had no concern in. That assembly has allarmed and alienated Quakers, Anabaptists, Mennonists, Moravians, Swedenborgians, Methodists, Catholicks, protestant Episcopalians, Arians, Socinians, Armenians, & & &, Atheists and Deists might be added. A general Suspicion prevailed that the Presbyterian Church was ambitious and aimed at an Establishment of a National Church. I was represented as a Presbyterian and at the head of this political and ecclesiastical Project. The secret whisper ran through them "Let us have Jefferson, Madison, Burr, any body, whether they be Philosophers, Deists, or even Atheists, rather than a Presbyterian President." This principle is at the bottom of the unpopularity of national Fasts and Thanksgivings. Nothing is more dreaded than the National Government meddling with Religion.

John Adams to Benjamin Rush, June 12, 1812. *Old Family Letters*, 392–93.

A philosopher may regard the present course of things in Europe as some great providential dispensation. A Christian can hardly view it in any other light. Both these descriptions of persons must approve a national appeal to Heaven for protection. The politician will consider this as an important mean of influencing Opinion, and will think it a valuable resource in a contest with France to set the Religious Ideas of his Countrymen in active Competition with the Atheistical tenets of their enemies. This is an advantage which we shall be very unskilful, if we do not improve to the utmost. And the impulse cannot be too early given. I am persuaded a day of humiliation and prayer besides being very proper would be extremely useful.

Alexander Hamilton to William Loughton Smith, April 10, 1797. Syrett, *Papers of Alexander Hamilton*, 21:41.

That the government of a State should have authority to appoint "particular days for rendering thanks to God" for any signal blessing, or imploring his assistance "in any public calamity," is certainly proper.

John Jay to Edward Livingston, July 28, 1822. Johnston, *Correspondence of Jay*, 4:465.

I consider the government of the US. as interdicted by the constitution from intermedling with religious institutions, their doctrines, discipline, or exercises. This results not only from the provision that no law shall be made respecting the establishment, or free exercise of religion, but from that also which reserves to the states the powers not delegated to the US. Certainly no power to prescribe any religious exercise, or to assume authority in religious discipline, has been delegated to the general government. It must then rest with the states, as far as it can be in any human authority.

But it is only proposed that I should <u>recommend</u>, not prescribe a day of fasting & prayer. That is, that I should <u>indirectly</u> assume to the US. an authority over religious exercises which the constitution has directly precluded them from. . . . I do not believe it is for the interest of religion to invite the civil magistrate to direct it's exercises, it's discipline or it's doctrine: nor of the religious societies that the general government should be invested with the power of effecting uniformity of time or matter among them. Fasting & prayer are religious exercises: the enjoining them an act of discipline. Every religious society has a right to determine for itself the times for these exercises, & the objects proper for them, according to their own particular tenets: and this right can never be safer than in their own hands, where the constitution has deposited it.

Thomas Jefferson to Samuel Miller, January 23, 1808. Jefferson Papers, Library of Congress.

Religious proclamations by the Executive recommending thanksgivings & fasts . . . altho' recommendations only, they imply a religious agency, making no part of the trust delegated to political rulers. . . . The last & not the least objection is the liability of the practice to a subserviency to political views; to the scandal of religion, as well as the increase of party animosities. Candid or incautious politicians will not always disown such views. In truth it is difficult to frame such a religious Proclamation generally suggested by a political State of things, without referring to them in terms having some bearing on party questions.

James Madison, Detached Memoranda, 1819. Rakove, *Madison Writings*, 764–65.

God

From the Scriptures I learn that there is but one God to whom worship is due. That he is the Creator Preserver and Governor of universal Nature. Thou shalt have no other Gods before me is the first command after that of loving God. There is no other object of religious worship but the one Supreme Deity. There is no other Being of whom we have sufficient reason to think that he is constantly present with us and a witness of all our thoughts words and actions. And there is no other Being to whom our supplications ought to be addressed. The language of Jesus Christ is "thou shalt worship the Lord thy God, and him only shalt thou serve."

Abigail Adams to Louisa Catherine Adams, April 15, 1818. Adams Papers (microfilm), reel 443, Library of Congress.

God has infinite Wisdom, goodness and power. He created the Universe. His duration is eternal, a parte Ante, and a parte post. His presence is as extensive as Space. What is Space? An infinite, spherical Vaccuum. He created this Speck of Dirt and the human Species for his glory: and with the deliberate design of making, nine tenths of our Species miserable forever, for his glory. This is the doctrine of Christian Theologians in general: ten to one.

Now, my friend, can Prophecies, or miracles convince You, or Me, that infinite Benevolence, Wisdom and Power, created and preserves, for a time, innumerable millions to make them miserable, forever; for his own Glory? Wretch! What is his Glory? Is he ambitious? Does he want promotion? Is he vain? tickled with Adulation? Exulting and tryumphing in his Power and the Sweetness of his Vengeance? Pardon me, my Maker, for these Aweful Questions. My Answer to them is always ready: I believe no such Things. My Adoration of the Author of the Universe is too profound and too sincere. The Love of God and his Creation; delight, Joy, Tryumph, Exultation in my own existence, 'tho but an Atom, a Molecule Organique, in the Universe; are my religion. Howl, Snarl, bite, ye Calvinistick! Ye Athanasian Divines, if You will. Ye will say, I am no Christian: I say Ye are no Christians: and there the Account is ballanced. Yet I believe all the honest men among you are Christians in my sense of the Word. . . .

It has been long, very long a settled opinion in my Mind that there is now, never will be, and never was but one being who can Understand the Universe. And that it is not only vain but wicked for insects to pretend to comprehend it.

John Adams to Thomas Jefferson, September 14, 1813. Cappon, *Adams-Jefferson Letters*, 2:373–74.

When we say God is a Spirit, we know what we mean as well as we do when we say that the Pyramids of Egypt are

Matter. Let us be content therefore to believe Him to be a Spirit, that is, an Essence that we know nothing of, in which originally and necessarily reside all energy, all Power, all Capacity, all Activity, all Wisdom, all Goodness.

John Adams to Thomas Jefferson, January 20, 1820. Ibid., 2:560.

Question 1. Is this stupendous and immeasurable universe governed by eternal fate? 2. Is it governed by chance? 3. Is it governed by caprice anger resentment and vengeance? 4. Is it governed by intelligence wisdom and benevolence? The three first of these questions I have examined with as close attention as I am capable of & have decided them all forever in the negative. The 4th I have meditated with much more satisfaction & comfort to myself & decided unequivocally in the affirmative & from this last decision I have derived all my system of divinity.

John Adams to Louisa Catherine Adams, November 11, 1821.
Adams Papers (microfilm), reel 124, Library of Congress.

But what do we mean by the ideas, the thoughts, the reason, the intelligence, or the speech of God? His intelligence is a subject too vast, too incomprehensible for Plato, Philo, Paul or Peter, Jews, Gentiles, or Christians. Let us adore, not presume nor dogmatize. Even the great Teacher may not reveal this subject. There never was, is not, and never will be more than one Being in the universe capable of comprehending it. At least this is the humble adoring opinion of the writer of this note.

Moses says, God spoke the world into being. He said "Let there be Light" and there was Light. Plato and Philo seem to teach that God thought the world into existence. Which is the most sublime? Which the most incomprehensible? But if God's idea was of itself almighty and produced a world, the world must be eternal because God must have had an idea of it from eternity. These are all the effects of great minds grasping at ideas too vast for their comprehension. The will of God must come into consideration. Moses seems to have understood it best. God had the idea from eternity. At length he willed the existence of the world, expressed his will by a word, and it was done. The world existed and stood fast. Thinking, or willing a world into existence is as sublime as speaking it. A thought is more simple than a word! But these are incorrect figures to express inadequate ideas.

Admire and adore the Author of the telescopic universe, love and esteem the work, do all in your power to lessen ill, and increase good: but never assume to comprehend.

> John Adams, marginalia in Joseph Priestley's *Early Opinions Concerning Jesus Christ*. Haraszti, *Prophets of Progress*, 288.

God governs the world and all things <u>must</u> be right and just.

> Elias Boudinot to Susan Boudinot, October 22, 1781. Boudinot Papers, Princeton University Library.

Our God has provided for us hitherto, is the same yesterday, today & forever. His hand is not shortened: but is yet mighty to save.

> Elias Boudinot to James Milnor, March 22, 1820. Boudinot Papers, American Bible Society.

God is a spirit, from everlasting to everlasting, alone-self existent, invisible, unchangeable, infinitely powerful, wise, just, true, merciful, good, holy, who by his word created all things, and preserves, governs and disposes of them, according to his will.

> John Dickinson, "Religious Instruction for Youth," undated. R. R. Logan Papers, Historical Society of Pennsylvania.

Limited as our Capacities are, We are favored so far as to perceive, that the Sovereign of the Universe can deduce

Good out of Evil; and that he is inclined to do so. But our sentiments on this Head must be mingled with pure Humility, for "who hath known the Mind of the Lord? Or, who hath been his Councellor?"

John Dickinson to Mercy Otis Warren, December 22, 1806. *Warren-Adams Letters*, 2:349.

It might be judg'd an Affront to your Understandings should I go to prove this first Principle, the Existence of a Deity and that he is the Creator of the Universe, for that would suppose you ignorant of what all Mankind in all Ages have agreed in. I shall therefore proceed to observe: 1. That he must be a Being of great Wisdom: 2. That he must be a Being of great Goodness and 3. That he must be a Being of great Power. That he must be a Being of infinite Wisdom, appears in his admirable Order and Disposition of Things, whether we consider the heavenly Bodies, the Star and Planets, and their wonderful regular Motions, or this Earth compounded of such an Excellent mixture of all the Elements; or the admirable Structure of Animal Bodies of such an infinite Variety, and yet every one adopted to its Nature, and the Way of Life it is to be placed in, whether on Earth, in the Air or in the Waters, and so exactly that the highest and most exquisite human Reason, cannot find a fault. . . .

2. That the Deity is a Being of great Goodness, appears in his giving Life to so many Creatures, each of which acknowledge it a benefit by their unwillingness to leave it; in his providing plentiful Sustenance for them all, and making those Things that are most useful, most common and easy to be had; such as Water necessary for almost every Creature's Drink; Air without which few could subsist, the inexpressible Benefits of Light and Sunshine to almost all Animals in general. . . . 3. That he is a Being of infinite

Power appears, in his being able to form and compound such Vast Masses of Matter as this Earth and the Sun and innumerable Planets and Stars, and give them such prodigious Motion, and yet so to govern them in their greatest Velocity as that they shall not flie off out of their appointed Bounds nor dash one against another, to their mutual Destruction.

> Benjamin Franklin, "On the Providence of God in the Government of the World," [1732]. Labaree, *Papers of Benjamin Franklin*, 1:265–66.

... the benevolent and sublime reformer of that religion [Jesus—Ed.] has told us only that god is good and perfect, but has not defined him. I am therefore of his theology, believing that we have neither words nor ideas adequate to that definition. And if we could all, after his example, leave the subject as undefinable, we should all be of one sect, doers of good and eschewers of evil. No doctrines of his lead to schism.

> Thomas Jefferson to Ezra Stiles Ely, June 25, 1819. Adams, *Jefferson's Extracts*, 387.

I hold (without appeal to revelation) that when we take a view of the Universe, in it's parts general or particular, it is impossible for the human mind not to perceive and feel a conviction of design, consummate skill, and indefinite power in every atom of it's composition. The movements of the heavenly bodies, so exactly held in their course by the balance of the centrifugal and centripetal forces, the structure of our earth itself, with it's distribution of lands, waters and atmosphere, animal and vegetable bodies, examined in all their minutest particles, insects mere atoms of life, yet as perfectly organised as man or mammoth, the mineral substances, their generation and uses, it is impossible, I say, for the human mind not to believe that there is, in all this, design, cause and effect, up to an ultimate cause, a fabricator of all things from matter and motion, their preserver and regulator while permitted to exist in their present forms, and their regenerator into new and other forms. We see, too, evident proofs of the necessity of a superintending power to maintain the Universe in it's course and order. Stars, well known, have disappeared, new ones have come into view, comets, in their incalculable courses, may run foul of suns and planets and require renovation under other laws; certain races of animals are become extinct; and, were there no restoring power, all existences might extinguish successively, one by one, until all should be reduced to a shapeless chaos. So irresistible are these evidences of an intelligent and powerful Agent that, of the infinite numbers of men who have existed thro' all time, they have believed, in proportion of a million at least to Unit, in the hypothesis of an eternal pre-existence of a creator, rather than in that of a self-existent Universe. Surely this unanimous sentiment renders this more probable than that of the few in the other hypothesis.

> Thomas Jefferson to John Adams, April 11, 1823. Cappon, *Adams-Jefferson Letters*, 2:592.

I am persuaded that there is one omnipotent God, in whose hands the nations are Dust, who holdeth the reins of Government & ordereth the ways of Men. Therefore I shall not anticipate events, but in the regular course of my Life sing the song of the Fervirous Habbakuk. "Altho' the Fig Tree shall not blossom, &Ca., yet I will rejoice in the Lord, and joy in the God of my Salvation."

> Henry Laurens to James Habersham, May 25, 1769. Rogers, *Papers of Henry Laurens*, 6:573.

. . . it will probably always be found that the course of reasoning from the effect to the cause, "from Nature to Nature's God," Will be the more universal & persuasive application. The finiteness of the human understanding betrays itself on all subjects, but more especially when it contemplates such as involve infinity. What may safely be said seems to be, that the infinity of time & space forces itself on our conception, a limitation of either being inconceivable; that the mind prefers at once the idea of a self-existing cause to that of an infinite series of cause & effect, which augments, instead of avoiding the difficulty; and that it finds more facility in assenting to the self-existence of an invisible cause possessing infinite power, wisdom & goodness, than to the self-existence of the universe, visibly destitute of those attributes, and which may be the effect of them. In this comparative facility of conception & belief, all philosophical Reasoning on the subject must perhaps terminate.

> James Madison to Frederick Beasley, November 20, 1825. Gaillard Hunt, ed., *The Writings of James Madison* (New York: G. P. Putnam's Sons, 1910), 9:230–31.

The Supreme Being, for the same reasons, often assumes to himself the violent passions, and even the features and senses of men; and yet who can suppose it proper to ascribe either of them to a Being, one of whose perfections consists in his existing as a pure unchangeable spirit.

> Benjamin Rush, "An Enquiry into the Consistency of Oaths with Reason and Christianity," January 20, 1789. Rush, *Essays: Literary, Moral, and Philosophical*, 78.

No Man has a more perfect Reliance on the alwise, and powerful dispensations of the Supreme Being than I have nor thinks his aid more necessary.

> George Washington to William Gordon, May 13, 1776. Fitzpatrick, *Writings of Washington*, 37:526.

. . . the supreme Dispenser of every Good.

> George Washington to Philip Schuyler, January 27, 1776. Ibid., 4:281.

Grief

Religion my Friend does not forbid us to weep and to mourn for our departed friends. But it teaches us to cast our Sorrows upon that Being in whose hands and at whose disposal we are and who can heal the wounded bosom and bind up the broken heart.

> Abigail Adams to ——, January 19, 1811. Adams Papers (microfilm), reel 411, Library of Congress.

You my dear son have learnt from the Scriptures which you so faithfully study those lessons of . . . duty and of submission to the dispensations of heaven. Yet this does not forbid us to sorrow for our great Teacher wept, altho cloathed with the power of raising him whom he loved from the dead and this to shew his disciples and followers that he took our infirmities upon him.

> Abigail Adams to John Quincy Adams, January 25, 1813. Ibid., reel 415, Library of Congress.

I should have expressed my sincere sympathy with you and your whole family on the loss of your amiable Grand Child. We who have lost all our ancestors and collaterals and several of our children and Grand Children well know the pungency of grief in younger life under such tender deprivations. A gloomy Philosophy or a more melancholy Religion disposes men to misery and despair but a more cheerful confidence in the wisdom and benevolence that governs the universe ought to dispose us not only to submit but to make the best of everything. I can neither applaud nor approve of the lamentations over "Few and evil days." "Days in which there is no pleasure." "Vale of tears." "Miseries of life," etc. etc. etc. I have seen no such days and those who think they have, I fear have made them such by want of reflection.

John Adams to Mercy Otis Warren, March 24, 1814. Ibid., reel 95.

Grief drives Men into habits of serious Reflection sharpens the Understanding and softens the heart; it compells them to arrouse their reason, to assert its Empire over their Passions Propensities and Prejudices; to elevate them to a Superiority over all human Events; to give them the Felicis Annimi immotan tranquilitatem [the imperturbable tranquility of a happy heart—Ed.]; in short to make them Stoicks and Christians.

John Adams to Thomas Jefferson, May 6, 1816. Cappon, *Adams-Jefferson Letters*, 2:473.

The Stoicks, the Christians the Mahometans and our North American Indians all agree, that complaint is unmanly, unlawful and impious. To bear torment without a murmur, a sigh, a groans, or a distortion of face and feature or a writhe, or contortion of the body is consummate virtue, heroism and piety. . . . I see nothing but pride, vanity, affectation and hypocrisy in these pretended stoical apathies. I have so much sympathy and compassion for human nature, that a man or a woman may grunt and groan, screech and scream, weep, cry, or roar as much as nature dictates under extreme distress, provided there be no affectation; for there may be hypocrisy even in these expressions of torture.

John Adams to Francis van der Kemp, May 16, 1816. Adams Papers (microfilm), reel 122, Library of Congress.

But you may answer, you are sorely bereaved and deeply afflicted, and shall you not mourn your irretrievable loss. Yes my dear Friend, you not only may, but it is your duty to feel your loss, and mourn under the mighty hand of a righteous God, and shed tears of sorrow & great distress. Jesus, your great Example and Redeemer, taught you this duty at the Tomb of Lazarus his beloved Friend. . . . Altho He foreknew that he should immediately restore Lazarus to Life, yet the Brother was dead. The Sister and it may be a Mother were sunk in Sorrow & inexpressible Trouble. All his Friends were deeply afflicted. Did Jesus, the compassionate Jesus, forbid the expression of the deepest distress in the flood of Tears that flowed on the Occasion. No he felt all the sinless effects of sudden separation and irreparable loss in so dear a friend. He did feel and soon joined the mourning & tearful throng. For it is said with great Emphasis "and Jesus wept." He acknowledged as a Man, all that was so distressful in the death of a beloved Brother. A Friend & Protector, and as an Example to his followers, manifested his sympathy with his pious Friends. Blessed effect of pure and unadulterated Love! When notwithstanding the dignity of his person & the excellence of his glory, yet he condescended to partake in the sufferings of his Friends. Sweet and consoling Instance of social feelings & of the workings of sincere Friendship in the Son of God. Thus did the immaculate Jesus, manifest himself in the flesh, to be both God & Man. But Jesus wept and mourned, as one who had hope in death.

Elias Boudinot to Catherine Harris, June 7, 1818. Boudinot Papers, Princeton University Library.

Indeed, I have sustained an afflicting Deprivation [the death of his wife—Ed.]. I am stunn'd by it. My mind is continually engaged in contemplating it and seems to delight in sorrow. Yet I am perfectly convinced that I ought not to grieve as those "who have no hope," for the departed Spirit was truely excellent and has gone to an Eternity of

Happiness. I will bear the Deprivation as a dependent Creature favored by the Light of the Gospel should do.

John Dickinson to Tench Coxe, May 22, 1804. Coxe Papers (microfilm), reel 77, Library of Congress.

By Indulgence both Cheerfulness and Dejection will become Habits, but of very different Characters. They who neglect to cultivate the one and resist the other, are not wise. Our Religion, however serious from its Objects and their Importance, gives no countenance to habitual Melancholy. The Faith, Trust, Gratitude, Love, and Joy which it inculcates can not be associated with such an Inmate. Our Religion not only permits, but directs us to rejoice; and altho' it does not forbid occasional Sorrow or Grief, yet it marks the Limits beyond which they are not be indulged. Beyond these Limits they are Temptations and are to be treated accordingly. While prudential Truths and Principles remain inactive in speculation, they are as unproductive as Gold locked up in a Misers Chest. Until used and employed, neither of them do any good. I rejoice that you not only have sound Principles, but that you bring them into Practice. Virtuous Exertions are never neglected by Providence; and I am persuaded that yours will be blessed, if you persevere.

John Jay to Maria Jay Banyar, January 3, 1812. Jay Papers (online edition), Columbia University Library.

Be assured however my Dear Son, I will do all that is proper to shake off excess of grief [at the death of his young son, James—Ed.]. Thank God, in the midst of irresistible moaning & weeping I feel also an irresistible inclination to transmit to Heaven sentiments of gratitude & thankfulness for blessings past & present_the stroke indeed lies heavy & affects me more than doubly_that precious Limb torn from my Soul_the aggravated sense of this total seperation from all my Children, from all my family, the absence of every one who could alleviate by participation leaves the burthen upon my mind barely supportable__but it is mine it is the Will of God to lay it upon me & I will bear it with all possible Patience. . . . let every Young Man take heed & let us every day pray__"so teach us to number our days that we may apply our Hearts unto wisdom."__ten thousand thousand ways there are in which Men employ their time & to which they apply their Hearts, but in the event it will be found that none are equal to the ways of Wisdom. "for Wisdom is a defence & Money is a defence, but the excellency of knowledge is that Wisdom giveth Life to them that have it"__we too often however find verified in our selves the humble acknowledgement by the same Author__"I said I will be wise but it was far from me"__let us not be discouraged but earnestly strive & we shall obtain.

Henry Laurens to John Laurens, January 8, 1776. Rogers, *Papers of Henry Laurens*, 11:12–13.

Hell

Without Religion this World would be Something not fit to be mentioned in polite Company, I mean Hell.

John Adams to Thomas Jefferson, April 19, 1817. Cappon, *Adams-Jefferson Letters*, 2:509.

I think Bekker[20] might have demanded a truce from his antagonists, on the question of a Hell, by desiring them first

---

[20] Possibly a reference to Balthasar Bekker (1634–1698), a Dutch writer, some of whose works on the supernatural were translated into English.

to fix its geography, but wherever it be, it is certainly the best patrimony of the church, and procures them in exchange the solid acres of this world.

Thomas Jefferson to Francis van der Kemp, May 1, 1817. Jefferson Papers, Library of Congress.

What makes the review of life so short to most people is it has been spent upon the whole happily. In hell each moment will be like the duration of a thousand years.

Benjamin Rush, "Commonplace Book," 1809. Corner, *Autobiography of Rush*, 335.

Indians: see Native Americans

Islam

Napoleon is a military Fanatic like Achilles, Alexander, Caesar, Mahomet, Zingis Kouli, Charles 12th etc. The Maxim and Principle of all of them was the same "Jura negat sibi cata, nihil non arrogat armis" [he denies that laws were made for him; he arrogates everything to himself by force of arms—Ed.].

John Adams to Thomas Jefferson, July 16, 1814. Cappon, *Adams-Jefferson Letters*, 2: 435–36.

Predestination, eternal decrees, everlasting Counsels . . . I
can see no Liberty in the Universe consistent with these The-
ories and consequently no fault, no blame, no crime, no
sin, and no punishment and no reward, no merit nor de-
merit. Edwards, Hopkins, Priestley, Diderot, Jacques de Fa-
talist, Mahomet, Horace Virgil all held the same Dogma.
The Calvinists and the Atheists differ in nothing but this; the
former believe in eternal Misery; the latter not . . . Greeks
Romans Christians and Mahometans held Predestination.

> John Adams to John Quincy Adams, June 6, 1816. Adams Papers
> (microfilm), reel 432, Library of Congress.

Mahomet aimed to establish his pretensions to divine authority, by the power of the sword and the terrors of his
government; while he carefully avoided any attempts at
miracles in the presence of his followers, and all pretences
to foretell things to come. His acknowledging the divine
mission of Moses and Christ confirms their authority as far
as his influence will go, while their doctrines entirely destroy all his pretensions to the like authority. His doctrines
and precepts, are calculated to gratify the prejudices of
every party, and to confirm them in the established principles of a fanciful religion. To the Jews he was a disciple of
Moses—to Christians, he was a believer in the prophetic
character of Jesus Christ, while he indulged the heathen in-
habitant of Arabia in sensual ideas, that were most captivat-
ing and pleasing to the human heart. Instead of doctrines
and precepts inculcating the entire renovation of our
natures—the becoming a new creature and overcoming the
world Instead of a Felicity consisting of pure and spiritual
pleasures, "did he not establish a system of carnal indul-
gences, ever grateful to the natural man, founded in the
fascinating allurements of its promised rewards?—In their
agreeableness to the propensities of corrupt nature in

general, and to those of the inhabitants of warm climates in particular,—in the artful accommodation of its doctrines and its rites to the preconceived opinions, the favourite passions, and the deep routed prejudices of those to whom it was addressed."

Elias Boudinot, *The Age of Revelation* (Philadelphia: Asbury Dickins, 1801), 36–37.

And I saw three unclean spirits, like frogs, come out of the mouth of the dragon [the Roman temporal government] and out of the mouth of the beast [with seven heads and ten horns] and out of the mouth of the false prophet (it may be either the ecclesiastical powers of Rome, which are so-called after the reign of the antichrist, or the Mahometan power, now in possession of the eastern part of the old Roman empire), for they are the spirits of devils working miracles.

Elias Boudinot, *The Second Advent* (Trenton, N.J.: D. Fenton & S. Hutchinson, 1815), 517–18.

I rejoice exceedingly that I have been thus usefully engaged in following your steps by sending the Gospel of the Son of God, the Saviour of Men, to enlighten the dark abodes of Sin and Misery with the bright shining of the Sun of Righteousness, even in the utmost corners of pagan darkness and Mahometan superstition (and degrading Idolatry.)

Elias Boudinot to Emperor Alexander of Russia, June 29, 1818. Boudinot Papers, American Bible Society.

When the Portuguese arrived in the East Indies, the Mahometans, at the very period formidable enemies, were strongly establishing themselves there. Had a little more time been allowed them, it is highly probable their wishes would have been realized, by their being immoveably fixed in possession of all the wealth and power continually flowing, as the experience of ages has proved, from these inexhaustible sources. Nor is there the least reason to question, that they would have strenuously employed the increase of wealth and power in their favourite design of reducing all Christendom to the same miserable slavery, with which by their oppressive superstition, so many celebrated parts of it, including the Birthplace of its religion, have already been overwhelmed.

> John Dickinson, notes, undated. R. R. Logan Papers, Historical Society of Pennsylvania.

Every religion consists of moral precepts, and of dogmas. In the first they all agree. All forbid us to murder, steal, plunder, bear false witness &ca. and these are the articles necessary for the preservation of order, justice, and happiness in society. In their particular dogmas all differ; no two professing the same. These respect vestments, ceremonies, physical opinions, and metaphysical speculations, totally unconnected with morality, and unimportant to the legitimate objects of society. Yet these are the questions on which have hung the bitter schisms of Nazarenes, Socinians, Arians, Athanasians in former times, and now of Trinitarians, Unitarians, Catholics, Lutherans, Calvinists, Methodists, Baptists, Quakers &c. Among the Mahometans we are told that thousands fell victims to the dispute whether the first or second toe of Mahomet was the longest; and what blood, how many human lives have the words "this do in remembrance of me" cost the Christian world! . . . It is time then to become sensible how insoluble these questions are by minds like ours, how unimportant, and how mischievous; and to consign them to the sleep of death, never to be awakened from it. The varieties in the structure and actions of the human mind, as in those of the human body, are the work of the creator, against which it can not be a religious duty to erect the standard of uniformity. The practice of morality being necessary for the well being of society, he has taken care to impress it's precepts so indelibly on our hearts, that they shall not be effaced by the whimsies of our brain. Hence we see good men in all religions, and as many in one as another.

Thomas Jefferson to James Fishback, September 27, 1809. Adams, *Jefferson's Extracts*, 344 n.

Suppose a Man, under the guidance of his Passions & Appetites, a Lover of much & mixed Company, a Sensualist, or Slothful & a bad Oeconomist, taking the Koran instead of the New Testament for his Compass, and you will find no difficulty in granting, that such a Man is in continual danger of submitting to Bribery, by a Variety of Instruments. If his Bank of Cash stands unimpaired, a Title, a Wench, a Nod, or fulsome flattery, shall be his price. But in failure of the Fund, he will even *offer* himself to Sale to replenish it, as the only possible means for keeping up his sham happiness.

Henry Laurens to John Laurens, February 21, 1774. Rogers, *Papers of Henry Laurens*, 9:303.

Such is my veneration for every religion that reveals the attributes of the Deity, or a future state of rewards and punishment, that I had rather see the opinions of Confucius or Mohammed inculcated upon our youth than see them grow up wholly devoid of a system of religious principles.

Benjamin Rush, *A Plan for the Establishment of Public Schools*. Frederick Rudolph, ed., *Essays on Education in the Early Republic* (Cambridge, Mass.: Harvard University Press, 1965), 10.

"The bosom of America," he [Washington] declared a few months later, was "open to receive . . . the oppressed and persecuted of all Nations and Religions; whom we shall welcome to a participation of all our rights and privileges ... if they are good workmen, they may be of Asia, Africa, or Europe. They may be Mohometans, Jews or Christians of any Sect, or they may be Atheists."

Boller, *Washington*, 118.

Jesus

[Jesus] was, as you say, "the most benevolent Being that ever appeard on Earth."

John Adams to Thomas Jefferson, February 2, 1816. Cappon, *Adams-Jefferson Letters*, 2:462.

An incarnate God ! ! ! An eternal, self-existent, omnipresent omniscient Author of this stupendous Universe, suffering on a Cross ! ! ! My Soul starts with horror, at the Idea, and it has stupified the Christian World. It has been the Source of almost all the Corruptions of Christianity.

John Adams to John Quincy Adams, March 28, 1816. Adams Papers (microfilm), reel 430, Library of Congress.

The suffering Messiah known to the whole angelic host, as lying in the father's bosom from eternity, and as the great object of their love and adoration from their first existence; and who alone was capable of knowing and contemplating the Divinity in his pure essence, and who had seen the Father, being the express image of his person, and who thought it no robbery to claim an equality with God: this glorious being, becoming an expiatory sacrifice and propitiatory victim for the sins of the world, magnified the law of

God; demonstrated his infinite justice and love to being in general, and made it known to the universe, when he declared, "That God so loved the world, as to give his only begotten Son, that whosoever should believe in him should not perish, but have everlasting life." All this fully proved the infinite wisdom of the amazing plan, designed to subdue all things to, and keep them in the love of order and obedience, discovering to men and angels "the exceeding sinfulness of sin," and the awful consequences of it, even when the sacred humanity of the eternal Son of God was to be the victim, as a substitute for the aggressor.

> Elias Boudinot, *The Age of Revelation* (Philadelphia: Asbury Dickins, 1801), 217–18.

It is the example of him, who being in the form of God, came down from heaven for our sakes, took upon him the form of a servant and sealed his love to us by greater suffering than any man ever endured for his friend. This example is easy and familiar, conveying instruction in instances frequently occurring in human life. Upon all occasions the conduct of our blessed saviour was open meek patient sincere kind tender friendly and courteous, marking out a plain path for us to "walk even as he walked." He was the modestest humblest best natured most self denying and disinterested man that ever appeared in the world.

> John Dickinson, undated note. R. R. Logan Papers, Historical Society of Pennsylvania.

As to Jesus of Nazareth, my Opinion of whom you particularly desire, I think the System of Morals and his Religion, as he left them to us, the best the World ever saw or is likely to see; but I apprehend it has received various corrupting Changes, and I have, with most of the present Dissenters in England, some Doubts as to his Divinity; tho' it is a question I do not dogmatize upon, having never studied it, and think it needless to busy myself with it now when I expect soon an Opportunity of knowing the Truth with less Trouble [Franklin was eighty-four—Ed.]. I see no harm, however, in its being believed, if that Belief has the good Consequence, as probably it has, of making his Doctrines more respected and better observed.

> Benjamin Franklin to Ezra Stiles, March 9, 1790. Smyth, *Writings of Franklin*, 10:84.

His character and doctrines have received still greater injury from those who pretend to be his special disciples, and who have disfigured and sophisticated his actions and precepts, from views of personal interest, so as to induce the unthinking part of mankind to throw off the whole system in disgust, and to pass sentence as an imposter on the most innocent, the most benevolent the most eloquent and sublime character that ever has been exhibited to man.

> Thomas Jefferson to Joseph Priestley, April 19, 1803. Adams, *Jefferson's Extracts*, 328.

I am indeed . . . sincerely attached to his doctrines, in preference to all others; ascribing to himself every human excellence, and believing he never claimed any other.

> Thomas Jefferson to Benjamin Rush, April 21, 1803. Ibid., 331.

In this state of things among the Jews, Jesus appeared. His parentage was obscure, his condition poor, his education null, his natural endowments great, his life correct, and innocent; he was meek, benevolent, patient, firm, disinterested, and of sublime eloquence. The disadvantages under which his doctrines appear are remarkable.

1. Like Socrates and Epictetus, he wrote nothing himself.
2. But he had not, like them, a Xenophon or an Arrian to

write for him. On the contrary, all the learned of his country, entenched in it's power and riches, were opposed to him lest his labours should undermine their advantages: and the committing to writing his life and doctrines, fell on the most unlettered, and ignorant of men: who wrote too from memory, and not till long after the transactions had passed.

3. According to the ordinary fate of those who attempt to enlighten and reform mankind, he fell an early victim to the jealousy and combination of the altar and the throne; at about 33. years of age, his reason having not yet attained the maximum of it's energy, nor the course of his preaching, which was but of about 3. years, presented occasions for developing a compleat system of morals.

4. Hence the doctrines which he really delivered were defective as a whole. And fragments only of what he did deliver have come to us, mutilated, mistated, and often unintelligible.

5. They have been still more disfigured by the corruptions of schismatising followers, who have found an interest in sophisticating and perverting the simple doctrines he taught, by engrafting on them the mysticisms of a Graecian Sophist, frittering them into subtleties, and obscuring them with jargon, until they have caused good men to reject the whole in disgust, and to view Jesus himself as an imposter.

Notwithstanding these disadvantages, a system of morals is presented to us, which, if filled up in the true style and spirit of the rich fragments he left us, would be the most perfect and sublime that has ever been taught by man.

The question of his being a member of the god-head, or in direct communication with it, claimed for him by some of his followers, and denied by others, is foreign to the present view, which is merely an estimate of the intrinsic merits of his doctrines.

1. He corrected the Deism of the Jews, confirming them in their belief of only one god, and giving them juster notions of his attributes and government.

2. His moral doctrines relating to kindred and friends were more pure and perfect, than those of the most correct of the philosophers, and greatly more so than those of the Jews. And they went far beyond both in inculcating universal philanthropy, not only to kindred and friends, to neighbors and countrymen, but to all mankind, gathering all into one family, under the bonds of love, charity, peace, common wants, and common aids. A development of this head will evince the peculiar superiority of the system of Jesus over all others.

3. The precepts of Philosophy, and of the Hebrew code, laid hold of actions only. He pushed his scrutinies into the heart of man; erected his tribunal in the region of his thoughts, and purified the waters at the fountain head.

4. He taught, emphatically, the doctrine of a future state: which was either doubted or disbelieved by the Jews: and wielded it with efficacy, as an important incentive, supplementary to other motives to moral conduct.

> Thomas Jefferson, "Syllabus of an Estimate of the Merit of the Doctrines of Jesus, Compared with Those of Others," [April 21, 1803]. Adams, *Jefferson's Extracts*, 332–34.

Let us examine what our knowledge of Jesus Christ, the author of our salvation, is. Do we consider him as God and man, united in two distinct natures and one person forever? Do we rightly understand the mediatorial character, and the office Jesus Christ is invested with, that he was appointed by the Father to undertake the work of redeeming lost sinners; and for this purpose was constituted a prophet to reveal the counsels of grace; a priest, by the sacrifice of himself to atone for our sin, and plead for pardon; and a king, to rule or reign over us and defend us. Have we right apprehensions of the covenant of redemption and grace; that the Father from all eternity, upon the foresight of the fall, determined to rescue and save a chosen number; and to this end appointed his own Son to be mediator of the new covenant; to take upon him our nature, to be made under the law, and as the sinner's substitute, to obey the precepts and to endure the penalty thereof; thus fulfilling all the righteousness of it, for the justifying of the ungodly; and as an encouragement hereto, promised to furnish for, assist and succeed him in the undertaking, and give him a seed to serve him? The Son accepted the proposal, answering, "Lo I come to do thy will O God!" and in the appointed time was made man, became subject to the law, lived a holy and exemplary life, and died a cursed death on the cross; that so by completely answering the demand of the law, he might ransom us from hell, and purchase pardon, reconciliation, with God, the adoption of children, the sanctifying, quickening and strengthening influences of the holy spirit, and eternal life in heaven for all his people.

Roger Sherman, *Short Sermon*, 4–5.

Jews

As much as I love, esteem, and admire the Greeks, I believe the Hebrews have done more to enlighten and civilize the world. Moses did more than all their legislators and philosophers.

John Adams, undated marginalia in Condorcet's *Outlines of an Historical View of the Progress of the Human Mind*. Haraszti, *Prophets of Progress*, 246.

I have had occasion to be acquainted with several Gentlemen of your Nation and to transact Business with some of
them, whom I found to be Men of as liberal Minds, as
much honor Probity Generosity and good Breeding as any I
have known in any Sect of Religion or Philosophy. I wish
your Nation may be admitted to all the Privileges of Citizens in every Country of the World. This Country has done
much. I wish it may do more; and annul every narrow Idea
in Religion, Government and Commerce. Let the Wits joke;
the Philosophers sneer! What then? It has pleased the
Providence of the first Cause, the Universal Cause, that
Abraham should give Religion not only to Hebrews but to
Christians and Mahomitans, the greatest part of the modern civilized World.

> John Adams to Mordecai Noah, July 31, 1818. Adams Papers
> (microfilm), reel 123, Library of Congress.

I really wish the Jews again in Judea an independent nation.
For as I believe the most enlightened men of it have participated in the amelioration of the philosophy of the age, once
restored to an independent government & no longer persecuted they would soon wear away some of the asperities
and peculiarities of their character [and] possibly in time
become liberal unitarian Christians for your Jehovah is our
Jehovah & your God of Abraham Isaac & Jacob is our God.

> John Adams to Mordecai Noah, March 15, 1819. Ibid., reel 123.

However despised the nation of the Hebrews were among
the Greeks, Romans and others of their neighbours, during
the existence of their civil government, and by all the
nations of the earth ever since, there can be no doubt now,
that they have been and still are the most remarkable people that have existed since the first century after the
flood. . . . For while dispersed through the world without a
spot of land they could properly call their own, and de-

spised and persecuted in every part of it, yet they have continued a separate people, known by their countenances, while their enemies and conquerors have wasted away and are, as it were, lost from the earth, in fulfilment of the declarations of their prophets, inspired by God, to the astonishment of all nations.

This people was also a living example to the world of the dealings of Divine Providence towards the workmanship of his hands, by rewarding their obedience in a very extraordinary manner, and punishing their wilful transgressions by the most exemplary sufferings. . . .

God has acknowledged them by express revelation—by prophecies, forewarning them of what should befall them in the world, accordingly as they kept his commandments, or were disobedient to them, until their final restoration to the promised land. In short, their long dispersed state, with their severe persecutions, and still continuing a separate people among all nations, are standing, unanswerable and miraculous proofs of their sacred writings, and a complete fulfilment of the many prophecies concerning them, some thousands of years past.

> Elias Boudinot, *A Star in the West: or a Humble Attempt to Discover the Long Lost Ten Tribes of Israel* (Freeport, N.Y.: Books for Libraries Press, 1970), 23–25.

Let all then, carefully attend to the word of the Lord, as spoken by his prophets, and watch the signs of the times, seeking to know the will of God, and what he expects from those who are awakened to see their error. Much is to be done when the signal is set up for the nations; and these children of God's watchful providence shall be manifestly discovered. They are to be converted to the faith of Christ, and instructed in their glorious prerogatives, and prepared and assisted to return to their own land and their ancient

city, even the city of Zion, which shall become a praise in all
the earth. Let not our unbelief, or other irreligious conduct,
with a want of a lively, active faith in our Almighty Redeemer, become a stumbling block to these outcasts of Israel, wherever they may be. They will naturally look to the
practice and example of those calling themselves christians
for encouragement. Who knows but God has raised up these
United States in these latter days, for the very purpose of accomplishing his will in bringing his beloved people to their
own land.

Ibid., 297.

It does not appear to Me likely, that any of the Actors in the
present Tragedies will establish the Jews in the Land of
Canaan. The best Commentators I have met with, when
speaking only of their general Conversion, represented that
Event as two or three Centuries remote. That Nation is indeed, to use thy Expression, "a standing Miracle," and most
certainly and wonderfully will be instrumental in accomplishing the divine purpose. Connected with their general
Conversion will be the mighty Revolution in papal Christendom, and the fall of the Turkish Empire.

John Dickinson to Mercy Otis Warren, December 22, 1806.
Warren-Adams Letters, 2:348.

We observe a strange and general alteration in the feelings
of Christians towards the heathen; and one still more
strange and unprecedented has taken place in their feelings
towards the *Jews*; feelings very different from those which
so many centuries have universally prevailed. Although, as
it were, *sifted*, over all nations, yet, unlike the drops of rain
which blend with the waters on which they fall, those scat-
tered exiles have constantly remained in a state of separation from the people among whom they were dispersed;

obstinately adhering to their peculiarities, and refusing to coalesce with them. By thus fulfilling the prophecies, every Jew is a living witness to their truth.

The same prophecies declare, that a time will come when all twelve tribes shall be restored to their country, and be a praise in the earth; but the precise time is not specified. By declaring that "blindness in part hath happened unto Israel, *until* the fulness of the Gentiles be come in, and that Jerusalem shall be trodden down of the Gentiles until the times of the Gentiles be fulfilled," they lead us to conclude, that their blindness will not be sooner removed, and therefore that their conversion is not to be sooner expected. Individual Jews have, from time to time, been relieved from their blindness, and become Christians; and there are expressions in the Scriptures, which favour the prevailing opinion, that the conversion of a large portion, and perhaps the whole of the tribe of Judah, may precede that of the other tribes. They are now experiencing less oppression, less contempt, and more compassion than formerly. Their obduracy is softening, and their prejudices abating. These changes have the appearance of incipient preparatives for their conversion.

John Jay to the American Bible Society, May 8, 1823. Johnston, *Correspondence of Jay*, 4:489–90

Your sect by its sufferings has furnished a remarkable proof of the universal spirit of religious intolerance, inherent in every sect, disclaimed by all while feeble and practised by all when in power. Our laws have applied the only antidote to this vice, protecting our religious, as they do our civil rights by putting all on an equal footing. But more remains to be done, for altho' we are free by the law, we are not so in practice. Public opinion erects itself into an Inquisition and exercises it's office with as much fanaticism as fans the flames of an Auto da fé. The prejudice still scowling on your section of our religion, altho' the elder one, cannot be unfelt by yourselves. It is to hoped that individual dispositions will at length mould themselves to the model of the law and consider the moral basis on which all our religions rest, as the rallying point which unites them in a common interest; while the peculiar dogmas branching from it are the exclusive concern of the respective sects embracing them and no rightful subject of notice to any other. Public opinion needs reformation on this point.

> Thomas Jefferson to Mordecai Noah, May 20, 1818. Jefferson Papers, Library of Congress.

Thomas Jefferson presents to Mr. Marx his compliments & thanks for the Transactions of the Paris Sanhedrin, which he shall read with great interest, and with the regret he has ever felt at seeing a sect the parent and basis of all those of Christendom, singled out by all of them for a persecution and oppression which prove they have profited nothing from the benevolent doctrines of him whom they profess to make the model of their principles and practice.

> Thomas Jefferson to Joseph Marx, July 8, 1820. Ibid.

I was carried back to the ancient world and was led to contemplate the passovers, the sacrifices, the jubilees, and other ceremonies of the Jewish Church. After this, I was led forward into futurity and anticipated the time foretold by the prophets when this once-beloved race of men shall again be restored to the divine favor and when they shall unite with Christians with one heart and one voice in celebrating the praises of a common and universal Saviour.

> Benjamin Rush to Julia Rush, June 27, 1787. Butterfield, *Letters of Rush*, 1:431.

May the same wonder-working Deity, who long since delivering the Hebrews from their Egyptian oppressors [and] planted them in the promised land—whose providential agency has lately been conspicuous in establishing these United States as an independent nation—still continue to water them with the dews of Heaven and to make the inhabitants of every denomination participate in the temporal and spiritual blessings of that people whose God is Jehovah.

> George Washington to the Hebrew Congregation of the City of Savannah, [May 1790]. Boller, *Washington*, 185.

Law

To him who believes in the Existence and Attributes physical and moral of a God, there can be no obscurity or perplexity in defining the Law of Nature to be his wise benign and all powerful Will, discovered by Reason. A Man who disbelieves the Being of a God, will have no perplexity or obscurity in defining Morality or the Law of Nature, natural Law, natural Right or any such Things to be mere Maxims of Convenience, to be Swifts[21] pair of Breeches to be put on upon occasion for Decency or Conveniency and to be put off at pleasure for either.

> John Adams to Thomas Boylston Adams, March 19, 1794. Adams Papers (microfilm), reel 377, Library of Congress.

Good and wise men, in all ages . . . have supposed, that the deity, from the relations, we stand in, to himself and to each

---

[21] Jonathan Swift (1667–1745), the famous British satirist; author of *Gulliver's Travels*. DNB.

other, has constituted an eternal and immutable law, which is, indispensibly, obligatory upon all mankind, prior to any human institution whatever.

This is what is called the law of nature, "which, being co-eval with mankind, and dictated by God himself, is, of course, superior in obligation to any other. It is binding over all the globe, in all countries, and at all times. No human laws are of any validity, if contrary to this."

> Alexander Hamilton, "The Farmer Refuted," February 1775. Syrett, *Papers of Alexander Hamilton*, 1:87.

The moral or natural law was given by the Sovereign of the universe to all mankind; with them it was co-eval, and with them it will be co-existent. Being founded by infinite wisdom and goodness on essential right, which never varies, it can require no amendment or alteration.

> John Jay to John Murray, Jr., April 15, 1818. Johnston, *Correspondence of Jay*, 4:403.

. . . who now can question but that the whole Bible and Testament are a part of the Common law? And that Connecticut, in her blue laws, laying it down as a principle that the laws of god should be the laws of the land, except where their own contradicted them, did anything more than express, with a salvo, what the English judges had less cautiously declared without any restriction?

> Thomas Jefferson to John Adams, January 14, 1814. Cappon, *Adams-Jefferson Letters*, 2:423.

Liberty of Conscience

I have well fixed it in my Mind as a Principle, that every Nation has a Right to that Religion and Government which it chooses, and as long as any People please themselves in these great Points, I am determined they shall not displease me.

> John Adams to Abigail Adams, June 3, 1778. Butterfield, *Adams Family Correspondence*, 3:32.

I assert the divine right and sacred duty of private individual judgment and deny all human authority in matters of faith. . . . Now I know of no divine authority for Lords Parsons Lords Brethren, Lords Councils, Lords Synods, Lords Associations Lords Consociations or Lords General Assemblies, any more than in Lords Bishops, Lords Cardinals or Lords Kings or Gods Popes, to deliver a man over to Satan to be buffeted than there is in a Quincy Braintree or a Randolph Town Meeting.

> John Adams to Francis van der Kemp, January 23, 1813. Adams Papers (microfilm), reel 121, Library of Congress.

I will not condescend to employ the word Toleration. I assert that unlimited freedom of religion, consistent with morals and property, is essential to the progress of society and the amelioration of the condition of mankind.

> John Adams to Francis van der Kemp, October 2, 1818. Ibid., reel 123.

To obtain religious and civil liberty, I entered zealously into the Revolution, and observing the Christian religion divided into many sects, I founded the hope that no one would be so predominant as to become the religion of the state. That hope was thus early entertained, because all of them joined in the same cause, with few exceptions of individuals. God grant that this religious liberty may be preserved in these states, to the end of time, and that all believing in the religion of Christ may practice the leading principle of charity, the basis of every virtue.

> Charles Carroll of Carrollton to John Stanford, October 9, 1827. Kate Rowland, *The Life of Charles Carroll of Carrollton, 1737–1832* (New York: G. P. Putnam's Sons, 1898), 2:358.

Adequate security is also given to the rights of conscience and private judgment. They are by nature subject to no control but that of the Deity and in that free situation they are now left. Every man is permitted to consider, to adore, to worship his Creator in the manner most agreeable to his conscience. No opinions are dictated, no rules of faith prescribed, no preference given to one sect to the prejudice of others. The constitution, however, has wisely declared, that the "liberty of conscience thereby granted shall not be so construed as to excuse acts of licentiousness, or justify practices inconsistent with the peace or safety of the State."[22] In a word, the convention by whom that constitution was formed were of the opinion that the gospel of Christ, like the ark of God, would not fall, though unsupported by the arm of flesh; and happy would it be for mankind if that opinion prevailed more generally.

> John Jay, "Charge to the Ulster County Grand Jury," September 9, 1777. Johnston, *Correspondence of Jay*, 1:162–63.

. . . Almighty God hath created the mind free, and manifested his supreme will that free it shall remain by making it

---

[22] Jay is quoting, with minor alterations, Article 38 of the New York Constitution of 1777.

altogether insusceptible of restraint; that all attempts to influence it by temporal punishments, or burthens, or by civil incapacitations, tend only to beget habits of hypocrisy and meanness, and are a departure from the plan of the holy author of our religion, who being lord both of body and mind, yet chose not to propagate it by coercions on either, as was in his Almighty power to do, but to extend it by the influence of reason alone.

> Thomas Jefferson, "A Bill for Establishing Religious Freedom," 1777. Boyd, *Papers of Thomas Jefferson*, 2:545.

The clergy [had] a very favorable hope of obtaining an establishment of a particular form of Christianity thro' the US. And as every sect believes it's own form the true one, every one perhaps hoped for it's own: but especially the Episcopalians and the Congregationalists. The returning good sense of our country threatens abortion to their hopes, and they believe that any portion of power confided to me will be exerted in opposition to their schemes. And they believe truly. For I have sworn upon the altar of god eternal hostility against every form of tyranny over the mind of man.

> Thomas Jefferson to Benjamin Rush, September 23, 1800. Adams, *Jefferson's Extracts*, 320.

I never will, by any word or act, bow to the shrine of intolerance, or admit a right of enquiry into the religious opinions of others. On the contrary we are bound, you, I, and every one, to make common cause, even with error itself, to maintain the common right of freedom of conscience.

> Thomas Jefferson to Edward Dowse, April 19, 1803. Ibid., 330.

Our country has been the first to prove to the world two truths, the most salutary to human society, that man can govern himself, and that religious freedom is the most effective anodyne against religious dissension: the maxims of civil government being reversed in that of religion, where it's true form is "divided we stand, united we fall."

Thomas Jefferson to Jacob Delamotta, September 1, 1820. Jefferson Papers, Library of Congress.

The Religion then of every man must be left to the conviction and conscience of every man; and it is the right of every man to exercise it as these may dictate. This right is in its nature an unalienable right. It is unalienable, because the opinions of men, depending only on the evidence contemplated by their own minds cannot follow the dictates of other men; It is unalienable also, because what is here a right towards men, is a duty towards the Creator. It is the duty of every man to render to the Creator such homage and such only as he believes to be acceptable to him.

James Madison, "Memorial and Remonstrance," June 20, 1785. Rakove, *Madison Writings*, 30.

If I could have entertained the slightest apprehension that the Constitution framed in the Convention, where I had the honor to preside, might possibly endanger the religious rights of any ecclesiastical Society, certainly I would never have placed my signature to it; and if I could now conceive that the general Government might ever be so administered as to render the liberty of conscience insecure, I beg you will be persuaded that no one would be more zealous than myself to establish effectual barriers against the horrors of spiritual tyranny, and every species of religious persecution— For you, doubtless, remember that I have often expressed my sentiments, that every man, conducting himself as a good citizen, and being accountable to God alone for his religious opinions, ought to be protected in worshipping the Deity according to the dictates of his own conscience.

George Washington to the General Committee Representing the United Baptist Churches in Virginia, May 1789. Boller, *Washington*, 170.

The Citizens of the United States of America have a right to applaud themselves for having given to Mankind examples of an enlarged and liberal policy, a policy worthy of imitation. All possess alike liberty of conscience and immunities of citizenship. It is now no more that toleration is spoken of, as if it was by the indulgence of one class of people, that another enjoyed their inherent natural rights. For happily the Government of the United States, which gives to bigotry no sanction, to persecution no assistance, requires only that they who live under its protection should demean themselves as good citizens, in giving it on all occasions their effectual support.

> George Washington to the Hebrew Congregation of Newport, Rhode Island, [August 17, 1790]. Ibid., 186.

There is not a single instance in history in which civil liberty was lost, and religious liberty preserved entire.

> John Witherspoon, "The Dominion of Providence over the Passions of Man," May 17, 1776. *Works of Witherspoon*, 3:37.

Marriage

By discharging all the duties of conjugal life from religious principles, we enjoy a kind of exclusive happiness suited to the perfection and dignity of our natures: a happiness which involves in it all the inferior pleasures of reason and sense and which can never be equally relished by those animal machines, who are governed in all their actions by instinct only, or by the vulgar maxims and fashions of the world.

Benjamin Rush to Julia Stockton, November 12, 1775. Benjamin Rush, *My Dearest Julia: The Love Letters of Dr. Benjamin Rush to Julia Stockton* (New York: N. Watson Academic Publications, 1979), 13–14.

Marriage was instituted in Paradise before the Fall. All its pleasures therefore are free from sin. It is essential to the order and happiness of society—it must therefore be agreeable to the will of God. It is the most natural and successful mode of multiplying human beings. —It must therefore be necessary to bring into existence the objects of the great covenant of redemption. Our Saviour's conduct while he was in the world accords in everything with these general propositions. He honored a wedding with his first miracle, and he rebuked the woman of Samaria for living with a man who was <u>not</u> her husband. Could a single life have been proper in any one person in the world, it certainly must have been in his mother Mary. But no. Even her body does not become sacred by bearing the Son of God. She afterwards publicly becomes the wife of Joseph and has children by him. St. Paul pronounces "marriage honorable in all, and the bed undefiled." He likewise ranks "forbidding to marry among the doctrines of devils." These general assertions overset every insinuation to the contrary that time and circumstances introduced into his writings.

Benjamin Rush to Mary Stockton, September 7, 1788. Butterfield, *Letters of Rush*, 1:484–85.

Millennium

However it is a matter of little consequence, whether the great event shall come in 10–20 or 50 years. We know it is approaching. We plainly see the signs of the times and therefore we have a right to lift up our heads and rejoice, knowing that our redemption is drawing nigh. The signal of the great catastrophe is the downfall of the Pope and the destruction of the great city. Blessed be God that, whenever the time comes, let it be sooner or be it later, Jesus shall reign king of nations as he is king of saints and all the earth shall be covered with the knowledge of God as the waters cover the sea.

> Elias Boudinot to Elisha Boudinot, January 6, 1798. Boudinot Papers, Princeton University Library.

May we not now ask, as the sum of this whole matter, does not this great question, relative to the second advent of the glorified Saviour (as applicable to America as Europe) from the signs of the times, herein before described and held up to view, appear to be fully established, by its having been shewn that this all important event is drawing nigh, if not at the very door? And do not the facts that have been developed in this work, call upon all the servants of Jesus Christ, by whatever name distinguished, to be found ready for the marriage supper of the Lamb? I know that this is not a singular opinion of mine: it is the voice of reason, founded on revelation.

> Elias Boudinot, *The Second Advent* (Trenton, N.J.: D. Fenton & S. Hutchinson, 1815), 545.

The restoration of this suffering and despised nation [the Jews—Ed.] to their ancient city and their former standing in the favour of God, with a great increase of glory and happiness, are expressly foretold by Christ, his prophets and apostles, as immediately preceding the second coming of our Lord and Saviour Jesus Christ, to this our earth, with his saints and angels, in his own glory as mediator, and the glory of the father, or of his divine nature, plainly distinguished from that humility and abasement attending his first coming in the flesh.

Elias Boudinot, *A Star in the West; or, a Humble Attempt to Discover the Long Lost Ten Tribes of Israel* (Freeport, N.Y.: Books for Libraries Press, 1970), 25.

Many pious people expect we are upon the eve of the millennium. I am not of that opinion. There is a great deal of preparatory work to be done before that event can take place.

Benjamin Rush to John Montgomery, June 6, 1801. Butterfield, *Letters of Rush*, 2:834.

Miracles

Most of his [Jesus'—Ed.] miracles were such objects of sense, that he could not have been deceived himself, by enthusiasm or other false principle. They all come within the first two rules, laid down by an excellent writer of the last century, relative to the proof of ancient facts, on which he justly challenges all the enemies to revelation, as to every other system but that of the bible, viz. First—"That the matters of fact shall be such, as the reality of them may be ascertained by external evidence." Second—"That they shall be performed publicly." Thirdly—"That not only public monuments shall be maintained in memory of them, but some external deeds should be performed." Fourthly—"That such monuments, deeds or observances, shall be instituted and commence from the period in which the matters of fact shall be transacted."

Jesus Christ walked upon the waters—he healed the sick, openly and publickly, before all the people, by a word, and often at a distance—he raised the dead at his first approach to them—he cast out devils, and once permitted them to enter into a herd of 2000 swine, which were near at hand—he rebuked the winds and the waves, and they obeyed him— he fed multitudes with a few loaves and small fishes. He therefore could not mistake these events, or be deceived by an enthusiastic temper of mind; but the miracles he wrought, and the predictions he declared, must have been honestly intended as evidences, conclusive evidences, of his divine mission, and for the good of mankind; the truth of which he sealed with his blood, premeditatedly and deliberately, with his own foreknowledge, having frequently forewarned his disciples, and declared to his enemies, that such would be the issue of his ministry.

Elias Boudinot, *The Age of Revelation* (Philadelphia: Asbury Dickins, 1801), 194–95.

Missionary and Bible Societies

According to the pamphlet you sent me, we must all pay, voluntarily or involuntarily, Tithes or Fifths or thirds, or halves, or all we have, to send Bibles and Missionaries, to convert all Men and save their Souls. I am confident that all

the property of Europe and America would not be suffi-
cient to convert Asia and Africa. Mankind must have a
Crusade, a War of Reformation, a French Revolution, or
Anti-Revolution, to amuse them and preserve them from
Ennui.

> John Adams to Benjamin Waterhouse, December 19, 1815. Adams
> Papers (microfilm), reel 122, Library of Congress.

We have now, it seems a National Bible Society,[23] to propagate King James's Bible, through all Nations. Would it not be
better, to apply these pious subscriptions, to purify Christendom from the corruptions of Christianity, than to propagate
these corruptions in Europe, Asia, Africa and America!

> John Adams to Thomas Jefferson, November 4, 1816. Cappon,
> *Adams-Jefferson Letters*, 2:493–94.

One of the zealous mendicants for contributions to the
funds of the Missionary Societies called upon a gentleman
in Haverhill and requested his charity. The gentleman de-
clined contributing, but added there are, in and about the
town of Newburyport nine Clergymen Ministers of nine
Congregations not one of whom lives on terms of civility
with any other, will admit none other into his pulpit nor be
permitted to go into the pulpit of any other. Now if you will
raise a fund to send Missionaries to Newburyport to convert these nine Clergymen to Christianity I will contribute
as much as any Man.

> John Adams to Aaron Bancroft, January 24, 1823. Adams Papers
> (microfilm), reel 124, Library of Congress.

Thus my beloved friends, hath God in his condescending
grace appointed us to become his humble instruments in
opening the eyes of the blind; in cheering the abodes of

---

[23] Adams is referring to the American Bible Society, formed in 1816.

primeval darkness with the joyful sounds of redeeming
love; in fulfilling the encouraging prophecy of the angel fly-
ing through the midst of heaven, having the everlasting
Gospel in his hands, to preach to all nations, languages,
tongues, and people on the earth.

> Elias Boudinot, President, American Bible Society, to the Managers
> of the American Bible Society, May 5, 1817. W. P. Strickland, *History
> of the American Bible Society* (New York, 1849), 349–50.

We now see Christians, in different countries, and of different denominations, spontaneously and cordially engaged in
conveying the Scriptures, and the knowledge of salvation,
to the heathen inhabitants of different regions. . . . From the
nature, the tendency, and the results of these recent and singular changes, events, and institutions; from their coin-
cidence, and admirable adjustment, as means for making
known the Holy Scriptures, and inculcating the will of their
Divine and merciful Author, throughout the world; and
from the devotedness with which they are carrying into operation, there is reason to conclude that they have been produced by Him in whose hand are the hearts of all men. . . .
They who march under the banners of Emmanuel have God
with them; and consequently have nothing to fear.

> John Jay to the American Bible Society, May 8, 1823. Johnston,
> *Correspondence of Jay*, 4:489–92.

[New England] is now looking to the fleshpots of the South
and aiming at foothold there by their missionary teachers.
They have lately come forward boldly with their plan to establish "a qualified religious instructor over every thousand
souls in the US" and they seem to consider none as qualified but their own sect. Thus, in Virginia, they say there are
but 60 qualified, and that 914 are still wanting of the full
quota. All besides the 60 are "mere nominal ministers unac-

quainted with theology." Now the 60 they allude to are exactly in the string of counties at the western foot of the Blue Ridge, settled originally by Irish presbyterians, and comprising precisely the tory district of the state. There indeed is found, in full vigor, the hypocrisy, the despotism, and anti-civism of the New England qualified religious instructors. The country below the mountains, inhabited by Episcopalians, Methodists & Baptists (under mere nominal ministers unacquainted with theology) are pronounced "destitute of the means of grace, and as sitting in darkness and under the shadow of death." They are quite in despair too at the insufficient means of New England to fill this fearful void "with Evangelical light, with catechetical instructions, weekly lectures, & family visiting.["] That Yale cannot furnish above 80 graduates annually, and Harvard perhaps not more. That there must therefore be an immediate universal, vigorous & systematic effort made to evangelize the nation to see that there is a bible for every family, a school for every district, and a qualified (i.e. Presbyterian) "pastor for every thousand souls; that newspapers, tracts, magazines, must be employed; the press be made to groan, & every pulpit in the land to sound it's trumpet long and loud a more homogeneous" (i.e. New England) "character must be produced thro' the nation." That section then of our union having lost it's political influence by disloyalty to it's country is now to recover it under the mask of religion.

Thomas Jefferson to Horatio Spafford, January 10, 1816. Jefferson Papers, Library of Congress.

These Incendiaries, finding that the days of fire and faggot are over in the Atlantic hemisphere, are now preparing to put the torch to the Asiatic regions. What would they say were the Pope to send annually to this country colonies of Jesuit priests with cargoes of their Missal and translations of their Vulgate, to be put gratis into the hands of every one who would accept them? And to act thus nationally on us as a nation?

Thomas Jefferson to John Adams, November 25, 1816., Cappon, *Adams-Jefferson Letters*, 2:496

Morality

. . . you know that I look upon Religion as the most perfect System, and the most awfull Sanction of Morality.

John Adams to Abigail Adams, November 18, 1775. Butterfield, *Adams Family Correspondence*, 1:327.

There is no such thing [morality] without a supposition of a God. There is no right or wrong in the universe without the supposition of a moral government and an intellectual and moral governor.

John Adams, marginal note in Condorcet's *Outlines of an Historical View of the Progress of the Human Mind.* Haraszti, *Prophets of Progress*, 252.

The ominous dissolution of Morality both in Theory and Practice throughout the civilized World, threatens dangers and calamities of a novel species, beyond all Calculation: because there is no Precedent or Example in History that can shew us the Consequences of it. Perhaps you may say Tyre and Sidon, Sodom and Gomorra are examples in Point. But we have no relations of their rise, progress or decline. You may say the old World, when it repented God that he had made Man, when it grieved him in his heart that he had made so vile a Creature is a Case in Point. I know not what to say in answer to this, only that the same authority we have for the fact, assures us that the World shall never be again drowned.

John Adams to Benjamin Rush, May 21, 1787. *Old Family Letters*, 142.

Religion I hold to be essential to morals. I never read of an irreligious character in Greek or Roman history, nor in any other history, nor have I known one in life, who was not a rascal. Name one if you can, living or dead.

John Adams to Benjamin Rush, April 18, 1808. Ibid., 179.

No point of Faith is so plain, as that <u>Morality</u> is our Duty; for all Sides agree in that. A virtuous Heretick shall be saved before a wicked Christian.

Benjamin Franklin, "Dialogue between Two Presbyterians," April 10, 1735. Labaree, *Papers of Benjamin Franklin*, 2:33.

Can we in prudence suppose that national morality can be maintained in exclusion of religious principles? Does it not require the aid of a generally received and divinely authoritative Religion?

Alexander Hamilton, draft of Washington's Farewell Address, [1796]. Hamilton Papers, Library of Congress.

He who made us would have been a pitiful bungler if he had made the rules of our moral conduct a matter of science. For one man of science, there are thousands who are not. What would have become of them? Man was destined for society. His morality therefore was to be formed to this object. He was endowed with a sense of right and wrong merely relative to this. This sense is as much a part of his nature as the sense of hearing, seeing, feeling; it is the true foundation of morality. . . . The moral sense, or conscience, is as much a part of man as his leg or arm. It is given to all human beings in a stronger or weaker degree, as force of members is given them in a greater or less degree. It may be strengthened by exercise, as may any particular limb of the body. . . . This sense is submitted indeed in some degree to the guidance of reason; but it is a small stock which is required for this: even a less one than what we call Common sense. State a moral case to a ploughman and a professor. The former will decide it as well, and often better than the latter, because he has not been led astray by artificial rules.

Thomas Jefferson to Peter Carr, August 10, 1787. Boyd, *Papers of Thomas Jefferson*, 12:14–15.

As to myself, my religious reading has long been confined to the moral branch of religion, which is the same in all religions; while in that branch which consists of dogmas, all differ, all have a different set. The former instructs us how to live well and worthily in society; the latter are made to interest our minds in the support of the teachers who inculcate them. Hence for one sermon on a moral subject, you hear ten on the dogmas of the sect.

Thomas Jefferson to Thomas Leiper, January 21, 1809. Jefferson Papers, Library of Congress.

Nothing is more certain than that a general profligacy and corruption of manners make a people ripe for destruction. A good form of government may hold the rotten materials together for some time, but beyond a certain pitch, even the best constitution will be ineffectual, and slavery must ensue. On the other hand, when the manners of a nation are pure, when true religion and internal principles maintain their vigor, the attempts of the most powerful enemies to oppress them are commonly baffled and disappointed.

John Witherspoon, "The Dominion of Providence over the Passions of Man," May 17, 1776. *Works of Witherspoon*, 3:41.

Native Americans

Dr. Jarvis[24] in his seventh page has truly observed that the Indians can not communicate in relation to their religion. I have made the same observation. I have seen a strong and marked aversion to converse or say anything upon the subject. . . . In 1789 there occurred an occasion which gave me great hopes. A large deputation of Kings Warriors and Sachims from the Creek Nations came to New York with Mr. McGillivray[25] at their Head to treat with the government. They were lodged near my house in Richmond Hill. They frequently visited me and some of them dined with me. But I could learn nothing from them. Mr. McGillivray was the son of a Scotchman by an Indian Queen. His Father had given him a good Education and he spoke and wrote very well in English. From him I was confident [of] much information but he was as close as a miser. I asked him many questions concerning the religion of the Indians but when I pressed him pretty closely for some time he said with an arch smile—"why we used to say that our customs most resembled the Jews." When I urged him with questions concerning their belief in a future state he still betrayed great reluctance and would be silent. When I asked him whether they had any ideas of an existence after death? He answered with a malignant scornful kind of smile, "Why I believe very little. I have heard them say that men

[21] Samuel Jarvis, *A Discourse on the Religion of the Indian tribes of North America* (New York: C. Wiley & Co., 1820).

[25] Alexander McGillivray (1759–1793), was the son of a Scotch father and a Koasati mother. A leader of the Creek confederation, who resisted American incursions into Georgia, McGillivray participated in the Treaty of New York (August 7, 1790), which ceded substantial Creek lands to the United States. *ANB.*

are like trees, when a tree dies it rots." This is all I could obtain from him.

John Adams to William Smith Shaw, June 21, 1821. Adams Papers (microfilm), reel 124, Library of Congress.

It is a fact well attested, that a preacher went among them before the revolutionary war, and in a sudden discourse to them, began to tell them that there was a God, who created all things—that it was exceedingly sinful and offensive to him, to get drunk, or lie, or steal—Ball of which they must carefully avoid. They answered him—"Go about your business, you fool! Do not we know that there is a God, as well as you! Go to your own people and preach to them; for who gets drunk, and lies and steals more than you white people?" . . . The Indians are filled with great spiritual pride—we mean their chiefs and best men. They consider themselves as under a theocracy, and that they have God for their governor and head. They therefore hold all other people, comparatively, in contempt. They pay their religious worship, as Mr. Adair assures us and he had a great opportunity of knowing) to <u>Loak-Ishto, Hoolo-Abba</u>, or the great, beneficent, supreme, holy spirit of fire, who resides above the clouds, and on earth with unpolluted, holy people.

Elias Boudinot, *A Star in the West; or, a Humble Attempt to Discover the Long Lost Ten Tribes of Israel* (Freeport, N. Y.: Books for Libraries Press, 1970), 189.

These wandering nations of Indians are the long lost tribes of Israel; but kept under the special protection of Almighty God, though despised by all mankind, for more than two thousand years, separated from and unknown to the civilized world. Thus wonderfully brought to the knowledge of their fellow men, they may be miraculously prepared for instruction, and stand ready, at the appointed time, when God shall raise the signal to the nations of Europe, to be restored to the land and country of their fathers, and to Mount Zion the city of David, their great king and head, and this in direct, positive and literal fulfillment of the numerous promises of the God of Abraham, Isaac and Jacob, to their pious progenitors and founders, near four thousand years ago.

Ibid., 280.

They were all drunk Men and Women, quarrelling and fighting. Their dark-colour'd Bodies, half naked, seen only by the gloomy Light of the Bonfire, running after and beating one another with Firebrands, accompanied by their horrid Yellings, form'd a Scene the most resembling our Ideas of Hell that could well be imagin'd. There was no appeasing the Tumult, and we retired to our Lodging. At Midnight a Number of them came thundering at our Door, demanding more Rum; of which we took no Notice. The next Day, sensible they had misbehav'd in giving us that Disturbance, they sent three of their old Counsellors to make their Apology. The Orator acknowledg'd the Fault, but laid it upon the Rum; and then endeavour'd to excuse the Rum, by saying, "<u>The great Spirit who made all things made every thing for some Use, and whatever Use he design'd any thing for, that Use it should always be put to; Now, when he made Rum, he said</u>, LET THIS BE FOR INDIANS TO GET DRUNK WITH. <u>And it must be so</u>." And indeed if it be the Design of Providence to extirpate these Savages in order to make room for Cultivators of the Earth, it seems not improbable that Rum may be the appointed Means. It has already annihilated all the Tribes who formerly inhabited the Sea-coast.

Benjamin Franklin, *Autobiography*, post-1788. Labaree, *Autobiography of Franklin*, 198–99.

You ask further, if the Indians have any order of priesthood among them, like the Druids, Bards or Minstrels of the Celtic nation? Adair alone, determined to see what he wished to see in every object, metamorphoses their Conjurors into an order of priests, and describes their sorceries as if they were the great religious ceremonies of the nation. Lafitau calls them by their proper names, Jongleurs, Devins, Sortileges; De Bry praestigiatores, Adair[26] himself sometimes Magi, Archimagi, cunning men, Seers, rain makers, and the modern Indian interpreters, call them Conjurors and Witches. They are persons pretending to have communications with the devil and other evil spirits, to foretel future events, bring down rain, find stolen goods, raise the dead, destroy some, and heal others by enchantment, lay spells etc. And Adair, without departing from his parallel of the Jews and Indians, might have found their counterpart, much more aptly, among the Soothsayers, sorcerers and wizards of the Jews, their Jannes and Jambres, their Simon Magus, witch of Endor, and the young damsel whose sorceries disturbed Paul so much; instead of placing them in a line with their High-priest, their Chief priests, and their magnificent hierarchy generally. In the solemn ceremonies of the Indians, the persons who direct or officiate, are the chiefs, elders, and warriors, in the civil ceremonies or in those of war; it is the Head of the Cabin, in their private or particular feasts or ceremonies; and sometimes the Matrons, as in their Corn feasts. And, even here, Adair might have kept up his parallel, with ennobling his Conjurers. For the antient Patriarchs, the Noahs, the Abrahams, Isaacs and Jacobs, and, even after the consecration of Aaron, the Samuels and Elijahs, and we may

[26] James Adair, *The History of the American Indians* . . . (London: Charles and Edward Dilly, 1775), a book which argued that the Indians were descended from the ancient Israelites.

say further every one for himself, offered sacrifices on the altars. The true line of distinction seems to be, that solemn ceremonies, whether public or private, addressed to the Great Spirit, are conducted by the worthies of the nation, Men, or Matrons, while Conjurers are resorted to only for the invocation of evil spirits. The present state of the several Indian tribes, without any public order of priests, is proof sufficient that they never had such an order. Their steady habits permit no innovations, not even those which the progress of science offers to increase the comforts, enlarge the understanding, and improve the morality of mankind. Indeed so little idea have they of a regular order of priests, that they mistake ours for their Conjurers, and call them by that name.

Thomas Jefferson to John Adams, June 11, 1812. Cappon, *Adams-Jefferson Letters*, 2:306–7.

You do well to wish to learn our arts and ways of life, and above all, the religion of Jesus Christ. These will make you a greater and happier people than you are.

George Washington to the Delaware Chiefs, May 12, 1779. Fitzpatrick, *Writings of Washington*, 15:55.

. . . permit me to add that if an event so long and so earnestly desired as that of converting the Indians to Christianity and consequently to civilization, can be effected, the Society of Bethlehem bids fair to bear a very considerable part in it.

George Washington to John Ettwein, May 2, 1788. Ibid., 29:489.

New England

I anticipate nothing but suffering to the human race while the present system of paganism, deism, and atheism prevail in the world. New England may escape the storm which impends our globe, but if she does, it will only be by adhering to the religious principles and moral habits of the first settlers of that country.

Benjamin Rush to Noah Webster, July 20, 1797. Butterfield, *Letters of Rush*, 2:799.

Recollect here your definition of a New Englander given to one of your friends in Amsterdam. It was: "He is a meeting-going animal."

Benjamin Rush to John Adams, August 20, 1811. Ibid., 2, 1096.

Oaths

Designing and selfish men invented religious tests to exclude from posts of profit and trust their weaker or more conscientious fellow subjects; thus to secure to themselves all the emoluments of government: Wharton's[27] saying was a true as well as witty one—The oaths of government were

---

[27] Carroll is probably referring to Philip Wharton, 4th Baron Wharton (1613–1696), privy councillor of William III, well known for his opposition to oaths. *DNB*.

so framed as to damn one part of the nation, & to shame the other.

Charles Carroll of Carrollton to Walter Graves, August 15, 1774.
Carroll Papers, Maryland Historical Society.

If Christian Preachers had continued to teach as Christ & his Apostles did, without Salaries, and as the Quakers now do, I imagine Tests would never have existed: For I think they were invented not so much to secure Religion itself, as the Emoluments of it. When a Religion is good, I conceive that it will support itself; and when it cannot support itself, and God does not take care to support, so that its Professors are oblig'd to call for the help of the Civil Power, 'tis a Sign, I apprehend, of its being a bad one.

Benjamin Franklin to Richard Price, October 9, 1780. Labaree, *Papers of Benjamin Franklin*, 33:390.

The very Heathen held an Oath as a Thing of so great Force and of such sacred Authority, that they believed the Sin of Perjury was pursued with the severest Vengeance; such as extended itelf to the Posterity of the Offender.

Christians of all Denominations and in all Ages have held the solemn Obligation of an Oath in the same Light, and in the highest Degree of Veneration, as being the Touchstone of Truth, whereupon the Properties, Characters, and Lives of worthy Citizens do often depend.

Henry Laurens, "Reflections arising from a Retrospect of a late Case,"
1769. Rogers, *Papers of Henry Laurens*, 6:376.

There can be no doubt of christians having uniformly refused to take an oath in the first ages of the church; nor did they conform to this pagan custom, till after christianity was corrupted by a mixture with many other parts of the pagan and Jewish religions. . . . If oaths are contrary to reason, and have a pernicious influence upon morals and the order of society; and above all, if they are contrary to the precepts and spirit of the gospel; it becomes legislators and ministers of the gospel to consider how far they are responsible for all the falsehood, profane swearing and perjury that exist in society. It is in the power of legislators to abolish oaths, by expunging them from our laws; and it is in the power of ministers of the gospel, by their influence and example, to render truth so simple and obligatory, that human governments shall be ashamed to ask any other mode of declaring it, from <u>Christians</u>, than by a bare affirmation.

> Benjamin Rush, "An Enquiry into the Consistency of Oaths with Reason and Christianity," January 20, 1789. Rush, *Essays: Literary, Moral, and Philosophical*, 77–78.

Let it simply be asked where is the security for property, for reputation, for life, if the sense of religious obligation <u>desert</u> the oaths, which are the instruments of investigation in Courts of Justice?

> George Washington, Farewell Address, September 19, 1796. Rare Book and Special Collections Division, Library of Congress.

Patriotism

The patriot, like the Christian, must learn that to bear revilings & persecutions is a part of his duty; and in proportion as the trial is severe, firmness under it becomes more requisite & praiseworthy.

> Thomas Jefferson to James Sullivan, May 21, 1805. Jefferson Papers, Library of Congress.

The Amor Patriae is both a moral and a religious duty. It comprehends not only the love of our neighbors but of millions of our fellow creatures, not only of the present but of future generations.This virtue we find constitutes a part of the first characters in history. The holy men of old, in proportion as they possessed a religious were endowed with a public spirit. What did not Moses forsake and suffer for his countrymen! What shining examples of Patriotism do we behold in Joshua, Samuel, Maccabeus, and all the illustrious princes, captains, and prophets among the Jews! St. Paul almost wishes himself accursed for his countrymen and kinsmen after the flesh. Even our Saviour himself gives a sanction to this virtue. He confined his miracles and gospel at first to his own country. He wept at the prospect of her speedy desolation, and even after she had imbrued her hands in his blood, he commands his Apostles to begin the promulgation of his gospel at Jerusalem.

Benjamin Rush, "To His Fellow Countrymen: On Patriotism," October 20, 1773. Butterfield, *Letters of Rush*, 1:83.

Paul, the Apostle

Among the sayings and discourses imputed to him [Jesus— Ed.] by his biographers, I find many passages of fine imagination, correct morality, and of the most lovely benevolence: and others again of so much ignorance, so much absurdity, so much untruth, charlatanism, and imposture, as to pronounce it impossible that such contradictions should have proceeded from the same being. I separate therefore the gold from the dross: restore to him the former, and leave the latter to the stupidity of some and the roguery of others of the disciples. Of this band of dupes and imposters, Paul was the great Coryphaeus, and the first corrupter of the doctrines of Jesus.

> Thomas Jefferson to William Short, April 13, 1820. Adams, *Jefferson's Extracts*, 392.

Persecution

Why do you single out poor Calvin and Servetus? Luther would not tolerate Zwinglius because he did not believe in Consubstantiation. Peter Portellus was condemned for being a Zwinglian. Anabaptists also were put to death. Zwinglius also condemned an Anabaptist, to be drowned . . . . Why then do you single out Calvin? All the protestant leaders were intolerant, and all the Protestant Dissenters too when they had power. Even the settlers of Virginia and New England. If the Arminians are an exception, they never had power. The French Atheists, Deists, Philosophers in the late revolution were as intolerant as Christian Priests. What shall we say? Human nature is intolerant whenever it has power. Trust power then without a counterpoise to no church, to no sect, to no Party. Amen and Amen.

> John Adams to Francis van der Kemp, June 5, 1812. Adams Papers (microfilm), reel 118, Library of Congress.

Checks and Ballances, Jefferson, however you and your Party may have ridiculed them, are our only Security, for the progress of the Mind, as well as the Security of the Body. Every Species of these Christians would persecute Deists, as soon as either Sect would persecute another, if it had unchecked and unballanced Power. Nay, the Deists would persecute Christians and Atheists would persecute Deists, with as unrelenting Cruelty, as any Christians would persecute them or one another. Know thyself, human Nature!

John Adams to Thomas Jefferson, June 25, 1813. Cappon, *Adams-Jefferson Letters*, 2:334.

1. And it came to pass after these Things, that Abraham sat in the Door of his Tent, about the going down of the Sun.

2. And behold a Man, bowed with Age, came from the Way of the Wilderness, leaning on a Staff.

3. And Abraham arose and met him, and said unto him, Turn in, I pray thee, and wash thy Feet, and tarry all Night, and thou shalt arise early on the Morrow, and go on thy Way.

4. And the Man said, Nay, for I will abide under this Tree.

5. But Abraham pressed him greatly; so he turned, and they went into the Tent; and Abraham baked unleavened Bread, and they did eat.

6. And when Abraham saw that the Man blessed not God, he said unto him, Wherefore dost thou not worship the most high God, Creator of Heaven and Earth?

7. And the Man answered and said, I do not worship the God thou speakest of; neither do I call upon his Name; for I have made to myself a God, which abideth always in mine House, and provideth me with all Things.

8. And Abraham's Zeal was kindled against the Man; and he arose, and fell upon him, and drove him forth with Blows into the Wilderness.

9. And at Midnight God called unto Abraham, saying, Abraham where is the Stranger?

10. And Abraham answered and said, Lord, he would not worship thee, neither would he call upon thy Name; therefore have I driven him out before my Face into the Wilderness.

11. And God said, Have I born with him these hundred ninety and eight Years, and nourished him, and cloathed him, notwithstanding his Rebellion against me, and couldst not thou, that art thyself a Sinner, bear with him one Night?

12. And Abraham said, Let not the Anger of my Lord wax hot against his Servant. Lo, I have sinned: forgive me, I pray Thee:

13. And Abraham arose and went forth into the Wilderness, and sought diligently for the Man, and found him, and returned with him to his Tent; and when he had entreated him kindly, he sent him away on the Morrow with Gifts.

14. And God spake again unto Abraham, saying, For this thy Sin shall thy Seed be afflicted four Hundred Years in a strange Land:

15. But for thy Repentance will I deliver them; and they shall come forth with Power, and with Gladness of Heart, and with much Substance.

Benjamin Franklin, "A Parable against Persecution," July 1755. Labaree, *Papers of Benjamin Franklin*, 6:122–24.

If we look back into history for the character of present sects in Christianity, we shall find few that have not in their turns been persecutors, and complainers of persecution. The primitive Christians thought persecution extremely wrong in the Pagans, but practised it on one another. The first Protestants in the Church of England, blamed persecution in the Roman church, but practised it against the Puritans:

these found it wrong in the Bishops, but fell into the same practice themselves both here and in New England. To account for this we should remember, that the doctrine of <u>toleration</u> was not then known, or had not prevailed in the world. Persecution was therefore not so much the fault of the sect as of the times. It was not in those days deemed wrong <u>in itself</u>. The general opinion was only, that those <u>who are in error</u> ought not to persecute <u>the truth</u>: But the <u>possessors of truth</u> were in the right to persecute <u>error</u>, in order to destroy it. Thus every sect believing itself possessed of <u>all truth</u>, and that every tenet differing from theirs was <u>error</u>, conceived that when the power was in their hands, persecution was a duty required of them by that God whom they supposed to be offended with heresy. By degrees more moderate <u>and more modest</u> sentiments have taken place in the Christian world; and among Protestants particularly all disclaim persecution, none vindicate it, and few practise it. We should then cease to reproach each other with what was done by our ancestors, but judge of the present character of sects or churches by their <u>present conduct</u> only.

Benjamin Franklin, "Toleration in Old and New England," June 3, 1772. Labaree, *Papers of Benjamin Franklin*, 19:164.

Plato

Your employment in translating Plato has excited I know not what feelings in me. Curiosity, astonishment, and excuse me, when I say risibility. You could not have hit upon a subject more to my taste. It must compel your boys sooner or later to master Plato in his original Greek. They will find him a John Jacks Rousseau. Eloquence in perfection, fantastical in substance but strange to tell, and horrible to contemplate the original corrupter, by means of his disciples of the Divine Christian Religion.

John Adams to Louisa Catherine Adams, June 11, 1819. Adams Papers (microfilm), reel 447, Library of Congress.

[Plato] is one of the race of genuine Sophists, who has escaped the oblivion of his brethren, first by the elegance of his diction, but chiefly by the adoption and incorporation of his whimsies into the body of artificial Christianity. His foggy mind is for ever presenting the semblances of objects which, half seen thro' a mist, can be defined neither in form or dimension. Yet this which should have consigned him to early oblivion really procured him immortality of fame and reverence. The Christian priesthood, finding the doctrines of Christ levelled to every understanding, and too plain to need explanation, saw, in the mysticisms of Plato, materials with which they might build up an artificial system which might, from its indistinctness, admit everlasting controversy, give employment for their order, and introduce it to profit, power and pre-eminence. The doctrines which flowed from the lips of Jesus himself are within the comprehension of a child; but thousands of volumes have not yet explained the Platonisms engrafted on them: and for this obvious reason that nonsense can never be explained.

Thomas Jefferson to John Adams, July 5, 1814. Adams, *Jefferson's Extracts*, 359.

The Poor

I have heard it remarked that the Poor in Protestant Countries on the Continent of Europe, are generally more industrious than those of Popish Countries, may not the more numerous foundations in the latter for the relief of the poor have some effect towards rendering them less provident. To relieve the misfortunes of our fellow creatures is concurring with the Deity, 'tis Godlike, but if we provide encouragements for Laziness, and supports for Folly, may it not be found fighting against the order of God and Nature, which perhaps has appointed Want and Misery as the proper Punishments for, and Cautions against as well as necessary consequences of Idleness and Extravagancy.

Benjamin Franklin to Peter Collinson, May 9, 1753. Labaree, *Papers of Benjamin Franklin*, 4:480.

"The poor," said Dr. Boerhaave, "are my best patients, because God is their paymaster." I wish at all times to be under the influence of this heavenly and benevolent sentiment.

Benjamin Rush to Julia Rush, September 25, 1793. Butterfield, *Letters of Rush*, 2:683.

Prayer

Certainly the sincere Prayers of good Men, avail much.

John Adams to Abigail Adams, May 8, 1775. Butterfield, *Adams Family Correspondence*, 1:196.

If I were a Calvinest, I might pray that God by a Miracle of Divine Grace would instantaneously convert a whole Contaminated Nation from turpitude to purity, but even in this I should be inconsistent, for the fatalism of Mahometnism, Materialists, Atheists, Pantheists and Calvinests, and Church of England Articles, appear to me to render all prayer futile and absurd.

> John Adams to Thomas Jefferson, December 21, 1819. Cappon, *Adams-Jefferson Letters*, 2:551.

Set aside some time in every day (I do mean any particular hour, as this might be inconvenient & a snare) if it is but five Minutes, to lift up your Heart to God in Secret. This may season your whole Time & put you on your Guard against Sin of every kind, even in the wandering of your Thoughts. Be not content to live one day, without some sensible Communion between God and your Soul. Learn the sacred Art & Mystery of making Religion, or daily converse with God, an agreeable Business. It ought to be the most cheerful & delightful part of our Time. To have a God, who is Almighty, all wise, all good & merciful to go to as your constant Friend, as your continual Benefactor, as your Safeguard & Guide it should, it must sweeten every bitter Draught of Life.

> Elias Boudinot to Susan Bradford, December 29, 1784. Boudinot Papers, Princeton University Library.

The prayers of God's People, rich and poor of every denomination, all ranks and orders of his Children in every part of the great Sheepfold never cease night and day surrounding the Throne of the Eternal, for Blessings on their Labors. When Zion prays, God will hear and listen.

> Elias Boudinot to John Pintard, July 6, 1818. Boudinot Papers, American Bible Society.

The prayers of the innocent are all powerful.

Charles Carroll of Carrollton to Elizabeth Harper, December 22, 1820.
Carroll Papers (microfilm), reel 3, Library of Congress.

Our Saviour "spoke two Parables to this End, that Men ought allways to pray and not faint," besides repeated Commands to the same purport. . . . Tis true God needs not to be informed by Us of our Wants: But he knows that Prayer is useful for purifying our Hearts, and inclining Us to Obedience. Therefore his Wisdom and Goodness are both displayed in requiring Us to seek for his Mercies, and he is kind when he demands to be asked for them, as when he grants them to Us. . . .

Q[uestion]. With what Disposition or Temper of Mind should our Prayers be offered that they may be acceptable?

A[nswer]. With the deepest Humility under a Sense of the adorable Perfection of the Glorious Being, whom by his Condescension we are permitted to address, and a Conviction of our Guilt and Nothingness—a filial Submission to his Will as his Right and our Duty—the strictest Engagement to keep his Commandments throughout our whole Lives—the sincerest Goodwill to all Mankind & the warmest wishes for their spiritual & temporal Welfare, without the Exception of a single Individual—the firmest Resolution to do no Injuries to any of them in future, and to make Reparation for those we have allready done.

John Dickinson, "Religious Instruction for Youth," undated.
R. R. Logan Papers, Historical Society of Pennsylvania.

And conceiving God to be the Fountain of Wisdom, I thought it right and necessary to solicit his Assistance for obtaining it; to this End I form'd the following little Prayer . . . for daily Use.

O Powerful Goodness! bountiful Father! merciful Guide!
Increase in me that Wisdom which discovers my truest In-
terests; Strengthen my Resolutions to perform what that
Wisdom dictates. Accept my kind Offices to thy other
Children, as the only Return in my Power for thy continual
Favours to me.

Benjamin Franklin, *Autobiography*, post-1784. Labaree,
Autobiography of Franklin, 153.

Old Version	New Version, by BF
1. Our Father which art in Heaven.	1. Heavenly Father,
2. Hallowed be thy Name.	2. May all revere thee,
3. Thy Kingdom come.	3. And become thy dutiful Children and faithful Subjects.
4. Thy Will be done on Earth as it is in Heaven.	4. May thy Laws be obeyed on Earth as perfectly as they are in Heaven.
5. Give us this Day our daily Bread.	5. Provide for us this day as thou hast hitherto daily done.
6. Forgive us our Debts as we forgive our Debtors.	6. Forgive us our trespasses, and enable us likewise to forgive those that offend us.
7. And lead us not into temptation, but deliver us from Evil.	7. Keep us out of Temptation, and deliver us from Evil.

REASONS FOR THE CHANGE OF EXPRESSION

Old Version. *Our Father which art in Heaven*
New V. *Heavenly Father*, is more concise, equally expressive, and better modern English.

Old. *Hallowed be thy Name.* This seems to relate to an Observance among the Jews not to pronounce the proper or peculiar Name of God, they deeming it a Profanation so to do. We have in our Language no *proper Name* for God; the Word *God* being a common or general Name, expressing all chief Objects of Worship, true or false. The word *hallowed* is almost obsolete: People now have but an imperfect Conception of the Meaning of the Petition. It is therefore proposed to change the Expression into
New. *May all revere thee.*

Old V. *Thy Kingdom come.* This Petition seems suited to the then Condition of the Jewish Nation. Originally their State was a Theocracy: God was their King. Dissatisfied with that kind of Government, they desired a visible earthly King in the manner of the Nations round them. They had such King's accordingly; but their Happiness was not increased by the Change, and they had reason to wish and pray for a Return of the Theocracy, or Government of God. Christians in these Times have other Ideas when they speak of the Kingdom of God, such as are perhaps more adequately express'd by
New V. *And become thy dutiful Children and faithful Subjects.*

Old V. *Thy will be done on Earth as it is in Heaven.* More explicitly,
New V. *May thy Laws be obeyed on Earth as perfectly as they are in Heaven.*

Old V. *Give us this Day* our *daily Bread.* Give us what is *ours,* seems to put in a Claim of Right, and to contain too little of the grateful Acknowledgment and Sense of Dependance that becomes Creatures who live on the daily Bounty of their Creator. Therefore it is changed to
New V. *Provide for us this Day, as thou hast daily done.*

Old V. *Forgive us our debts as we forgive our Debtors.* Matthew. *Forgive us our Sins, for we also forgive every one that is indebted to us.* Luke.
Offerings were *due* to God on many Occasions by the Jewish Law, which when People could not pay, or had forgotten as debtors are apt to do, it was proper to pray that those debts might be forgiven. Our Liturgy uses neither the *Debtors* of Matthew, nor the *indebted* of Luke, but instead speaks of *thosethat trespass against us.* Perhaps the Considering it as a Christian Duty to forgive debtors, was by the Compilers thought an inconvenient Idea in a trading Nation. There seems however something presumptious in this Mode of Expression, which has the Air of proposing ourselves as an Example of Goodness fit for God to imitate. *We hope you will at least be as good as we are;* you see we forgive one another, and therefore we pray that you would forgive us. Some have considered it in another Sense, *Forgive us as we forgive others;* i. e., if we do not forgive others we pray that thou wouldst not forgive us. But this being a kind of conditional *Imprecation* against ourselves, seems improper in such a Prayer; and therefore it may be better to say humbly and modestly
New V. *Forgive us our Trespasses, and enable us likewise to forgive those that offend us.* This instead of assuming that we have already in and of ourselves the Grace of Forgiveness, acknowledges our Dependance on God, the Fountain of Mercy, for any Share we may have of it, praying that he would communicate it to us.

Old V. *And lead us not into Temptation.* The Jews had a Notion, that God sometimes tempted, or directed or permitted the Tempting of People. Thus it was said that he tempted Pharaoh; directed Satan to tempt Job; and a false Prophet to tempt Ahab, &. Under this Persuasion it was natural for them to pray that he would not put them to such severe Trials. We now suppose that Temptation, so far as it is supernatural, comes from the Devil only; and this Petition continued, conveys a Suspicion which in our present Conceptions seem unworthy of God, therefore might be altered to
New V. Keep *us* out of *Temptation.*

Benjamin Franklin, "New Version of the Lord's Prayer," [late 1768?]. Labaree, *Papers of Benjamin Franklin*, 15:301–3.

In this situation of this Assembly [the Constitutional Convention of 1787—Ed.], groping as it were in the dark to find political truth, and scarce able to distinguish it when presented to us, how has it happened, Sir, that we have not hitherto once thought of humbly applying to the Father of lights to illuminate our understandings? In the beginning of the Contest with G. Britain, when we were sensible of danger we had daily prayer in this room for the divine protection. Our prayers, Sir, were heard, and they were graciously answered. All of us who were engaged in the struggle must have observed frequent instances of a Superintending providence in our favor. To that kind providence we owe this happy opportunity of consulting in peace on the means of establishing our national felicity. And have we now forgotten that powerful friend? Or do we imagine that we no longer need his powerful assistance? I have lived, Sir, a long time, and the longer I live, the more convincing proofs I see of this truth—that God governs in the affairs of Men. And if a sparrow cannot fall to the ground without his notice, is it probable that an empire can rise without his aid? We have been assured, Sir, in the sacred writings, that "except the Lord build the House they labour in vain that build it." I firmly believe this; and I also believe that without his concurring aid we shall succeed in this political building no better than the Builders of Babel: We shall be divided by our little partial local interests; our projects will be confounded, and we ourselves shall become a reproach and bye word down to future ages. And what is worse, mankind may hereafter from this unfortunate instance, despair of establishing Governments by Human Wisdom and leave it to chance, war and conquest.

I therefore beg leave to move that henceforth prayers imploring the assistance of Heaven, and its blessings on our deliberations, be held in this Assembly every morning before we proceed to business.

> Benjamin Franklin, speech, Federal Constitutional Convention, June 28, 1787. Max Farrand, ed., *The Records of the Federal Convention of 1787* (New Haven, Conn.: Yale University Press, 1937), 1:451–52.

Prayers to heaven, the only contribution of old age.

> Thomas Jefferson to George Logan, October 15, 1815. Jefferson Papers, Library of Congress.

Man is as necessarily a praying as he is a sociable, domestic, or religious animal. As "no man liveth and sinneth not," so no man liveth and prayeth not. Distress and terror drive even atheists to call upon God. Worldly men pray for the success of their worldly schemes. Men in deep distress even call for the prayers of their friends. . . . Prayer is an instinct of nature in man, as much so as his love of society. He cannot, he does not live without it, except in a morbid or unnatural state of his mind.

> Benjamin Rush, "Commonplace Book," August 14, 1811. Corner, *Autobiography of Rush*, 339.

I now make it my earnest prayer, that God would have you, and the State over which you preside, in his holy protection, that he would incline the hearts of the Citizens to cultivate a spirit of subordination and obedience to Government, to entertain a brotherly affection and love for one another, for their fellow Citizens of the United States at large, and particularly for their brethren who have served in the Field, and finally, that he would most graciously be pleased to dispose us all, to do Justice, to love mercy, and to demean ourselves with that Charity, humility and pacific temper of mind, which were the Characteristicks of the Divine Author of our blessed Religion, and without an humble imitation of whose example in these things, we can never hope to be a happy Nation.

> George Washington, Circular to the Chief Executives of the States,
> June 8, 1783. Fitzpatrick, *Writings of Washington*, 26:496.

Presbyterians

I can not concur, however, in your preference in Presbyterianism. The presbytery have too much priestly Authority in matters of faith like that which is claimed by the Episcopal Church. And the doctrine of both the Churches are too Calvinistical for me as well as too hierarchical.

> John Adams to Alexander Johnson, March 21, 1823. Adams Papers
> (microfilm), reel 124, Library of Congress

The Presbyterian clergy are the loudest, the most intolerant of all sects, the most tyrannical, and ambitious; ready at the word of the lawgiver, if such a word could now be obtained, to put the torch to the pile, and to rekindle in this virgin hemisphere, the flames in which their oracle Calvin consumed the poor Servetus,[28] because he could not find in his Euclid the proposition which has demonstrated that three are one, and one is three, nor subscribe to that of Calvin that magistrates have a right to exterminate all heretics to Calvinistic creed. They pant to reestablish <u>by law</u> that holy inquisition, which they can now only infuse into <u>public opinion.</u>

> Thomas Jefferson to William Short, April 13, 1820. Adams, *Jefferson's Extracts*, 393.

Proclamations: see Fast and Thanksgiving Days

Profanity

The General is sorry to be informed that the foolish, and wicked practice, of profane cursing and swearing (a Vice heretofore little known in an American Army) is growing

---

[28] Michael Servetus (1511–1553), Spanish theologian, whose anti-Trinitarian views led to his being burned at the stake, at Calvin's insistence, in Geneva, October 27, 1553.

into fashion; he hopes the officers will, by example, as well as influence, endeavour to check it, and that both they, and the men will reflect, that we can have little hopes of the blessing of Heaven on our Arms, if we insult it by our impiety, and folly; added to this, it is a vice so mean and low, without any temptation, that every man of sense, and character, detests and despises it.

> George Washington, General Orders, August 3, 1776. Fitzpatrick, ed., *Writings of Washington*, 5:367.

There in nothing more rueful to think of, than that those whose trade is war should be dispisers of the name of the Lord of hosts, and that they should expose themselves to the imminent danger of being immediately sent from cursing and cruelty on earth, to the blaspheming rage and despairing horror of the infernal pit.

> John Witherspoon, "A Pastoral Letter from the Synod of New York and Philadelphia," June 29, 1775. *Works of Witherspoon*, 3:11.

Prophecy

The Crusades were commenced by the Prophets and every Age since, when ever any great Turmoil happens in the World, has produced fresh Prophets. The Continual Refutation of their Prognostications by Time and Experience has no Effect in extinguishing or dampning their Ardor.

I think these Prophecies are not only unphilosophical and inconsistent with the political Safety of States and Nations; but that the most sincere and sober Christians in the World ought upon their own Principles to hold them impious, for nothing is clearer from their Scriptures than that Their Prophecies were not intended to make Us Prophets.

John Adams to Thomas Jefferson, February 10, 1812. Cappon, *Adams-Jefferson Letters*, 2:297

He was obliged to keep a short diary of what was passing on the theatre of Europe. The many instances of exact conformity with the words and spirit of the Scriptures, convinced the author that the wonderful transactions daily passing in the kingdoms of Europe, were an exact fulfilment of the predictions of the Sacred record. That the antichrist foretold, as coming on the earth after the Man of Sin, had literally appeared in the new government of France, having Napoleon Bonaparte for her head, can scarcely be denied by any observing mind, who has become acquainted with the late history of that nation since 1790 and compared it with the language of holy writ.

Elias Boudinot, *The Second Advent* (Trenton, N.J.: D. Fenton & S. Hutchinson, 1815), iv.

In short, the present generation are so highly favoured with light and knowledge, that they have no excuse for the obstinate infidelity that prevails among them. Most of the old objections to Revelation are done away, by the exact fulfilment of events in these latter days, foretold in the prophetic declarations of the Scriptures. The testimony is still increasing, and the truth of prophesy is manifesting every day. As miracles, at the first commencement of Christianity, so the precise accomplishments of prophesy in these latter ages of it, confirms its truth and certainty, beyond rational objection and doubt.

Ibid., 554

Perilous times have descended upon all Europe, and Bonaparte seems to be the Nebuchadnezzar of the day. Divines say that in prophetic language nations are called seas. According to that language, Europe is a tempestuous and a raging ocean; and who can tell which of the governments afloat upon it will escape destruction or disaster?

John Jay to William Peters, July 24, 1809. Johnston, *Correspondence of Jay*, 4:318.

No man on earth has less taste or talent for criticism than myself, and least and last of all should I undertake to criticise works on the Apocalypse. It is between 50. and 60. years since I read it, and I then considered it as merely the ravings of a Maniac, no more worthy, nor capable of explanation than the incoherences of our own nightly dreams. . . . There is not coherence enough in them to countenance any suite of rational ideas. You will judge therefore from this how impossible I think it that either your explanation, or that of any man in the heavens above, or on the earth beneath, can be a correct one. What has no meaning admits no explanation.

Thomas Jefferson to Alexander Smyth, January 17, 1825. Adams, *Jefferson's Extracts*, 415–16.

For wise purposes it has pleased God to conceal from us the precise times in which the prophecies are to be accomplished. The attempts of bad men to defeat them and of good men to accelerate them would probably have increased in a great degree the miseries of our world from human ambition and folly.

Benjamin Rush to John Adams, January 13, 1809. Butterfield, *Letters of Rush*, 2:993.

Providence

. . . however the Belief of a particular Providence may be exploded by the Modern Wits, and the Infidelity of too many of the rising generation deride the Idea, yet the virtuous Mind will look up and acknowledge the great first cause, without whose notice not even a sparrow falls to the ground.

Abigail Adams to John Adams, October 15, 1780. Butterfield, *Adams Family Correspondence*, 4:6.

. . . but there is one consolation to which I must ever resort, in all my anxietyes. I thank Heaven who has given me to believe in a superintending providence Guiding and Governing all things in infinate wisdom and "to look through and trust the Ruler of the Skye."

Abigail Adams to John Adams, October 15, 1780. Ibid, 4:229.

But I must submit all my Hopes and Fears, to an overruling Providence, in which, unfashionable as the Faith may be, I firmly believe.

John Adams to Abigail Adams, July 3, 1776. Ibid., 2:28.

General Inferences should never be drawn from single Facts, or even from several Instances, especially in contemplating the inscrutable and incomprehensible Councils of Providence.

John Adams to Benjamin Rush, June 23, 1807. *Old Family Letters*, 151.

In the month of March last I was called to the house in another part of the town which was built by my father, in which he lived and died and from which I buried him; and in the chamber in which I was born I could not forbear to weep over the remains of a beautiful child of my son Thomas that died of the whooping cough. Why was I preserved 3/4 of a century, and that rose cropped in the bud? I, almost dead at the top and in all my limbs and wholly useless to myself and the world? Great Teacher, tell me.

John Adams to Benjamin Rush, July 19, 1812. Schutz and Adair, *Spur of Fame*, 239.

Every attempt to improve the late glorious Success, in a war so unequal; to the best Interests of the Citizens of these States, meets my hearty Concurrence and warmest Approbation. I have been in the midst of the principle Scenes of Action, during the whole Contest. I have not been a bare Spectator. I have carefully and attentively watched & Compared the Steps of divine Providence thro' the whole; and as the result, I can assure you, that our Success, has not been the effect of either our Numbers—Power—Wisdom or Art. It has been manifestly the Effect (I was going to say the miraculous Effect) of the astonishing and unparalleled Interposition of a holy God in our favour—of that God who speaketh & it is done—who commandeth and it cometh to pass.

I do not mean in the least, to derogate from the Bravery, wisdom, Patience & Perseverence of one of the most deserving Armies that ever graced any Country. As well might we decry the Merit of Moses, in conducting the Children of Israel thro the Wilderness, as I am clear that our political Salvation is not at all inferior to theirs. My Meaning is that in no Instance has our Numbers, Power, Wisdom or Art been such, that in the Judgment of rational, enlightened Judges, Success could have been reasonably depended on, independent of the special aid & overruling direction of Heaven.

Elias Boudinot to Samuel Mather, August 20, 1783. Paul Smith, ed., *Letters of Delegates to Congress, 1774–1789* (Washington, D.C.: Government Printing Office, 1993), 20:565–66.

The adorable Creator of the World is infinitely benevolent, tho it is impossible for our finite Capacities to comprehend all of his dispensations. However, we know enough to excite our warmest gratitude and firmest confidence. My belief is unhesitating, that by his superintending Providence a Period greatly favorable is commencing in the Destinies of the Human Race. That he may be pleased to honour Thee, as an Instrument for advancing his gracious Purposes, and that he may be thy Guide and Protector, is the ardent Wish, the fervent Prayer, of thy truly affectionate Friend.

> John Dickinson to Thomas Jefferson, February 21, 1801. Jefferson Papers, Library of Congress.

Without the Belief of a Providence that takes Cognizance of, guards and guides and may favour particular Persons, there is no Motive to Worship a Deity, to fear its Displeasure, or to pray for its Protection.

> Benjamin Franklin to ——, [December 13, 1757]. Labaree, *Papers of Benjamin Franklin*, 7:294.

And now I speak of thanking God, I desire with all Humility to acknowledge, that I owe the mention'd Happiness of my past Life to his kind Providence, which led me to the Means I us'd and gave them Success. My Belief of this, induces me to hope, tho' I must not presume, that the same Goodness will still be exercis'd towards me in continuing that Happiness, or in enabling me to bear a fatal Reverse, which I may experience as others have done, the Complexion of my future Fortune being known to him only: and in whose Power it is to bless to us even our Afflictions.

> Benjamin Franklin, *Autobiography*, 1771. Labaree, *Autobiography of Franklin*, 45.

But after all, my dear Friend, do not imagine that I am vain enough to ascribe our Success to any superiority in any of these Points. I am too well acquainted with all the Springs and Levers of our Machine, not to see, that our human means were unequal to our undertaking, and that, if it had not been for the Justice of our Cause, and the consequent Interposition of Providence, in which we had Faith, we must have been ruined. If I had ever before been an Atheist, I should now have been convinced of the Being and Government of a Deity! It is he who abases the Proud and favours the Humble. May we never forget his Goodness to us, and may our future Conduct manifest our Gratitude.

Benjamin Franklin to William Strahan, August 19, 1784. Smyth, *Writings of Franklin*, 9:262.

A proper history of the United States would have much to recommend it: in some respects it would be singular, or unlike all others; it would develop the great plan of Providence, for causing this extensive part of our world to be discovered, and these "uttermost parts of the earth" to be gradually filled with civilized and <u>Christian</u> people and nations. The means or second causes by which this great plan has long been and still is accomplishing, are materials for history, of which the writer ought well to know the use and bearings and proper places. In my opinion, the historian, in the course of the work, is never to lose sight of that great plan.

John Jay to Jedediah Morse, August 16, 1809. Johnston, *Correspondence of Jay*, 4:322.

They who ascribe all of this to the guidance and protection of Providence do well; but let them recollect that Providence seldom interposes in human affairs, but through the agency of human means.

John Jay to Richard Peters, March 29, 1811. Ibid., 4:351.

And for the support of this Declaration, with a firm reliance on the protection of divine Providence, we mutually
pledge to each other our Lives, our Fortunes, and our sacred Honor.

> Thomas Jefferson, Declaration of Independence, July 4, 1776. Boyd,
> *Papers of Thomas Jefferson*, 1:432.

. . . enlightened by a benign religion, professed, indeed, and
practiced in various forms, yet all of them inculcating hon-
esty, truth, temperance, gratitude and love of man; acknowledging and adoring an overruling Providence, which
by all of its dispensations proves that it delights in the happiness of man here and his greater happiness hereafter. . . .

> Thomas Jefferson, First Inaugural Address, March 4, 1801.
> Richardson, *Messages and Papers of the Presidents*, 1:311.

We are not in a world ungoverned by the laws and power of
a superior agent. Our efforts are in his hand and directed by
it; and he will give them their effect in his own time.

> Thomas Jefferson to David Barrow, May 1, 1815. Jefferson Papers,
> Library of Congress.

I agree that God's perceptive will ought to be obeyed in all
things, and his providential will submitted to as far as it is
made known by revelation, or the event; but no particular
person while in a state of probation can know that it is the
providential will of God that he shall finally perish, but he
knows that it is his perceptive will that he shall turn and
live.

> Roger Sherman to Samuel Hopkins, October 1790. American
> Antiquarian Society, *Proceedings* 5 (October 1887–October 1888),
> 459–60.

As I have heard since my arriv'l at this place, a circumstan-
tial acc[oun]t of my death and dying speech, I take this early

oppertunity of contradicting both, and of assuring you
that I now exist and appear in the land of the living by
the miraculous care of Providence, that protected me beyond all human expectation; I had 4 Bullets through my
Coat, and two Horses shot under me, and yet escaped un-
hurt.

> George Washington to John Augustine Washington, July 18, 1755.
> Fitzpatrick, *Writings of Washington*, 1:152.

I go fully trusting in that providence, which has been more
bountiful to me than I deserve. . . .

> George Washington to Martha Washington, June 23, 1775. Ibid., 3:301.

. . . however, it is to be hoped, that if our cause is just, as I do
most religiously believe it to be, the same Providence,
which has in many Instances appear'd for us, will still go on
to afford its aid.

> George Washington to John Washington, May 31, 1776. Ibid., 5, 93.

The hand of Providence has been so conspicuous in all this,
that he must be worse than an infidel that lacks faith, and
more than wicked, that has not gratitude enough to acknowledge his obligations, but, it will be time enough for
me to turn preacher, when my present appointment ceases;
and therefore, I shall add no more on the Doctrine of Providence.

> George Washington to Thomas Nelson, August 20, 1778. Ibid., 12, 343.

Divine Service is to be performed tomorrow [ed. following
the victory at Yorktown]. in the several Brigades or Divi-
sions. The Commander in Chief earnestly recommends that
the troops not on duty should universally attend with that
seriousness of Deportment and Gratitude of Heart which

the recognition of such reiterated and astonishing interpositions of Providence demands of us.

George Washington, General Orders, October 20, 1781. Ibid., 23:247.

When I contemplate the interposition of Providence, as it was visibly manifested, in guiding us through the Revolution, in preparing us for the reception of a general government, and in conciliating the good will of the People of America towards one another after its' adoption, I feel myself oppressed and almost overwhelmed with a sense of divine munificience. I feel that nothing is due to my personal agency in all these complicated and wonderful events, except what can simply be attributed to an honest zeal for the good of my country.

George Washington to the Mayor, Recorder, Aldermen, and Common Council of Philadelphia, April 20, 1789. Washington Papers, Library of Congress.

... it would be peculiarly improper to omit in this first official Act, my fervent supplications to that Almighty Being who rules over the Universe, who presides in the Councils of Nations, and whose providential aids can supply every human defect.... No People can be bound to acknowledge and adore the invisible hand, which conducts the Affairs of men more than the People of the United States. Every step, by which they have advanced to the character of an independent nation, seems to have been distinguished by some token of providential agency.

George Washington, Inaugural Address, April 30, 1789. Fitzpatrick, *Writings of Washington*, 30:292–93.

In passing down the vale of time, and in journeying through such a mutable world as that in which we are placed, we must expect to meet with a great and continual mixture of afflictions and blessings. This is a mingled cup which an overruling providence undoubtedly dispences to us for the wises and best purposes.—and as you justly observe, shall we shortsighted mortals dare to arraign the decrees of eternal wisdom.

Martha Washington to Mercy Otis Warren, June 12, 1790. *Papers of Martha Washington*, 226.

Quakers

We have been obliged to attempt to humble the Pride of some Jesuits who call themselves Quakers, but who love Money and Land better than Liberty or Religion. The Hypocrites are endeavouring to raise the Cry of Persecution, and to give this Matter a religious Turn, but they cant succeed. The World knows them and their Communications. Actuated by a land jobbing Spirit, like that of William Penn, they have been soliciting Grants of immense Regions of Land on the Ohio. American Independence has disappointed them, which makes them hate it. Yet the Dastards dare not avow their Hatred to it, it seems.

John Adams to Abigail Adams, September 8, 1777. Butterfield, *Adams Family Correspondence*, 2:337–38.

Quakers are like all other Sects. I would trust Presbyterians, Congregationalists, English Episcopalians, Anabaptists, nay Papists, as soon. I have witnessed a Quaker despotism in Pennsylvania.

John Adams to Francis van der Kemp, May 20, 1813. Adams Papers (microfilm), reel 95, Library of Congress.

The Friends [Quakers—Ed.] are men, formed with the same passions, and swayed by the same natural principles and prejudices as others. In cases where the passions are neutral, men will display their respect for the religious *professions* of their sect. But where their passions are enlisted, these *professions* are no obstacle. You observe very truly that both the late and present administration conducted the government on principles *professed* by the Friends. Our efforts to preserve peace, our measures as to the Indians, as to slavery, as to religious freedom, were all in consonance with their *professions*. Yet I never expected we should get a vote from them, and in this I was neither deceived nor disappointed. There is no riddle in this to those who do not suffer themselves to be duped by the *professions* of religious sectaries. The theory of American Quakerism is a very obvious one. The Mother-society is in England. It's members are English by birth and residence, devoted to their own country as good citizens ought to be. The Quakers of these states are colonies or filiations from the mother society, to whom the society sends it's yearly lessons. On these the filiated societies model their opinions, their conduct, their passions and attachments. A Quaker is essentially an Englishman, in whatever part of the world he is born or lives. The outrages of Great Britain on our navigation and commerce have kept us in perpetual bickerings with her. The Quakers here have taken side against their own government; not on their *profession* of peace, for they saw that peace was our object also; but from devotion to the views of the Mother-society. In 1797. and 8. when an administration sought war with France the Quakers were the most clamorous for war. Their principle of peace, as a secondary one, yielded to the primary one of Adherence to the Friends in England, and what was patriotism in the Original became Treason in the Copy.

Thomas Jefferson to William Baldwin, January 19, 1810. Adams, *Jefferson's Extracts*, 345–46.

No Man has more Love for the Society of Quakers than I have, they are good friends good Neighbours good Citizens in times of peace & tranquility & in time of War exceedingly useful in their own ways to the Side to which they are attached—but they are the most dangerous Enemies in the World—they now profess themselves to be "real & true friends to America" . . . Can there be more dangerous Inmates than Men who are in close correspondence with & giving intelligence to, the open Enemies of those with whom they dwell & to whom they outwardly profess Love & friendship? Can there be an instance produced of more refined insulting hypocrisy than an artful declaration of Specious truth calculated to deceive? "We profess Love & Friendship to you in our open Addresses, but in our Secret testimonials we declare the Strongest attachment to your inveterate Enemies, we there call you unjust—tyrants usurpers of power & authority & we demonstrate that the true meaning of our Love & friendship for you is, opposition to you, & an ardent desire that you may be Subdued by your Enemies who we know will imprison Some of you put others to death & confiscate your Estates—and this you are also to understand to be the genuine interpretation of our professed, real friendship to America."—the Devil himSelf would be too honest, none but a thorough bred Jesuit would have the hardiness to call Such duplicity, that "Wisdom from above which is first pure, then peaceable, gentle & easy to be intreated, full of Mercy & good fruits, without partiality & without hypocrisy" . . . The calling God who is the fountain of truth; or the quoting his Holy Scriptures, which are the Oracles of Truth—to witness a Lie, or any Species of deceit, is blasphemy—And to Such Men as we have in view it may very fairly be retorted—"they wrest the holy Scriptures to their own damnation."

Henry Laurens to John Lewis Gervais, September 5, 1777. Rogers, *Papers of Henry Laurens*, 11:496–97.

Your principles and conduct are well known to me; and it is doing the people called Quakers no more than justice to say, that (except their declining to share with others the burthen of common defence) there is no denomination among us, who are more exemplary and useful citizens.

George Washington to the Society of Friends, September 1789.
Washington Papers, Library of Congress.

Reason

Not the least intimation in history or tradition that religion was discovered by reason. But the contrary—that is—by revelation.

The great question as to reason is this—whether reason since the introduction of sin into the world is sufficient to discover our duty and incline us to enforce its performance. Denied.

John Dickinson, miscellaneous papers on religion, undated.
R. R. Logan Papers, Historical Society of Pennsylvania.

After the astonishing catastrophe at Babel . . . Men "sought out many inventions" and true religion was supplanted by fables and idolatrous rites. Their mythology manifests the inability of <u>mere</u> human reason, even when combined with the learning of Egypt, and the philosophy of Greece and Rome, to acquire the knowledge of our actual state and future destiny, and of the conduct proper to be observed in relation to both.

John Jay to the American Bible Society, May 9, 1822. Johnston, *Correspondence of Jay*, 4:479.

Certain other commentators, doubtless from a sincere desire to increase Christian knowledge by luminous expositions of abstruse subjects, have attempted to penetrate into the recesses of profound mysteries, and to dispel their obscurity by the light of reason. It seems they did not recollect that <u>no man can explain what no man can understand</u>. Those mysteries were revealed to our faith, to be believed on the credit of Divine testimony; and were not addressed to our mental abilities for explication.

John Jay to the American Bible Society, May 12, 1825. Ibid., 4:502.

Reason and free inquiry are the only effectual agents against error. Give a loose to them, they will support the true religion, by bringing every false one to their tribunal, to the test of their investigation. . . . Reason and experiment have been indulged, and error has fled before them. It is error alone which needs the support of government.

Thomas Jefferson, *Notes on the State of Virginia*, 1781. Peden, *Notes on Virginia*, 159–60.

Fix reason firmly in her seat, and call to her tribunal every fact, every opinion. Question with boldness even the existence of a god because, if there be one, he must more approve the homage of reason, than that of blindfolded fear. . . . I repeat that you must lay aside all prejudice on both sides, and neither believe nor reject any thing because any other person, or description of persons have rejected or believed it. Your own reason is the only oracle given you by heaven, and you are answerable not for the rightness but uprightness of the decision.

Thomas Jefferson to Peter Carr, August 10, 1787. Boyd, *Papers of Thomas Jefferson*, 12:15–17.

. . . a devoted friend myself to freedom of religious enquiry and opinion, I am pleased to see others exercise the right,

without reproach or censure; and I respect their con-
clusions, however different from my own. It is their own
reason, not mine, nor that of any other, which has been
given them by their creator for the investigation of truth,
and of the evidences, even of those truths, which are presented to us as revealed by himself. Fanaticism, it is true, is
not sparing of her invectives against those who refuse
blindly to follow her dictates, in abandonment of their own
reason. For the use of this reason however every one is responsible to the god who has placed it in his breast as a light
for his guidance, and that by which alone he will be judged.

> Thomas Jefferson to William Carver, December 4, 1823. Jefferson
> Papers, Library of Congress.

I fear all our attempts to produce political happiness by the
solitary influence of human reason will be as fruitless as the
search for the philosopher's stone. It seems to be reserved to
Christianity alone to produce universal, moral, political,
and physical happiness. Reason produces, it is true, great
and popular truths, but it affords motives too feeble to induce mankind to act agreeably to them. Christianity
unfolds the same truths and accompanies them with motives, agreeable, powerful, and irresistible.

> Benjamin Rush to Noah Webster, July 20, 1798. Butterfield, *Letters of
> Rush*, 2:799.

Religion, Freedom of: see Liberty of Conscience

Religion: Propensity of Humans for

There is in human Nature a solid, unchangeable and eternal Foundation of Religion. There is also a germ of superstition, seemingly a fungous growth or a spurious sprout, which the grossest Blockheads and most atrocious Villains are able to cultivate into Systems and Sects to deceive millions and cheat and pillage hundreds and thousands of their fellow Creatures.

John Adams to John Quincy Adams, May 10, 1816. Adams Papers (microfilm), reel 431, Library of Congress.

Religion always has and always will govern mankind. Man is constitutionally, essentially and unchangeably a religious animal. Neither philosophers or politicians can ever govern him in any other way.

John Adams to Francis van der Kemp, October 2, 1818. Ibid., reel 123.

There is in all Men something like a natural Principle which enclines them to DEVOTION or the Worship of some unseen Power.

Benjamin Franklin, "Articles of Belief and Acts of Religion," November 20, 1728. Labaree, *Papers of Benjamin Franklin*, 1:102.

There appears to be in the nature of man, what ensures his belief in an invisible cause of his present existence, & an anticipation of his future existence. Hence the propensities & susceptibilities, in the case of religion, which, with a few doubtful or individual exceptions, have prevailed throughout the world.

James Madison to Jasper Adams, September 1833. Dreisbach, *Religion and Politics*, 117.

We are all necessarily Religious as we are reasoning and musical animals. It is true we are disposed to false Religions; so we are to false reasoning and false music, but this shows the depth of each of those principles in the human mind.

Benjamin Rush, "Commonplace Book," 1809. Corner, *Autobiography of Rush*, 335.

Religion: Social Utility of

. . . the design of Christianity was not to make men good Riddle Solvers or good mystery mongers, but good men, good magestrates and good Subjects. . . .

John Adams, Diary, February 18, 1756. Butterfield, *Diary and Autobiography of John Adams*, 1:8.

My Opinion of the Duties of Religion and Morality, comprehends a very extensive Connection with society at large, and the great Interest of the public. Does not natural Morality, and much more Christian Benevolence, make it our indispensible Duty to lay ourselves out, to serve our fellow Creatures to the Utmost of our Power, in promoting and supporting those great Political systems, and general

Regulations upon which the Happiness of Multitudes depends. The Benevolence, Charity, Capacity and Industry which exerted in private Life, would make a family, a Parish or a Town Happy, employed upon a larger Scale, in Support of the great Principles of Virtue and freedom of political Regulations might secure whole Nations and Generations from Misery, Want and Contempt.

John Adams to Abigail Adams, October 29, 1775. Butterfield, *Adams Family Correspondence*, 1:316–17.

Religion and Virtue are the only Foundations, not only of Republicanism and of all free Government, but of social felicity under all Governments and in all Combinations of human Society.

John Adams to Benjamin Rush, August 28, 1811. *Old Family Letters*, 354.

Our country should be preserved from the dreadful evil of becoming enemies to the religion of the Gospel, which I have no doubt, but would be the introduction of the dissolution of government and the bonds of civil society.

Elias Boudinot, *The Age of Revelation* (Philadelphia: Asbury Dickins, 1801), xxii.

Without morals a republic cannot subsist any length of time; they therefore, who are decrying the Christian religion, whose morality is so sublime and pure, which denounces against the wicked, the eternal misery, and insures to the good eternal happiness, are undermining the solid foundation of morals, the best security for the duration of free governments.

Charles Carroll of Carrollton to Charles Carroll, Jr., November 4, 1800. Alf J. Mapp, Jr., *The Faiths of Our Fathers* (Lanham, Md.: Rowman & Littlefield, 2003), 140–41.

<u>History</u> will also afford frequent Opportunities of showing the Necessity of a <u>Publick Religion</u>, from its Usefulness to the Publick.

> Benjamin Franklin, "Proposals Relating to the Education of Youth in Pennsylvania," 1749. Labaree, *Papers of Benjamin Franklin*, 3:413.

The politician who loves liberty sees . . . a gulph that may swallow up the liberty to which he is devoted. He knows that morality overthrown (and morality <u>must</u> fall without religion) the terrors of despotism can alone curb the impetuous passions of man, and confine him within the bounds of social duty.

> Alexander Hamilton, *The Stand*, no. 3 (April 7, 1798). Syrett, *Papers of Alexander Hamilton*, 21:405.

I am not so much alarmed as at the apprehension of her [France] destroying the great pillars of all government and of social life—I mean virtue, morality and religion. This is the armor, my friend, and this alone, that renders us invincible.

> Campbell, *Henry*, 407.

. . . the Christian religion when divested of the rags in which they have inveloped it, and brought to the original purity and simplicity of it's benevolent institutor, is a religion of all others most friendly to liberty. . . .

> Thomas Jefferson to Moses Robinson, March 23, 1801. Adams, *Jefferson's Extracts*, 325.

Jefferson was walking "with his large red prayer book under his arm when a friend querying him after their mutual good morning said which way are you walking Mr. Jefferson. To which he replied to Church Sir. You going to Church

Mr. J. You do not believe a word in it. Sir said Mr. J. No nation has ever yet existed or been governed without religion. Nor can be. The Christian religion is the best religion that has been given to man and I as chief Magistrate of this nation am bound to give it the sanction of my example. Good morning Sir."

> Anecdote recorded by the Reverend Ethan Allen, "Washington Parish, Washington City." Manuscript Division, Library of Congress.

It is foreign to my purpose to hint at the arguments which establish the truth of Christian revelation. My only business is to declare, that all its doctrines and precepts are calculated to promote the happiness of society, and the safety and well being of civil government.

> Benjamin Rush, "Of the Mode of Education Proper in a Republic." Rush, Essays:Literary, Moral, and Philosophical, 6.

True religion affords to government its surest support.

> George Washington to the Synod of the Reformed Dutch Church of North America, October 1789. Washington Papers, Library of Congress.

Of all the dispositions and habits which lead to political prosperity, Religion and morality are indispensable supports. In vain would that man claim the tribute of Patriotism, who should labour to subvert these great Pillars of human happiness, these firmest props of the duties of Men and citizens. The mere Politician, equally with the pious man ought to respect and to cherish them. A volume could not trace all their connections with private and public felicity.

> George Washington, Farewell Address, September 19, 1796. Rare Book and Special Collections Division, Library of Congress.

The United States in Congress assembled . . . do further recommend to all ranks, to testify their gratitude to God for his goodness, by a cheerful obedience to his laws, and by promoting, each in his station, and by his influence, the practice of true and undefiled religion, which is the great foundation of public prosperity and national happiness.

> John Witherspoon, "Thanksgiving Day Proclamation," October 11, 1782. *Journals of the Continental Congress* (Washington, D.C.: Government Printing Office, 1904), 23:647.

Republicanism

The Goodness of the Common parent . . . has invested all his rational Creatures with equal rights and with propensities favorable to mutual felicity. Actual republicanism is a system of human convention, for carrying these benevolent and sacred principles into effect by the diffusion of happiness.

> John Dickinson to Thomas Jefferson, June 27, 1801. Jefferson Papers, Library of Congress.

I look upon Republicanism to be the Gospel of policy. It embraces its several objects with mildness and benevolence. In primitive times the <u>heathen</u> used to say—"Behold! How these Christians love one another." Let the <u>heathens</u>—I mean the enemies of truth—in our day be forced to exclaim—"Behold! how the Republicans love one another."

> John Dickinson to Caesar Rodney, November 9, 1803. Milton Flower, *John Dickinson:Conservative Revolutionary* (Charlottesville: University Press of Virginia, 1983), 292–93.

A Christian can not fail of being a republican. The history of the creation of man, and of the relation of our species to each other by birth, which is recorded in the Old Testament, is the best refutation that can be given to the divine rights of kings, and the strongest argument that can be used in favor of the original and natural equality of all mankind. A Christian, I say again, cannot fail of being a republican, for every precept of the Gospel inculcates those degrees of humility, self-denial, and brotherly kindness, which are directly opposed to the pride of monarchy and the pageantry of a court. A Christian cannot fail of being useful to the republic, for his religion teacheth him, that no man "liveth to himself." And lastly, a Christian cannot fail of being wholly inoffensive, for his religion teacheth him, in all things to do to others what he would wish, in like circumstances, they should do to him.

Benjamin Rush, "Of the Mode of Education Proper in a Republic."
Rush, *Essays: Literary, Moral, and Philosophical*, 6.

I have always considered Christianity as the <u>strong ground</u> of republicanism. The spirit is opposed, not only to the splendor, but even to the very forms of monarchy, and many of its precepts have for their objects republican liberty and equality as well as simplicity, integrity, and economy in government. It is only necessary for republicanism to ally itself to the Christian religion to overturn all the corrupted political and religious institutions in the world.

Benjamin Rush to Thomas Jefferson, August 22, 1800. Butterfield,
Letters of Rush, 2:820–21.

Rights

The great . . . have accordingly laboured, in all ages, to wrest from the populace, as they are contemptuously called, the knowledge of their rights and wrongs, and the power to assert the former or redress the latter. I say RIGHTS, for such they have, undoubtedly, antecedent to all earthly government—Rights that cannot be repealed or restrained by human laws—Rights derived from the great legislator of the universe.

> John Adams, "A Dissertation on the Canon and Feudal Law," 1765. Taylor et al., *Papers of John Adams*, 1:111–12.

"The Science of the Rights of Man is a new science. The Americans have invented it." . . . The Americans did not invent this foundation of Society. They found it in their religion.

> John Adams to Thomas Boylston Adams, March 19, 1794. Adams Papers (microfilm), reel 377, Library of Congress.

Kings or parliaments could not give the rights essential to happiness—we claim them from a higher source—from the King of Kings and the Lord of all the Earth. They are not annexed to us by parchments or seals. They are created in us by the decrees of Providence, which establish the laws of our nature. They are born with us; and cannot be taken from us by any human power.

> John Dickinson, *The letters of Fabius, in 1788, on the federal Constitution, and in 1797, on the present situation of public affairs* (Wilmington: W. C. Smyth, 1797), 184 n.

The sacred rights of mankind are not to be rummaged for, among old parchments, or musty records. They are written, as with a sum beam, in the whole <u>volume</u> of human nature, by the hand of divinity itself; and can never be erased or obscured by mortal power.

> Alexander Hamilton, "The Farmer Refuted," February 1775. Syrett, *Papers of Alexander Hamilton*, 1:122.

<u>Real</u> Christians will abstain from violating the Rights of others.

> John Jay to John Murray, Jr., October 12, 1816. Johnston, *Correspondence of Jay*, 4:392.

I cannot forbear to embrace the opportunity afforded by the present occasion, to express my earnest hope, that the peace happiness & prosperity enjoyed by our beloved country, may induce those who direct her national councils to recommend a general & public return of praise & thanksgiving to Him from whose goodness these blessings descend.

The most effectual means of securing the continuance of our civil & religious liberties is always to remember with reverence & gratitude the source from which they flow.

> John Jay to the Committee of the Corporation of the City of New York, June 29, 1826. Jay Papers (online edition), Columbia University Library.

We hold these truths to be self-evident, that all men are created equal, that they are endowed by their Creator with certain unalienable Rights, that among these are Life, Liberty and the pursuit of Happiness.

> Thomas Jefferson, The Declaration of Independence, July 4, 1776. Boyd, *Papers of Thomas Jefferson*, 1:429.

. . . our civil rights have no dependance on our religious opinions, any more than our opinions in physics or geometry.

> Thomas Jefferson, "A Bill for Establishing Religious Freedom," 1777. Ibid., 2:545–46.

But our rulers can have authority over such natural rights only as we have submitted to them. The rights of conscience we never submitted, we could not submit. We are answerable for them to our God.

And can the liberties of a nation be thought secure when we have removed their only firm basis, a conviction in the minds of the people that these liberties are of the gift of God? That they are not to be violated but with his wrath?

Thomas Jefferson, *Notes on the State of Virginia*, 1781. Peden, *Notes on Virginia*, 159, 163.

Sabbath

. . . let me with great Sincerity assure you, and your own Experience in years to come will verify it, that as your Sabbath is, so will you find the Residue of the Week to be. Once obtain a spiritual Taste and relish for Communion with God and fellowship with Jesus Christ, and I will rest your Attachment to the Sabbath on this Basis. I know but one Way, that you will be likely to succeed in. Convince yourself, that the Day is specially the Lords, devoted by him & set apart for the purpose of his Worship & the transacting your spiritual Affairs & receiving the foretaste of his everlasting Love, and you will find a thousand difficulties removed, that will otherwise appear insurmountable. I do not think it worthwhile here, to enter into an investigation, whether the fourth

Commandment is obligatory on Christians or not . . . but this I will say, make the Experiment faithfully & religiously, and I will leave the decision of the Question to your Experience. This will be instead of a thousand subtle Arguments & nice Distinctions. I know you will have the violent Current of Custom & Fashion against you.

> Elias Boudinot to Susan Bradford, December 14, 1784. Boudinot Papers, Princeton University Library.

I should be glad to know what it is that distinguishes Connecticut Religion from common Religion: Communicate, if you please, some of those particulars that you think will amuse me as a Virtuoso. When I travelled in Flanders I thought of your excessively strict Observation of Sunday; and that a man could hardly travel on that day among you upon his lawful Occasions, without Hazard of Punishment; while where I was, every on[e] travell'd, if he pleas'd, or diverted himself any other way; and in the Afternoon both high and low went to the Play or the Opera, where there was plenty of Singing, Fiddling and Dancing. I look'd round for God's Judgments but saw no Signs of them. The Cities were well built and full of Inhabitants, the Markets fill'd with Plenty, the People well favour'd and well clothed; the Fields well till'd; the Cattle fat and strong; the Fences, Houses and Windows all in Repair; and no Old Tenor [depreciated paper money—Ed.] anywhere in the Country; which would almost make one suspect, that the Deity is not so angry at that Offence as a New England Justice.

> Benjamin Franklin to Jared Ingersoll, December 11, 1762. Labaree, *Papers of Benjamin Franklin*, 10:175–76.

Can any of our Governments be rightfully restrained from providing for the Observance of the Sabbath, which the Sovereign of the universe has assured us "was made for man?"

John Jay to Edward Livingston, July 28, 1822. Johnston, *Correspondence of Jay*, 4:465.

. . . the observance of the Sabbath, with which national prosperity has always been intimately connected.

Benjamin Rush to John Adams, August 20, 1811. Butterfield, *Letters of Rush*, 2:1096.

Sin

. . . there is Reason to be diffident of a Man who grossly violates the Principles of Morals, in any one particular habitually. This sentiment was conveyed to Us in one of the Paradoxes of the ancient Stoicks, that "all Sins were equal," and the same Idea is suggested from higher Authority. He that violates the Law in any one Instance is guilty of all.

John Adams to Abigail Adams, November 18, 1775. Butterfield, *Adams Family Correspondence*, 1:327.

I have read many of the Calvinistical Treatises on original sin and they have not convinced me of the total Depravity of human Nature. They go further than to say that human nature is destitute of benevolence. They say it is positively malevolent, altogether malicious and malignant. Je n'en crois rien [I do not believe it—Ed.].

John Adams to Francis van der Kemp, March 9, 1806. Adams Papers (microfilm), reel 118, Library of Congress.

The origin of mal moral [moral evil—Ed.] is liberty, the self determining power of free agents, endowed with reason & conscience & consequently accountable for their conduct. . . . I have read the Holy Fathers of the Hindus, of the disciples of Pythagoras of Frederick of Prussia of Soame Jenings[29] of Dr. Edwards & many others and am no more satisfied than with Eve's apple. I have no difficulty about it. I am answerable for my own sins because I know they were my own fault; and that is enough for me to know.

> John Adams to Francis van der Kemp, February 23, 1815. Ibid., reel 122.

That angels and men having sinned, and thus introduced a principle of disobedience into the creation of God, which must have proved of the most dangerous consequence to the whole extent of being; God of his infinite love and mercy, to prevent the awful catastrophe, determined to show to all worlds, his infinite disapprobation and abhorrence of sin.

It might be expected indeed, that our author [Thomas Paine—Ed.], with his incredulous temper, would have laughed at this doctrine of original sin, and the defection of angels; but on his own system, let him otherwise account in a rational manner, for the universal prevalence of evil, both in the moral and natural world—the sufferings of infants, with those of the best of men—the fury of animals and their devouring each other—the disregard and inattention in men to the great First Cause; and the blasphemies of those

---

[29] Soame Jenyns (1704–1787), a member of Parliament and bureaucrat who wrote on the taxation of the American colonies, published in 1776 *A View of the internal Evidence of the Christian Religion*, an apology for Christianity which went through ten editions by 1798 and was highly regarded by many of the Founders, especially by Patrick Henry. *DNB*.

who presumptuously deny the existence of any God but nature.

Elias Boudinot, *The Age of Revelation* (Philadelphia: Asbury Dickins, 1801), 216.

But lest they shou'd imagine that one of their strongest Objections hinted at here and elsewhere, is designedly overlook'd, as being unanswerable, viz., <u>our lost and undone State by Nature</u>, as it is commonly call'd, proceeding undoubtedly from the Imputation of old Father Adam's first Guilt. To this I answer once for all, that I look upon this Opinion every whit as ridiculous as that of Imputed Righteousness. 'Tis a Notion invented, a Bugbear set up by Priests (whether <u>Popish</u> or <u>Presbyterian</u> I know not) to fright and scare an unthinking Populace out of their Senses, and inspire them with Terror, to answer the little selfish Ends of the Inventors and Propagators. 'Tis absurd in it self, and therefore cannot be father'd upon the Christian Religion as deliver'd in the Gospel. Moral Guilt is so personal a Thing, that it cannot possibly in the Nature of Things be transferr'd from one Man to Myriads of others, that were no way accessary to it. And to suppose a Man liable to Punishment upon account of the Guilt of another, is unreasonable; and actually to punish him for it, is unjust and cruel.

Benjamin Franklin, "A Defense of Mr. Hemphill's Observations," 1735. Labaree, *Papers of Benjamin Franklin*, 2:114.

Among the strange things of this world, nothing seems more strange than that men pursuing happiness should knowingly quit the right and take a wrong road, and frequently do what their judgments neither approve nor prefer. Yet so is the fact; and this fact points strongly to the necessity of our being healed, or restored, or regenerated by a power more energetic than any of those which properly belong to the human mind. We perceive that a great breach has been made in the moral and physical systems by the introduction of moral and physical evil; how or why, we know not; so, however, it is, and it certainly seems proper that this breach should be closed and restored. For this purpose only one adequate plan has ever appeared in the world, and that is the Christian dispensation. In this plan I have full faith. Man, in his present state, appears to be a degraded creature; his best gold is mixed with dross, and his best motives are very far from being pure and free from earth and impurity.

John Jay to Lindley Murray, August 22, 1794. Johnston, *Correspondence of Jay*, 4:51–52.

To see Things as they are—to estimate them aright—and to act accordingly, is to be wise. But you know my dear Sir that most men, in order to become wise, have much to unlearn as well as to learn—much to undo as well as to do. The Israelites had little Comfort in Egypt, and yet they were not very anxious to go to the promised Land. Figuratively speaking, we are all at this Day in Egypt, and a Prince worse than Pharaoh reigns in it. Altho the Prophet "like unto Moses" offers to deliver from Bondage, and invites us to prepare and be ready to go with him, under divine Guidance and Instruction, to the promised Land; yet great is the number who prefer remaining in Slavery, and *dying* in Egypt.

John Jay to William Wilberforce, November 8, 1809. Jay Papers (online edition), Columbia University Library.

. . . may not moral evil be nothing positive, but an absence only of moral good? Does not this relieve our Systems of divinity from the awful charge against God of having created, or of being the author of Sin? He only withdrew his moral omnipresence or energy from the wills of Devils and man, and sin followed. Free will was necessary to happiness. It was abused. It can be held only by God himself. Therefore Jehovah commits the happiness of his creatures to the will of his Son, who has, in preferring good, established happiness for all of his creatures. Sin, like disease, is weakness. It is destroyed by power, or strength, as disease is by stimuli. Nothing is annihilated therefore in the destruction of sin. Good, in the form of power and love, fills its space. It is conveyed into the human mind by means of the holy Spirit. This Spirit expels nothing. It only restores strength to weakness and order to disorder, as stimuli cure weakness and convulsions in the human body.

> Benjamin Rush, "A Thought on the Origin of Evil," [1789–91].
> Corner, *Autobiography of Rush*, 193.

That he [God—Ed.] made man at first perfectly holy, that the first man sinned, and as he was the public head of his posterity, they all became sinners in consequence of his first transgression, are wholly indisposed to that which is good & inclined to evil, and on account of sin are liable to all the miseries of this life, to death, and to the pains of hell forever.

> Roger Sherman, "White Haven Church Confession of Faith" (draft), 1788. Sherman Papers, Library of Congress.

This may lead us to enquire further, whether we have right conceptions of the deplorable state in which the Gospel of God's grace supposes, and finds mankind? viz. a state of depravity, guilt and misery, exposed to the eternal curse of the law—dead in trespasses and sins—by nature prone to evil and averse to good, and entirely unable to deliver ourselves

Does all sin appear inexpressibly hateful in our eyes? Do we loath it and loath ourselves on account of it? So that we are ready with the leper to cry out unclean! unclean? And does this mourning for, and hatred of sin, manifest itself to be genuine by our forsaking it? And setting ourselves with all our might to oppose and destroy it? He is not a true penitent, who does not heartily renounce all his evil ways, and bid adieu to every thing which he knows to be sinful, with a fixed determination of soul never to indulge himself therein any more.

Roger Sherman, *Short Sermon*, 4–5, 7.

No propensities in animal nature are themselves sinful, if not indulged contrary to law. That moral good consists in rightful exercises of the natural powers and principles of the soul, in setting the affections on right objects & moral evil in placing the affections on the wrong objects. And mankind having the power of free agency are justly accountable for the exercise of their natural powers, and that any indisposition to do what they know to be their duty can be no excuse for not doing it.

Roger Sherman to Justus Mitchell. February 8, 1790. Sherman Papers, Library of Congress.

Without the shadow of reasoning, he [Thomas Paine, as the author of *Common Sense*—Ed.] is pleased to represent the doctrine of original sin as an object of contempt or abhorrence. . . . Was it modest or candid for a person without name or character, to talk in this supercilious manner of a doctrine that has been espoused and defended by many of the greatest and best men that the world ever saw, and makes an essential part of the established Creeds and Confessions of all the Protestant churches without exception? . . . Was it prudent, when he was pleading a public cause, to speak in such opprobrious terms of a doctrine, which he knew, or ought to have known, was believed and professed by, I suppose, a great majority of very different denominations.

> John Witherspoon, "The Dominion of Providence over the Passions of Man," May 17, 1776. *Works of Witherspoon*, 3:23–24 n.

Slavery

Poor Falmouth has shared the fate of Charlstown;[30] are we become a Sodom? I would fain hope we are not. Unsearchable are the ways of Heaven who permitteth Evil to befall a city and a people by those very hands who were by them constituted the Gaurdians and protectors of them. We have done Evil or our Enimies would be at peace with us. The Sin of Slavery as well as many others is not washed away.

> Abigail Adams to John Adams, October 25, 1775. Butterfield, *Adams Family Correspondence*, 1:313.

The Bible itself has not authority sufficient in these days to reconcile negro slavery to reason, justice & humanity. . . . I shudder when I think of the calamities which slavery is likely to produce in this country. You would think me mad if I were to describe my anticipations. If the gangrene is not stopped, I can see nothing but insurrections of the blacks

---

[30] Falmouth and Charlestown were Massachusetts towns burned by the British in 1775.

against the whites and massacres by the whites in their turn of the blacks.

John Adams to Louisa Catherine Adams, January 13, 1820. Adams Papers (microfilm), reel 449, Library of Congress.

Dr. Jarvis has assign'd some good causes of the too general inattention to the religion of the Indians. But those causes do not apply to the negroes. We have thousands if not millions of them domesticated with us. We might examine them. But who asks them a question? Or who studies their languages? They have probably as great a variety of tongues as the Indians. Nations which have neither records, nor histories, nor letters have fables and traditions and dogmas which have meanings or Allusions, worth searching if they can be found.

Why are not Bibles translated into negro and sent to the gold coast. My learn'd ingenious eloquent and amiable friend and next neighbour when I lived in the white house in Brattle Square, Dr. Samuel Cooper,[31] had a negro fellow named Glasgow, who seem'd as harmless and almost as mindless as an idiot.

Nevertheless his master endeavoured to instruct him in the Christian Religion. He began by reading and explaining the History in Genesis of the fall of Man. Glasgow listen'd with great attention and astonishment for a long time but at last he broke silence. Master! "We have a different account of this matter in my Country" Aye! Indeed what is that account? "We say that in the beginning, the lot of the world was put upon a race between a dog and a toad. If the dog came out first the world was to be good and happy. If the toad, all was to be wicked and sinful. Everybody rejoiced.

---

[31] Samuel Cooper (1725–1783), Congregational minister of the Brattle Street Church in Boston, was a close friend of many patriot leaders and an important proponent of American independence. *ANB.*

Surely the dog would win. But when they started the dog had run a great way before the toad had hopp'd a rod. But about half way the evil Spirit threw a bone before the Dog, who turn'd aside to gnaw it, while the toad hopp'd on and got out first." Dr. Cooper has repeatedly related this anecdote to me. Is not this the history of the loss of Paradise translated into Negro? There is the same dulness of Understanding, the imbecility of Virtue against Appetite in the dog that there was in Eve and Adam. The same ruin to the world though ascrib'd to chance and to fault. The same personification of Evil in the tempter. It is as rational an attempt to account for the Origin of Evil as that of the great Frederick, Soame Jennings, or Dr. Edward's [Jonathan Edwards—Ed.].

John Adams to William Smith Shaw, June 20, 1821. Ibid., reel 124.

Not only the practice of ancient nations, and that of all modern Europe, had been brought into view, but even the sacred Scriptures had been quoted to justify this iniquitous traffic [the slave trade—Ed.]. It is true, that the Egyptians held the Israelites in bondage for four hundred years, and Mr. B. doubted not, but much the same arguments as had been used on the present occasion, had been urged with great violence by the King of Egypt, whose heart, it is expressly said, had been extremely hardened to show why he should not consent to let the children of Israel go, who had now become absolutely necessary to him; but, said he, gentlemen cannot forget the consequences that followed; they were delivered by a strong hand and stretched out arm, and it ought to be remembered that the Almighty Power that accompanied their deliverance is the same yesterday, to-day, and forever. The New Testament has afforded a number of texts to countenance this doctrine, in the gentleman's opinion. One would have imagined that the uniform tenor of the Gospel, that breathes a spirit of love and universal philanthropy to our fellow creatures—that commands our love to our neighbor to be measured by our love to ourselves—that teaches us whatsoever we would that men should do to us to do so to them, would have prevented this misapplication. Surely the gentleman overlooked the prophecy of St. Peter, where he foretells that among other damnable heresies, "Through covetousness shall they, with feigned words, make merchandise of you."

> Elias Boudinot, Speech in the House of Representatives, March 22, 1790. Jane J. Boudinot, ed., *The Life, Public Services, Addresses and Letters of Elias Boudinot* (New York: DaCapo Press, 1971), 2:221–22.

How will you answer, in the great day of inquisition for blood, for the share you have had in that horrid traffic in the souls of men, called the Guinea trade? How will you account for the contradiction between your national declarations in a day of distress and humiliation, and your political conduct, under the smiles of divine Providence, since your deliverance has been effected. . . . Your declaration of Independence, of which you so justly boast, has these words, "We hold these truths to be self evident, that all men are created equal, that they are endowed by their Creator with certain unalienable rights; that among these are life, liberty, and the pursuit of happiness." However you may plead in your excuse, that this declaration found you in possession of this species of property, and the total relinquishment of it, would have been adding affliction to the afflicted, yet are you not, as a nation, answerable for every soul imported from Africa since that date, and who are daily imported into Georgia and South Carolina, by vessels, many of them from the eastern states, as well as for the children born since that time in your states? Were these declarations designed merely to deceive and mislead—will not the God of all the earth make inquisition for these things?

Elias Boudinot, *The Second Advent* (Trenton, N.J.: D. Fenton & S. Hutchinson, 1815), 534–35.

I take this opportunity to acknowledge the receit of Anthony Benezet's Book against the slave trade.[32] I thank you for it. It is not a little surprising that the professors of Christianity, whose chief excellence consists in softening the human heart, and in cherishing and improving its finer feelings, should encourage a practice so totally repugnant to the first impressions of right and wrong. What adds to the wonder is that this abominable practice has been introduced in the most enlightened ages. Times, that seem to have pretensions to boast of high improvements in the arts, and sciences, and refined morality, have brought into general use and guarded by many laws, a species of violence and tyranny, which our more rude and barbarous, but more honest ancestors detested. Is it not amazing, that at a time when the rights of Humanity are defined and understood with precision in a country above all others fond of liberty, that in such an age and in such a country, we find men professing a religion the most humane, mild, meek, gentle and generous, adopting a Principle as repugnant to humanity, as it is inconsistent with the Bible and destructive of liberty? Every thinking honest man rejects it in speculation, how few in practice from conscientious motives.

Would any one believe that I am a master of slaves of my own purchase! I am drawn along by the general inconve-

[32] It is not clear which of the polemics against slavery by the Quaker Anthony Benezet (1703–1784) Henry had received. Possibly it was Benezet's *Caution and warning to Great-Britain and her colonies, in a short representation of the calamitous state of the enslaved Negroes in the British dominions* (Philadelphia: Henry Miller, 1766).

nience of living without them. I will not, I cannot justify it. However culpable my conduct, I will so far pay my devoir to virtue, as to own the excellence and rectitude of her precepts and to lament my want of conformity to them.

I believe a time will come when an opportunity will be offered to abolish this lamentable evil. Everything we can do, is to improve it if it happens in our day; if not, let us transmit to our descendants, together with our slaves, a pity for their unhappy lot, and an abhorrence of slavery. If we cannot reduce this wished-for reformation to practice, let us treat the unhappy victims with lenity, it is the furthest advance we can make toward justice. It is a debt we owe to the purity of our Religion to show that it is at variance with that law which warrants slavery.

Patrick Henry to Robert Pleasants, January 18, 1773. Campbell, *Henry*, 99–100.

An excellent law might be made out of the Pennsylvania one for the gradual abolition of slavery. Till America comes into this Measure her Prayers to Heaven for Liberty will be impious. This is a strong expression but it is just.

John Jay to Egbert Benson, September 18, 1780. Jay Papers (online edition), Columbia University Library.

If a slave can have a country in this world, it must be any other in preference to that in which he is born to live and labour for another. ... I tremble for my country when I reflect that God is just: that his justice cannot sleep forever: that considering numbers, nature and natural means only, a revolution of the wheel of fortune, an exchange of situation, is among possible events: that it may become probable by supernatural interference! The Almighty has no attribute which can take side with us in such a contest. But it is impossible to be temperate and to pursue this subject through the

various considerations of policy, of morals, of history natural and civil. We must be contented to hope they will force
their way into every one's mind. I think a change already
perceptible, since the origin of the present revolution. The
spirit of the master is abating, that of the slave rising from
the dust, his condition mollifying, the way I hope preparing,
under the auspices of heaven, for a total emancipation, and
that this is disposed, in the order of events, to be with the
consent of the masters, rather than by their extirpation.

> Thomas Jefferson, *Notes on the State of Virginia*, 1781. Peden,
> *Notes on Virginia*, 163.

What a stupendous, what an incomprehensible machine is
man! Who can endure toil, famine, stripes, imprisonment or
death itself in vindication of his own liberty, and the next
moment be deaf to all those motives whose power supported him thro' his trial, and inflict on his fellow men a
bondage, one hour of which is fraught with more misery
than ages of that which he rose in rebellion to oppose. But
we must await with patience the workings of an overruling
providence, and hope that that is preparing the deliverance
of these our suffering brethren. When the measure of their
tears shall be full, when their groans shall have involved
heaven itself in darkness, doubtless a god of justice will
awaken to their distress, and by diffusing light and liberal-
ity among their oppressors, or at length by his exterminat-
ing thunder, manifest his attention to the things of this
world, and that they are not left to the guidance of a blind
fatality.

> Thomas Jefferson to Jean Nicolas Démeunier, June 26, 1786. Boyd.
> *Papers of Thomas Jefferson*, 10:63.

You know my Dear Sir I abhor Slavery, I was born in a
Country where Slavery had been established by British

Kings & Parliaments as well as by the Laws of that Country Ages before my existence. I found the Christian Religion & Slavery growing under the same authority & cultivation. I nevertheless disliked it. In former days there was no combatting the prejudices of Men supported by Interest, the day I hope is approaching when from principles of gratitude as well as justice every Man will strive to be foremost in shewing his readiness to comply with the Golden Rule; not less than 20,000 Sterling would all my Negroes produce if sold at public Auction tomorrow. I am not the Man who enslaved them, they are indebted to English Men for that favour, nevertheless, I am devising means for manumitting many of them & for cutting off the entail of Slavery—great powers oppose me, the Laws & Customs of my Country, my own & the avarice of my Country Men—What will my Children say if I deprive them of so much Estate? These are difficulties but not insuperable I will do as much as I can in my time & leave the rest to a better hand. I am not one of those who arrogate the peculiar care of Providence in each fortunate event, nor one of those who dare trust in Providence for defence & security of their own Liberty while they enslave & wish to continue in Slavery, thousands who are as well intitled to freedom as themselves. I perceive the work before me is great. I shall appear to many as a promoter not only of strange but of dangerous doctrines, it will therefore be necessary to proceed with caution. . . .

> Henry Laurens to John Laurens, August 14, 1776. Rogers,
> *Papers of Henry Laurens*, 11:224–25.

A Christian slave is a contradiction in terms.

But if, in the partial Revelation which God made, of his will to the Jews, we find such testimonies against slavery, what may we not expect from the Gospel, the Design of which was to abolish all distinctions of name and country. While the Jews thought they complied with the precepts of the law, in confining the love of their neighbor "to the children of their people," Christ commands us to look upon all mankind even our enemies as our neighbors and brethren, and "in all things, to do unto them whatever we would wish they should do unto us." He tells us further that his "kingdom is not of this world," and therefore constantly avoids saying anything that might interfere directly with the Roman or Jewish Governments: so that altho' he does not call upon masters to emancipate their slaves, or upon slaves to assert that liberty wherein God and Nature made them free, yet there is scarcely a parable or a sermon in the whole history of his life, but what contains the strongest arguments against slavery. Every prohibition of covetousness—intemperance—pride—uncleanness—theft—and murder which he delivered—every lesson of meekness, humility, forbearance, charity, self-denial, and brotherly love which he taught, are levelled against this evil;—for slavery, while it includes all the former vices, necessarily excludes the practice of all the latter virtues, both from the master and the slave. Let such, therefore, who vindicate the traffic of buying and selling souls, seek some modern system of religion to support it, and not presume to sanctify their crimes by attempting to reconcile it to the sublime and perfect religion of the Great Author of Christianity.

Benjamin Rush, *An Address to the Inhabitants of the British Settlements in America upon Slave-Keeping* (New York: Hodge and Shober, 1773), 14–15, 17.

Trinity

There is not any reasoning which can convince me, contrary to my senses, that three is one and one three. Is it possible for the humane mind to form an idea of the Supreme Being, without some visible qualities such as wisdom, power, and goodness. The creator, preserver and governor of the world. The first commandment forbids the worship of but one God. That Jesus Christ was sent into the world by the Father to take upon him humane nature, to exalt redeem and purify the world, to set an example to all his followers of sinless obedience and holiness of life and conversation, and to bring life and immortality to light, the scriptures fully testify, and that a conformity to his precepts and example, as far as humane nature is capable of it, will be rewarded by future happiness in the world to come, is my firm belief.

Is there not a subordination to the Father manifested in the whole life and character of Jesus Christ? Why said he call ye me good. There is none good but one that is God. Again, I do nothing of myself, but the Father in me. . . . From these and many other passages of scripture, I am led to believe in the unity of the Supreme Being.

Abigail Adams to John Quincy Adams, May 4, 1816. Adams Papers (microfilm), reel 431, Library of Congress.

The human Understanding is a revelation from its Maker which can never be disputed or doubted. There can be no Scepticism, Pyrrhonism or Incredulity or Infidelity here. No Prophecies, no Miracles are necessary to prove this celestial communication. This revelation has made it certain that two and one make three; and that one is not three; nor can three be one. . . . Had you and I been forty days with Moses on Mount Sinai and admitted to behold, the divine Shekinah, and there told that one was three and three, one: We might not have had the courage to deny it, but We could not have believed it. The thunders and Lightenings and Earthquakes and the transcendant Splendors and Glories, might have overwhelmed Us with terror and Amazement: but We could not have believed the doctrine. We should be more likely to say in our hearts, whatever We might say with our Lips, This is Chance. There is no God! No truth. This is all delusion, fiction, and a lie: or it is all Chance.

> John Adams to Thomas Jefferson, September 14, 1813. Cappon, *Adams-Jefferson Letters*, 2:373.

It is wholly beside my purpose, to proceed further in the important dispute relative to the Trinity. I am contented with knowing, that the Scriptures are the word of the ever-living God; and that therein he has revealed to me, that the Father, the Son, and the Holy Spirit, in whose name I was baptized, bear record in Heaven; and that these three are the one only infinite and eternal God, whom I am to worship, love and adore, in spirit and truth. It is sufficient in the present dispute, to have shown, that this doctrine (whether true or false) was the doctrine of the Jewish church before the coming of the Saviour; not invented first by Christian theory, but as old as the creation; I believe I may add, as eternity.

Had it been consistent with my plan, I should not have shrunk from a fuller inquiry into this great mystery, as far as the nature of the question would admit; which could be only to show, that however it may exceed, yet it is not contrary to human reason.

> Elias Boudinot, *The Age of Revelation* (Philadelphia: Asbury Dickins, 1801), 128.

Is there not an incongruity in saying that the Son, the second person, was conceived of the spirit, the third person?

Of the Difficulties of Understanding the Doctrine of the Trinity, see . . . what the admirable Locke says in his Treatise on Christianity page 239,[33] concerning the insufficiency of long and intricate deductions of Reason, for convincing and influencing mankind in general are also applicable to this perplexing system of theology. His words are: "you may as soon hope to have all the day labourers, tradesmen, the spinsters and dairy maids perfect mathematicians, as to have them perfect in ethics this way." Yet all of these have souls to be saved.

> John Dickinson, notes on religion, undated. R. R. Logan Papers, Historical Society of Pennsylvania.

It appeared to me that the Trinity was a Fact fully revealed and substantiated, but that the quo modo was incomprehensible and consequently inexplicable by human Ingenuity. According to sundry Creeds, the divine Being whom we denominate the second Person in the Trinity had before all worlds been so generated or begotten by the first Person in the Trinity, as to be his coeval, coequal and coeternal Son. For proof of this I searched the Scriptures diligently—but without Success. I therefore consider this Position of being at least of questionable Orthodoxy.

> John Jay to Samuel Miller, February 18, 1822. Jay Papers (online edition), Columbia University Library.

Ridicule is the only weapon which can be used against unintelligible propositions. Ideas must be distinct before reason

---

[33] John Locke, *The reasonableness of Christianity, as deliver'd in the scriptures* . . . 6th ed., (London: A. Bettesworth and C. Hitch, 1736), 239.

can act upon them; and no man ever had a distinct idea of the trinity. It is the mere Abracadabra of the mountebanks calling themselves the priests of Jesus. If it could be understood it would not answer their purpose. Their security is in their faculty of shedding darkness, like the scuttle fish, thro' the element in which they move, and making it impenetrable to the eye of a pursuing enemy. And there they will skulk, until some rational creed can occupy the void which the obliteration of their duperies would leave in the minds of our honest and unsuspecting brethren.

Thomas Jefferson to Francis van der Kemp, August 6, 1816.
Adams, *Jefferson's Extracts*, 375.

No historical fact is better established than that the doctrine of one god, pure and uncompounded was that of the early ages of Christianity; and was among the efficacious doctrines which gave it triumph over the polytheism of the antients, sickened with the absurdities of their own theology. Nor was the unity of the supreme being ousted from the Christian creed by the force of reason, but by the sword of civil government wielded at the will of the fanatic Athanasius. The hocus-pocus phantasm of a god like another Cerberus with one body and three heads had it's birth and growth in the blood of thousands and thousands of martyrs. And a strong proof of the solidity of the primitive faith is it's restoration as soon as a nation arises which vindicates to itself the freedom of religious opinion, and it's eternal divorce from the civil authority. . . . In fact the Athanasian paradox that one is three, and three but one is so incomprehensible to the human mind that no candid man can say he has any idea of it, and how can he believe what presents no idea. He who thinks he does only decieves himself. He proves also that man, once surrendering his reason, has no remaining guard against absurdities the most monstrous, and like a ship without rudder is the sport of every wind. With such persons gullability which they call faith takes the helm from the hand of reason and the mind becomes a wreck.

Thomas Jefferson to James Smith, December 8, 1822. Ibid., 409.

I am full of an humble confidence that after we have passed thro this Vale of Sin & misery we shall enjoy everlasting communion in the presence of the one ever blessed & adorable God, Father, Son & Spirit. These are my most comfortable thoughts. Amen!

Henry Laurens to John Ettwein, November 10, 1763. Rogers, *Papers of Henry Laurens*, 4:42.

The wisest plan of education that could be offered would be unpopular among 99 out of an 100 of the citizens of America if it opposed in any degree the doctrine of the Trinity.

Benjamin Rush to Richard Price, May 25, 1786. Butterfield, *Letters of Rush*, 1:389.

We believe without attempting to explain the Mystery of the Trinity. Why believe Three in One and not believe the derived and the independent life of our Saviour, His being raised from the grave by his Father, and being the Author of His own resurrection—the Union of liberty and necessity, and the agency of divine and human efforts in bringing about the Salvation of the soul. They all appear to be true, though opposed to each other. They are like the Trinity— mysteries intelligible only, perhaps to the Creator.

Benjamin Rush, "Commonplace Book," August 14, 1811. Corner, *Autobiography of Rush*, 340.

I believe that there is one only living and true God, existing in three persons, The Father, the Son, and the

Holy Ghost, the same in substance equal in power and glory.

Roger Sherman, "White Haven Church Confession of Faith" (draft), 1788. Sherman Papers, Library of Congress.

Unitarianism

I thank you for your favour of the 10th and the pamphlet enclosed, "American Unitarianism."[34] I have turned over its leaves and have found nothing that was not familiarly known to me.

In the preface Unitarianism is represented as only thirty years old in New England. I can testify as a Witness to its old age. Sixty five years ago my own minister the Reverend Samuel Bryant, Dr. Johnathan Mayhew of the west Church in Boston, the Reverend Mr. Shute of Hingham, the Reverend John Brown of Cohasset & perhaps equal to all if not above all the Reverend Mr. Gay of Hingham were Unitarians. Among the Laity how many could I name, Lawyers, Physicians, Tradesmen, farmers!

John Adams to Jedidiah Morse, May 15, 1815. Adams Papers (microfilm), reel 122, Library of Congress.

We Unitarians, one of whom I have had the Honour to be, for more than sixty Years, do not indulge our Malignity in

---

[34] Jedidiah Morse, *Review of American Unitarianism* (Boston: S. T. Armstrong, 1815).

profane Cursing and Swearing, against you Calvinists; one
of whom I know not how long you have been. You and I,
once saw Calvin and Arius, on the Plafond of the Cathedral
of St. John the Second in Spain roasting in the Flames of
Hell. We Unitarians do not delight in thinking that Plato
and Cicero, Tacitus Quintilian Plyny and even Diderot, are
sweltering under the scalding drops of divine Vengeance,
for all Eternity.

> John Adams to John Quincy Adams, March 28, 1816, Ibid., reel 430.

I trust that there is not a young man now living in the US.
who will not die an Unitarian.

> Thomas Jefferson to Benjamin Waterhouse, June 26, 1822. Adams,
> *Jefferson's Extracts*, 406.

Universalism

I believe too in a future state of rewards and punishments
too; but not eternal.

> John Adams to Francis van der Kemp, July 13, 1815. Adams Papers
> (microfilm), reel 122, Library of Congress.

At Dr. Finley's School,[35] I was more fully instructed in these
principles by means of the Westminster Catechism. I retained

---

[35] West Nottingham Academy, in extreme northeast Maryland. Founded
by Samuel Finley (1715–1766), an evangelical (New Side) Presbyterian
minister, who became president of Princeton in 1761.

them but without any affection for them 'till about the year 1780. I then read for the first time Fletcher's controversy with the Calvinists in favor of the Universality of the atonement. This prepared my mind to admit the doctrine of Universal salvation, which was then preached in our city by the Revd. Mr. Winchester.[36] It embraced and reconciled my ancient calvinistical, and newly adopted Armenian principles. From that time I have never doubted upon the subject of the salvation of all men. My conviction of the truth of this doctrine was derived from reading the works of Stonehouse, Seigvolk, White, Chauncey, and Winchester, and afterwards from an attentive perusal of the Scriptures. I always admitted with each of these authors future punishment, and of long, long duration.

> Benjamin Rush, "Travels through Life." Corner, *Autobiography of Rush*, 163–64.

I think Dr. Chauncey's[37] sentiments on that subject [universal salvation—Ed.] very erroneous, & if believed will tend to relax the restraints on vice arising from the threatnings of the divine law against impenitent sinners. It is true I did declare it to be my opinion at first in the case of Dr. Beardsley, that such an opinion ought not to exclude a person from communion, but on further consideration of the matter, & finding a former determination of our church in point against my opinion I have viewed it in different point of light from what I did at first. I think we are as much

---

[36] Elhanan Winchester (1751–1797), one of the founders of American Universalism. Originally a Baptist, Winchester was expelled from his church in Philadelphia and preached in a room at the University of Pennsylvania. *ANB.*

[37] Charles Chauncy (1705–1787), long time pastor of Boston's first Congregational Church and a leading opponent of the Great Awakening, published two books supporting Universalism late in his life. Ibid.

bound to believe the threatnings, as the promises of the gospel.

Roger Sherman to David Austin, March 1, 1790. Sherman Papers, Yale University Library.

Virgin Mary

The Trinity was carried in a general council by one vote against a quaternity; the Virgin Mary lost an equality with the Father, Son, and Spirit only by a single suffrage.

John Adams to Benjamin Rush, June 12, 1812. Schutz and Adair, *Spur of Fame*, 225.

If I understand the Doctrine, it is, that if God the first second or third or all three together are united with or in a Man, the whole Animal becomes a God and his Mother is the Mother of God.

It grieves me: it shocks me to write in this stile upon a subject the most adorable that any finite Intelligence can contemplate or embrace: but if ever Mankind are to be superior to the Brutes, sacerdotal Impostures must be exposed.

John Adams to Francis van der Kemp, October 23, 1816.
Adams Papers (microfilm), reel 122, Library of Congress.

And the day will come when the mystical generation of Jesus, by the supreme being as his father in the womb of a virgin will be classed with the fable of the generation of Minerva in the brain of Jupiter.

Thomas Jefferson to John Adams, April 11, 1823. Adams, *Jefferson's Extracts*, 412.

War

In a Time of Warr, and especially a War like this, one may see the Necessity and Utility, of the divine Prohibition of Revenge, and the Injunctions of forgiveness of Injuries and love of Enemies, which We find in the Christian Religion. Unrestrained, in some degree by those benevolent Laws, Men would be Devils, at such a Time as this!

> John Adams to Abigail Adams, March 14, 1777. Butterfield, *Adams Family Correspondence*, 2:175.

I believe with you that Wars are the natural and unavoidable effect of the constitution of human Nature and the fabric of the Globe it is destined to inhabit and to rule. I believe further that Wars, at times, are as necessary for the preservation and perfection, the Prosperity, Liberty, Happiness, Virtue and independence of Nations as Gales of Wind to the Salubrity of the Atmosphere, or the Agitations of the Ocean to prevent its Stagnation and putrification. As I believe this to be the constitution of God Almighty and the constant order of his Providence, I must esteem all the speculations of Divines and Phylosophers about universal and Perpetual Peace, as short sighted frivolous Romances.

> John Adams to Benjamin Rush, July 7, 1812. *Old Family Letters*, 401–2.

I most cordially agree with you, and with the oldest statesman in America, Governor MacKean,[38] who in a charming letter I received from him a few days ago said that: "God

---

[38] Thomas McKean (1734–1817), signer of the Declaration of Independence, chief justice of Pennsylvania (1777–99) and, beginning in 1799, three-term governor of the state. Ibid.

Almighty has always been our General and Commander in Chief," and we have never had any other.

John Adams to Benjamin Waterhouse, October 28, 1814. Worthington C. Ford, ed., *Statesman and Friend* (Boston: Little, Brown, and Company, 1927), 112.

I wish them heartily success in humanizing War—if that is possible—and Christianizing it too—for I believe that War in many cases is very consistent with Christianity and that a Military Education of Youth is by no means inconsistent with Philosophy, Equity, humanity, or Religion.

John Adams to David Sewall, November 23, 1819. Adams Papers (microfilm), reel 124, Library of Congress.

In what Light we are viewed by superior Beings, may be gathered from a Piece of late West India News, which possibly has not yet reached you. A young Angel of Distinction being sent down to this world on some Business, for the first time, had an old courier-spirit assigned him as a Guide. They arriv'd over the Seas of Martinico, in the middle of the long Day of obstinate Fight between the Fleets of Rodney and De Grasse.[39] When, thro' the Clouds of smoke, he saw the Fire of the Guns, the Decks covered with mangled Limbs, and Bodies dead or dying; the ships sinking, burning, or blown into the Air; and the Quantity of Pain, Misery, and Destruction, the Crews yet alive were thus with so much Eagerness dealing round to one another; he turn'd angrily to his Guide, and said, "You blundering Blockhead, you are ignorant of your Business; you undertook to conduct me to the Earth, and you have brought me into Hell!"

[39] Franklin is referring to the naval engagement off the Saints Passage, April 21–22, 1782, in which a British fleet under Admiral George Rodney defeated a French fleet commanded by Admiral deGrasse.

"No, Sir," says the Guide, "I have made no mistake; this is really the Earth, and these are men. Devils never treat one another in this cruel manner; they have more Sense, and more of what Men (vainly) call <u>Humanity</u>."

> Benjamin Franklin to Joseph Priestley, June 7, 1782. Smyth,
> *Writings of Franklin*, 8:452–53.

In my Opinion there have been just and lawfull Wars, as well as unjust and unlawful Wars. It certainly is desireable that wars should become less frequent, and the Recurrence of them in this country cannot probably be more efficaciously checked, than by promoting Christianity, and by electing Christian Rulers—Such Men will neither provoke War by Aggression, nor be guilty of waging war unjustly against other nations.

> John Jay to Eleazar Lord, February 7, 1817. Jay Papers (online
> edition), Columbia University Library.

You seem to doubt whether there ever was a <u>just</u> war, and that it would puzzle even Solomon to find one.

Had such a doubt been proposed to Solomon, an answer to it would probably have been suggested to him by a very memorable and interesting war which occurred in his day. I allude to the war in which his brother Absalom on the one side, and his father David on the other, were the belligerent parties. That war was caused by and proceeded from "the lusts" of Absalom, and was horribly wicked. But the war waged against him by David was not caused by, nor did it proceed from, "the lusts" of David, but was right, just, and necessary. Had David submitted to be dethroned by his detestable son, he would, in my opinion, have violated his moral duty and betrayed his official trust.

Although just war is not forbidden by the gospel in express terms, yet you think an implied prohibition of all war, without exception, is deducible from the answer of our Lord to Pilate, viz: "If my kingdom were of this world, then would my servants fight," etc. . . .

You and I understand the words in question very differently. . . . To the advancement and support of his spiritual sovereignty over his spiritual kingdom, soldiers and swords and corporeal exertions were inapplicable and useless. But, on the other hand, soldiers and swords and corporeal exertions are necessary to enable the several temporal rulers of the states and kingdoms of this world to maintain their authority and protect themselves and their people; and our Saviour expressly declares that if his kingdom had been of this world, then would his servants fight to protect him; or, in other words, that then, and in that case, he would not have restrained them from fighting. The lawfulness of such fighting, therefore, instead of being denied, is admitted and confirmed by that declaration.

Had the gospel regarded war as being in every case sinful, it seems strange that the apostle Paul should have been so unguarded as, in teaching the importance of faith, to use an argument which clearly proves the lawfulness of war, viz.: "That it was through faith that Gideon, David, and others waxed valiant in fight, and turned to flight the armies of aliens;" thereby confirming the declaration of David, that it was God who had "girded him with strength to battle; and had taught his hands to war, and his fingers to fight."

The gospel appears to me to consider the servants of Christ as having two capacities or characters, with correspondent duties to sustain and fulfil.

Being subjects of his spiritual kingdom, they are bound in that capacity to fight, pursuant to his orders, with spiritual weapons, against his and their spiritual enemies.

Being also subjects and partakers in the rights and interests of a temporal or worldly state or kingdom, they are in that capacity bound, whenever lawfully required, to fight with weapons in just and necessary war, against the worldly enemies of that state or kingdom.

John Jay to John Murray, Jr., April 15, 1818. Johnston, *Correspondence of Jay*, 4:407–14.

I admire your pious and grateful adorations to the Supreme Being for the success of our forces at Havannah. Let you and I (while the wild mob proclaim their enthusiastic joy in frantic acclamations) cry out perpetually in our hearts, "Glory to God in the Highest." How apt are we to extol the prudence and moderation of a general, and the bravery and resolution of the soldiery, but how little do we eye the finger of God in our most glorious and important events. 'Tis God that steels the gallant soul! 'Tis God that inspires with martial courage! 'Tis God that teaches our hands to war and our fingers to fight! 'Tis God that rules, protects, commands, and governs all.—Glory to God in the Highest!

Benjamin Rush to Ebenezer Hazard, September 27, 1762. Butterfield, *Letters of Rush*, 1:6.

Are we not the only nation in the world, France excepted, whether Christian, Mohamidan, pagan, or savage, that has ever dared to go to war without imploring supernatural aid, either by prayers, or sacrifices, or auspices, or libations of some kind? . . . How differently did the Congresses of 1774, 1775, and 1776 begin and conduct the war with Great Britain that ended in the establishment of the liberties and independence of our country! They appealed to the God of armies and nations for support, and he blessed both their councils and their arms.

Benjamin Rush to John Adams, June 4, 1812. Ibid., 2:1138.

Wars I believe are not only inevitable and necessary, but sometimes obligatory upon nations. . . . Nations in like manner can exist with all the prerogatives of nations only by war. It is the condition by which they navigate the ocean and preserve their territory from incursion. To neglect to contend for both by arms is to forfeit their right to them. The ocean has been called the highroad of nations. It might be called God's gift to all nations. Not to maintain the exercise and enjoyment of this gift is (I hope I do not say too much when I add) ingratitude and disobedience to him that gave it. To expect perpetual peace therefore among beings constituted as we are, is as absurd as to expect to discover perpetual motion.

> Benjamin Rush to John Adams, July 18, 1812. Ibid., 2:1154.

The blessing and protection of Heaven are at all times necessary but especially so in times of public distress and danger. The General hopes and trusts, that every officer and man, will endeavour so to live, and act, as becomes a Christian Soldier defending the dearest Rights and Liberties of his country.

> George Washington, General Orders, July 9, 1776. Fitzpatrick, *Writings of Washington*, 5:245.

To the various branches of the Army . . . he can only again offer in their behalf his recommendations to their grateful country, and his prayers to the God of Armies. May ample justice be done them here, and may the choicest of heaven's favours, both here and hereafter, attend those who, under the devine auspices, have secured innumerable blessings for others.

> George Washington, Farewell Orders to the Armies of the United States, November 2, 1783. Ibid., 27:227.

Success in any attempt is to be ultimately attributed to God. . . . That it is he who in cases of difficulty and danger, directs their hands to war and their fingers to fight, and finally crowns their endeavors with success.

> John Witherspoon, "Sermon delivered at a Public Thanksgiving after Peace," November 28, 1782. *Works of Witherspoon*, 3:63.

Women

. . . I long to hear that you have declared an independency—and by the way in the new Code of Laws which I suppose it will be necessary for you to make I desire you would Remember the Ladies, and be more generous and favourable to them than your ancestors. Do not put such unlimited power into the hands of the Husbands. Remember all Men would be tyrants if they could. If perticuliar care and attention is not paid to the Laidies we are determined to foment a Rebelion, and will not hold ourselves bound by any Laws in which we have no voice, or Representation.

That your Sex are Naturally Tyrannical is a Truth so thoroughly established as to admit of no dispute, but such of you as wish to be happy willingly give up the harsh title of Master for the more tender and endearing one of Friend. Why then, not put it out of the power of the vicious and the Lawless to use us with cruelty and indignity with impunity. Men of Sense in all Ages abhor those customs which treat us only as vassals of your Sex. Regard us then as Beings placed

by providence under your protection and in immitation of
the Supreem Being make use of that power only for our
happiness.

> Abigail Adams to John Adams, March 31, 1776. Butterfield, *Adams
> Family Correspondence*, 1:370.

The Bible . . . is the most Republican Book in the World, and
therefore I will still revere it. The Curses against Fornication
and Adultery, and the prohibition of every wanton glance
or libinous ogle at a woman, I believe to be the only system
that ever did or will preserve a Republick in the World.
There is a Paradox for you. But if I don't make it out you
may say if you please that I am an enthusiast. I say then that
national Morality never was and never can be preserved,
without the utmost purity and chastity in women: and
without national Morality a Republican Government cannot be maintained. Therefore my dear Fellow Citizens of
America, you must ask leave of your wives and daughters
to preserve your Republick. I believe I shall write a Book
upon this Topick before I die and if I could articulate a word
I don't know but I should go into the Pulpit and preach
upon it.

> John Adams to Benjamin Rush, February 2, 1807. *Old Family Letters*,
> 127–28.

Your Duty to Man, depends in the performance of it, on
the fulfillment of your duty to God. Your domestic Connections will call for your particular Attention. Here you
must not forget, that your Husband, should be the first Object of it. By your union, you have submitted to him as
your Head and Superior. I know that it is a favourite observation with many, that Husband and Wife are equal and
there should be no superiority. This is not true, but a dan-

gerous Error, from whence many disagreeable Consequences flow.

It is true, neither in Theory or Practice. In point of Merit,
perhaps it may be strictly true, but in point of Order, God
has thought proper to make it otherwise, and that for the
punishment of Sin; and in the End, as all his other dealings
with his People are, for the Happiness of both.

The Imperfection of all human Societies, renders it absolutely necessary, that there should be a Head and Chief,
whose will is to determine and be the final Resort. God hath
placed this in Man, not to tyrannize and lord it over his Wife
and Family, but for their protection, instruction, nourish-
ment and guidance. It will therefore become you, in all reasonable Things, to submit to him, as your Head and support. This will sweeten the Path of Life, will lead you to look
up to him and lean upon him as your Staff and Comfort. It
will promote and secure in him, all that Affection, Love and
Confidence, which must naturally arise from a generous esteem and approbation, nourished by daily observation and
rational Reflection. The flame of Love is like that of fire, it
must have a continual addition of fuel or it will go out,
however bright it may burn at present. You should early
learn to prefer domestic peace and Happiness to all other
Enjoyments of Life. You will find it, next to the love of God,
the great antidote to human ills.

> Elias Boudinot to Susan Bradford, December 1784. Boudinot Papers,
> Princeton University Library.

A clergyman of long experience in the instruction of youth
informed me, that he always found children acquired religious knowledge more easily than knowledge upon other
subjects; and that young girls acquired this kind of knowledge more readily than boys. The female breast is the natural soil of christianity; and while our women are taught to

believe its doctrines, and obey its precepts, the wit of Voltaire, and the stile of Bolingbroke, will never be able to destroy its influence upon our citizens.

Benjamin Rush, "Thoughts on Female Education, Accommodated to the Present State of Society, Manners, and Government, in the United States of America," July 28, 1787. Rush, *Essays: Literary, Moral, and Philosophical*, 48–49.

I write to you as a Christian and a philosopher, and not as a <u>woman</u>, In inquiries after divine truth, the distinction of sexes should be forgotten, for in this delightful exercise we "neither marry, nor are given in marriage, but are as the angels in heaven."

Benjamin Rush to Mary Stockton, September 7, 1788. Butterfield, *Letters of Rush*, 1:486.

Suggestions for Further Reading
★

Since many people ascribe to Thomas Jefferson the creation of the American system of the separation of church and state, it is not surprising that monographs have been written that focus exclusively on his religious life. A good recent example of this genre is Edwin S. Gaustad, *Sworn on the Altar of God: A Religious Biography of Thomas Jefferson* (Grand Rapids, Mich.: William B. Erdmans Publishing Company, 1996); still valuable is an older volume, Charles B. Sanford, *The Religious Life of Thomas Jefferson* (Charlottesville: University Press of Virginia, 1984). There is also a good study of George Washington's religious life: Paul Boller, *George Washington and Religion* (Dallas: Southern Methodist University Press, 1963). There have been several attempts to penetrate Benjamin Franklin's religious views: among others is Alfred O. Aldridge, *Benjamin Franklin and Nature's God* (Durham, N.C.: Duke University Press, 1967). For Hamilton and Madison, see the following articles: Douglass Adair, "Was Alexander Hamilton a Christian Statesman?" in Trevor Colbourn, ed., *Fame and the Founding Fathers: Essays by Douglass Adair* (New York: W. W. Norton, 1974), 141–59; and James Hutson, "James Madison and Religion: Radicalism Unbound," in James Hutson, *Forgotten Features of the Founding: The Recovery of Religious Themes in the Early American Republic* (Lanham, Md.: Rowman & Litlefield, 2003), 155–85.

There are several histories of religion in the Founding period that present information about the Founders' religious lives. Among them are Patricia Bonomi, *Under the Cope of Heaven: Religion, Society, and Politics in Colonial America* (New York: Oxford University Press, 1986); Jon Butler, *Awash in a Sea of Faith: Christianizing the American People* (Cambridge, Mass.: Harvard University Press, 1990); Thomas Curry, *Church and State in America to the Passage of the First Amendment* (New York: Oxford University Press, 1986); Ronald Hoffman and Peter Albert, eds., *Religion in a Revolutionary Age* (Charlottesville: University Press of Virginia, 1994); James H. Hutson, *Religion and the Founding of the American Republic* (Washington, D.C.: Government Printing Office, 1998); and Frank Lambert, *The Founding Fathers and the Place of Religion in America* (Princeton, N.J.: Princeton University Press, 2003).

Index

Native Americans: John Adams on,
149–50; Boudinot on, 150–51;
Franklin on, 151; Jefferson on,
152–53; and Jews, 149–52; Washington on, 153
new birth; Boudinot on, 50
New England: John Adams on, 60;
Jefferson on, 144–45; Rush on, 154

oaths: Carroll on, 154; Franklin on,
155; Laurens on, 155; Rush on,
155–56; George Washington
on, 156

Paine, Thomas, 201, 205
patriotism: Jefferson on, 156; Rush
on, 157
Pascal, Blaise, 44–45
Paul (the apostle): Jefferson on,
157–58; on separation of church
and state, 65; on war, 227
Plato: John Adams on, 31, 105,
161–62; Jefferson on, 162
poor: Franklin on, 163; Rush on, 163
prayer: John Adams on, 163–64;
Boudinot on, 164; at Constitutional Convention of 1787,
169–70; Dickinson on, 165;
Franklin on, 165–70; Jefferson on,
170; Rush on, 170; George Washington on, 171
Presbyterians: John Adams on, 96,
101, 171; Jefferson on, 171–72
Priestley, Joseph, 71
persecution: John Adams on,
158–59; Franklin on, 159–61
proclamations. See fast and thanksgiving days
profanity: George Washington on,
172–73; Witherspoon on, 173
prophecy: John Adams on, 173–74;
Boudinot on, 73, 174; Jay on, 175;
Jefferson on, 175; Rush on, 175

Protestant Reformation, relation of
to the United States, 15–16
Providence: Abigail Adams on, 176;
John Adams on, 16, 176–77; and
American history, 15–19, 77–78,
177, 179, 181–82; Boudinot on,
177; and the Constitution, 77–78;
Dickinson on, 178; Franklin on
169–70, 178–79; Hamilton on,
101; Jay on, 179; Jefferson on,
180; Sherman on, 180; George
Washington on, 180–82; Martha
Washington on, 182
Pythagoras, 31

Quakers: John Adams on, 183;
Jefferson on, 184; Laurens on,
185; Rush on, 69; George Washington on, 186

reason: Dickinson on, 186; Jay on,
186–87; Jefferson on, 187–88;
Rush on, 188
religion, freedom of. See liberty of
conscience
religion, propensity of humanity
for: John Adams on, 189;
Franklin on, 189; Madison on,
190; Rush on, 190
religion, social utility of: John
Adams on, 190–91; Boudinot on,
191; Carroll on, 191; Franklin on,
192; Hamilton on, 192; Jefferson
on, 192–93; Rush on, 193; George
Washington on, 193; Witherspoon on, 194
republicanism: Dickinson on, 194;
Rush on, 195
rights: John Adams on, 196; Dickinson on, 196; Hamilton on, 196;
Jay on, 197; Jefferson on, 197–98
Rush, Benjamin: on animals, 20;
on the Bible, 25–26, 30, 35;